G. W Horn

Sermons by Missouri Methodist Preachers

G. W Horn

Sermons by Missouri Methodist Preachers

ISBN/EAN: 9783744744201

Printed in Europe, USA, Canada, Australia, Japan

Cover: Foto ©Thomas Meinert / pixelio.de

More available books at **www.hansebooks.com**

SERMONS

—BY—

Missouri Methodist Preachers

REPRESENTING

The Missouri, the St. Louis and the West St. Louis Conferences of the M. E. Church, South.

PUBLISHED IN THE INTEREST OF CENTRAL COLLEGE.

COMPILED BY

REV. G. W. HORN.

"He that knoweth God, heareth us."—1 *John* iv. 6.

ST. LOUIS:
SOUTHWESTERN BOOK AND PUBLISHING COMPANY,
510 AND 512 WASHINGTON AVENUE.
1874.

PREFATORY.

The publication of this book of sermons will serve two purposes. The first is, to give to the reading public a *good book*. At no time is the appearance of a good book impertinent. The makers of such books are benefactors. The masses obtain knowledge from books, and not, strictly speaking, by original research. Clubs and conversations and lectures cannot be substituted for books; books, therefore, are a staple and a necessity.

A book of *sermons* is no less desirable than other literature. The best style of mind admires sermons in print. With no factitious merit to catch the lovers of the light and merely novel, they sift the general mind, and detect by attraction the sober and worthy. A book of proper sermons has in it always matter worthy of any mind, even the greatest. We claim that for this volume from Missouri preachers.

We claim a reading from our people from three considerations: The sermons are the production of able minds; they are plain and unambiguous; and they are serious, earnest, devout discussions of momentous truths. There is little attempt at mere display, no flippant dealing with sacred things, no perverted partisan presentation, but sincere, direct, unctious, apostolic *preaching*. But the sermons may speak for themselves.

One word to the reader or hearer. Jesus says, "Take heed, therefore, how ye hear." As much depends upon right hearing as upon right preaching. If preaching is ever ineffective, it is the fault of the hearers. They hear and do not. Many have "itching ears," and desire only novelty, or the display of mental power, or something other than personal profit. They like the preacher just as he is able to minister to this carnal taste, and he is to them as Ezekiel was to his people—" as a very lovely song of one that hath a pleasant voice and can play well on an instrument; for they hear thy words, but they do them not."

The preacher does not, can not, should not, always present "some new thing." In an important sense, "there is nothing new under the sun." The principles of religion, the preacher's theme, are ever of old, immutable and undying. He may and should present variety of phrase and illustration, and possibly new phases of truth, but no new truth. He makes his message as attractive as he can, and leads his hearers by ways they have not known, out into the green pastures and beside the still waters; but it is theirs to be led, and to pluck the rich fruits and drink of the waters that flow softly. They are by him to learn duty, discover grace, "suffer the word of exhortation," and be admonished, reproved, rebuked as they may need. Ezekiel's hearers were charmed with his oratory and method; they drank in his eloquence, were pleased with his gorgeous Hebrew poetry and Chaldaic imagery, but they were not edified. Their sin was that they would not DO, and they *did* not because their hearing was defective. "Take heed, therefore, how ye hear."

The second purpose in the issuance of this volume is, to procure a fund for Central College Library. The mentioning of this object is enough. Every intelligent Methodist, with a right heart beating in him, is ready to aid such a cause. On this ground again we challenge the loyalty of every member of our Church in Missouri for patronage to this enterprise. Will not each worthy member contribute the small sum that buys this book to so good a cause?

In reference to the men who furnish the sermons

herein, a word is sufficient. They are among the leaders of the Church in Missouri—not, indeed, the only leading minds, for there are as many more of the same character, but they are peers of the best in this State or any other. They are men of God, and mean the welfare of those for whom this volume is prepared.

The compiler confesses indebtedness to the brethren who have kindly aided to make the undertaking a success. He is under grateful obligation, not only to those whose names are in this book, but to others also whose generosity will not be forgotten.

G. W. HORN.

MACON, MO., JAN. 20, 1874.

CONTENTS.

	PAGE.

I. DWELLING IN LOVE—By Rev. W. M. RUSH, D. D., Agent for Central College.................... 9

II. THE CHOICE OF MOSES—By Rev. C. P. JONES, D. D., of West St. Louis Conference............. 25

III. PREACHING CHRIST—By Rev. J. H. PRITCHETT, of the Missouri Conference...................... 47

IV. THE TRIAL OF CHRIST, THEN AND NOW; BEFORE PILATE AND YOU—By Rev. W. M. PROTTSMAN, of the West St. Louis Conference. 65

V. THE GLORY OF THE CHURCH.—By Rev. H. A. BOURLAND, of the Missouri Conference........ 82

VI. THE LAWS OF SPIRITUAL DEATH AND LIFE.—By Rev. F. X. FORSTER, Prof. in Central College 101

VII. AMAZING LOVE.—By Rev. W. C. GODBEY, of the West St. Louis Conference 116

VIII. THE LAW OF SACRIFICES.—By Rev. M. B. CHAPMAN, of the Missouri Conference............ 134

IX. MORE LABORERS IN THE HARVEST.—By Rev. J. P. NOLAN, of the Missouri Conference.... 146

X. DOING THE SAYINGS OF CHRIST.—By Rev. C. C. WOODS, of West St. Louis Conference...... 166

XI. THE FOLLY OF SKEPTICISM.—By Rev. J. E. GODBEY, of the St. Louis Conference.......... 178

CONTENTS.

PAGE.

XII. HEAVEN: ITS INHABITANTS, THEIR CHARACTER AND EMPLOYMENT.— By Rev. S. W. COPE, of the Missouri Conference 190

XIII. BAPTISM OF JESUS CHRIST.—By Rev. J. A. MURPHY, of West St. Louis Conference.......... 205

XIV. TO THE YOUNG.—By Rev. C. I. VANDEVENTER, of the Missouri Conference...................... 221

XV. THE HIDDEN LIFE.—By Rev. B. H. SPENCER, of the Missouri Conference 230

XVI. SERMON.—Preached before the St. Louis Annual Conference, assembled at Lexington, Missouri, September 19, 1866 241

XVII. FAITHLESS HUSBANDS AND DISAPPOINTED WIVES.—By Rev. J. W. Cunningham, of the Missouri Conference......................... 265

XVIII. THE LIMITS OF HUMAN RESPONSIBILITY.—By Rev. C. D. N. CAMPBELL, D. D., of the St. Louis Conference.............................. 283

XIX. THE RESURRECTION.—Delivered on Easter Sunday, April 5th, 1874, in the Second Methodist Church, South St. Louis, by Rev. D. R. M'ANALLY, of the St. Louis Conference...................... 299

XX. PIETY PROGRESSIVE....................... 316

SERMONS.

I.

DWELLING IN LOVE.

BY REV. W. M. RUSH, D. D.,

Agent for Central College.

"God is love; and he that dwelleth in love dwelleth in God, and God in him." — 1 JOHN iv. 16.

What a sublime utterance! The nature of God and all spiritual relations are here expressed in love. The self-existence, immutability and eternity of God are the self-existence, immutability and eternity of love. His unity and omnipresence are a universal, immense and all-pervading love. The sovereignty of God is love enthroned with supreme authority. Creation was a sublime expression of love. God willed that other beings capable of knowing and loving him, and of being happy with himself forever, should exist; and angels, archangels, seraphim and cherubim, in shining ranks stood before him, and in adoring love worshiped at his feet. He garnished the skies with worlds and systems of worlds, the abodes, perhaps, of intelligent beings, members of his great family. O, what an infinite satisfaction must the great Father have realized in the midst of the children of his love—they dwelling in him, and he in them, each moving in its proper sphere, and all held together in sweetest, purest, holiest sympathy, by an infinite love!

Love is the law of the moral universe, and is of equal authority upon angels and upon men. Our Saviour Christ says: "Thou shalt love the Lord thy God with all thy heart, and with all thy soul, and with all thy mind. This is the first and the great commandment. And the second is like unto it: thou shalt love thy neighbor as thyself. On these two commandments hang all the law and the prophets." Paul says, "Therefore love is the fulfilling of the law." Whatever may be the outward form of the commandment, the principle is love. Is it said, "Thou shalt have no other gods before me?" It is because we are to love the Lord our God with all our heart. Is it said, "Thou shalt not take the name of the Lord thy God in vain?" It is for the same reason. Is it said, "Thou shalt not kill?" It is because we are to love our neighbor as ourself. And for the same reason it is said thou shalt not steal, etc. The first table of the Decalogue requires supreme love to God, and the second requires love to our neighbor.

Love is *religion*. How many there are, even among church members, in the daily habit of using the term religion without ever considering or apprehending its exact or proper meaning. It comes from the Latin *religio*, and signifies *to rebind, to bind again*. The essence of sin is *enmity*. It is directly opposed to the law of love, and hence Paul says, "Sin is the transgression of the law."

It is the nature of sin to disintegrate—it has separated man from his Maker. By trangression man is a wanderer from God. "All we, like sheep, have gone astray; we have forsaken the fountain of living waters—strangers from the covenants of promise, having no hope and without God in the world." Such is the sad picture that is presented us of man by the unerring truth of God, in his fallen, corrupt and sinful condition. But sin not only separates man from his Maker, it separates man from his fellow. The tendency of sin is to make Ishmaelites of every one of us—setting every man's hand against his fellow. It has filled the earth with wrong and oppression, with violence and bloodshed. Religion is that divine process by which man is recovered from his alienation and brought back to God; it is a *rebinding* of his spirit to his spiritual and unseen Creator. The whole system of recovery, from its inception to its consummation, is a system of love. Love is the rebinding; it is that ligature which holds man in allegiance to the divine throne, and in harmony with the divine government. But religion not only unites us to God, it unites us to one another. Human hearts once severed, the links of affection all shattered and gone, are, by the religion of Jesus Christ, bound together in a bundle of love—the Apostle says, "knitted together in love." If the knitting is anatomical, the cement is love; if it is as the process of forming a garment of many stitches, then the cord which binds them all together is love. This is spiritual religion, which has to do directly and primarily with man's spiritual nature, and which, like its divine Author, is unchangeable—"the same yesterday, to-day and forever." Spiritual religion develops, as its fruit, practical religion. This practical religion is mentioned by James when he says : " Pure religion and undefiled before God and the Father is this, to visit the fatherless and widows in their afflictions, and to keep himself unspotted from the world." This practical religion is the good fruit of a good tree; it is the outward manifestation of an inward grace; it is the outgrowth of love to God, and love to one another.

Love is the *essence of spiritual life*. Spiritual life is the highest form of life. It is of the nature of God himself. There may be spiritual existence without spiritual life. The spirit of the beast that descendeth downward has not spiritual life. The angels that "left their first estate, that sinned against God," and " were thrust down to hell," are spiritual beings, but they have not spiritual life. Spiritual life is a *moral condition*, and exists only in vital connection with God. This vital connection is ruptured by sin. " The soul that sinneth it shall die," not merely because justice demands it, but in the very nature of the case such is the necessary result. A very high degree of mental action may remain, as in the case of fallen angels and wicked men, but vital connection with God, in which alone this highest form of life exists, is broken up. The soul that is dead by reason of sin must be restored to that moral condition in which its vital connection with God is re-established. That moral condition is a condition of love. Moses said to the children of Israel: "And the Lord thy God will circumcise thy heart, and the heart of thy seed, to love the Lord thy God with all thy heart, and with all thy soul, that thou mayest live." The gracious work that is here spoken of is called a circumcision because of the striking significance of that ordinance, which was the token of the covenant and the representative ordinance of the Church under that dispensation. The same gracious work is under the present dispensation called baptism, because of the striking significance of baptism, which is the token of the covenant and representative ordinance of the Church under the present dispensation. Still, however, under the present dispensation it is sometimes called a circumcision of the heart. Paul says, For he is not a Jew, which is one outwardly; neither is that circumcision which is outward in the flesh: but he is a Jew which is one inwardly; and circumcision is that of the heart in the spirit, and not in the letter; whose praise is not of men, but of God." It will be observed that both Moses and Paul speak of the heart as the subject of this gracious work—this spiritual circumcision; and Moses tells us that the heart is *circumcised* to *love* that it may have *life*. Man's spiritual being is restored to that moral condition in which its vital connections are re-established. Paul tells us that "to be carnally-minded is death," and assigns as a sufficient reason, "because the carnal mind is enmity against God, for it is not subject to the law of God, neither indeed can be." The law of God is love; the carnal mind is enmity. Enmity does not, cannot love, and, therefore, it is impossible, in the nature of the case, that the carnal mind should be subject to the law of God. Those who are *carnal* are said to be "children of wrath," " sold under sin," " dead in trespasses." This gracious work, which by Moses and Paul is called a circumcision, is by David called a *creation*. He says: " Create in me a clean heart, O God, and renew a right spirit within me." Our Lord said to Nicodemus: " Except a man be born again he cannot see the kingdom of God." To be *born again* is to be *created anew*. Paul says: "Created in Christ Jesus unto good works;" "and that ye put on the new man, which, after God, is created in righteousness and true holiness." Ezekiel says : " Then will I sprinkle clean water upon you, and ye shall be clean; from all your filthiness and from all your idols will I cleanse you. A new heart also will I give you, and a new spirit will I put within you; and I will take away the stony heart out of your flesh, and I will give you a heart of flesh."

I have quoted thus largely from both the Old and the New Testaments, to show that in both, this great and gracious work is set forth in identical and corresponding terms; in both, man's spiritual being is the subject of it; in both, the work is thorough and complete, being a transformation and renewal of our nature, restoring us not only to the favor, but to the image of God; not only *rebinding* us in allegiance to the divine throne, but re-establishing our vital connections with the great fountain of spiritual life. It is not only a rebinding, but is a living connection. Life from the very heart of God pulsates in the renewed soul. How striking and fitting the similitude employed by our Saviour—I am the vine, ye are the branches." It is the richness and fatness of the vine flowing into the branch that gives to the branch life and fruitfulness; and even so, it is the love of God shed abroad in our hearts, permeating our whole spiritual being, that gives us life and fruitfulness.

In our physical economy the blood is called by the word of God, "*the life.*" The heart is said to be the seat of life, because from it issues the blood, the tide of life. This blood flows through the arterial system to every part of the body, and through the venous system it is returned to the heart again. This circulation is essential to the life, not only of the whole, but of each individual member; for if any member of the body should become so diseased or otherwise injured as neither to receive nor circulate the blood, and that disease or injury should become permanent, that member would pass into a state of mortification or death, and would have to be amputated to preserve the life of the body; so love is the life of our moral or spiritual constitution. God is the great fountain of spiritual life to the universe, and his love flows to every heart in vital connection with himself, and every heart in vital connection with him loves him in return. "We love him because he first loved us." The circulation of this life-principle is essential to the spiritual life, not only of the moral universe, but of each personal spiritual being. If any one should become so morally diseased or injured in his moral constitution that he neither received, circulated nor reciprocated the love of God, he would pass into a state of spiritual death, and that condition being, or becoming permanent, he must be cut off from the great body of the family of God. It is thus that spiritual death is a necessary result of sin. "The soul that sinneth it shall die," is a truth that expresses not only a decree of God, but a moral necessity. Sin necessarily obstructs the life-principle, and the incorrigibly wicked—they who persistently reject the only method or plan by which their vital connection with the great fountain of spiritual life could be re-established—must be cut off. The separation of such an one from God's family is as much an act of goodness and of mercy as it is an act of justice. It is no act of cruelty to amputate a dead member, a hand, or a foot, from a living body. The amputation must take place or the body will die. If the dead member cannot be restored to life, if the circulation be permanently cut off, it will do it no good to remain connected with the body; but such connection will work the destruction of the body. Neither is it an act of cruelty to turn a dead spirit, a spirit that has broken up its vital connection with the fountain of life, out of heaven. It could do the impure and carnal spirit no good to remain in heaven, the home of purity and love, but its remaining there would break up and destroy heaven itself. This must not be. The mercy of God, the goodness of God, the infinite love of the Father for his children, will not permit it. The family homestead must be preserved.

When the soul is renewed and brought into vital connection with God, it receives in *kind* that life with which the saints are crowned in heaven. "He that believeth on the Son hath everlasting life." It is the same love that shall be his forever, if he continue steadfast unto the end. " Be thou faithful unto death, and I will give thee a crown of life."

> " Beyond this vale of tears
> There is a life above,
> Unmeasured by the flight of years—
> And all that life is love.
> There is a death whose pang
> Outlasts the fleeting breath;
> O! what eternal horrors hang
> Around the second death."

Whatever may be the employments of heaven, whether in obedience to the divine will, on pinions of celestial light, the redeemed and glorified spirit shall speed from star to star on missions of love and mercy, until reaching the utmost limits of creation, it shall be able to look into nothing's strange abode; or whether nearest the throne, gazing upon the unclouded glory of God, it shall join in anthems of everlasting praise; or whether in Eden bowers, amid jasper walls and golden streets and gates of pearl; or by the banks of the river of life, in sweetest, holiest communion with kindred spirits, the vitalizing principle of every employment is love. The very atmosphere of heaven is redolent with love.

> "This is the grace that must live and sing
> When faith and hope shall cease;
> Must sound from every joyful string
> Through the sweet groves of bliss."

Love is the substance of human joy. There is not a joy that swells the human heart but that is the offspring of love. Even forbidden presence is the result of a forbidden affection. For a confirmation of this let us appeal to the natural affections. Do we not find that in all the relations of natural affection, the thought of the object of our love fills the heart with pleasure? Ask that mother who is so tenderly caressing her infant babe, "Mother, do you love your babe?" Without a moment's hesitation the answer will be: "O, yes! no language can tell how much I love my child." "But, mother, how do you know that you love your child?" She answers: "I have an inward consciousness of the love that I have for my child." But what is that consciousness of love of which the mother speaks? Is it not that unspeakable pleasure that swells within her heart and sweeps every cord of her maternal nature as she thinks of the child she loves so much? A father may think of his prodigal son with mingled feelings of pleasure and of pain. He loves his son, but he hates his vices, he hates his prodigality. The love gives pleasure, but the hatred gives pain. The heart that is full of love, with no enmity, is full of joy. We remember, through the lapse of long and numerous years, the hour of our conversion, when first from above we received the pledge of love—when first the full tide of spiritual life was poured into our souls—when first we realized that we did love God, because he first loved us; then were we happy—happy as we had never been before. O! who can ever forget the gladness of that happy hour! David celebrated it in sacred song. When God had removed his transgressions from him, as far as the East is from the West, he shouted: "Bless the Lord,

O my soul, and all that is within me bless his holy name." Again he says: "I love the Lord because he hath heard my voice and my supplications; because he hath inclined his ear unto me, therefore will I call upon him as long as I live." And yet again, out of a heart full of love, he says: "Whom have I in heaven but thee? And there is none upon the earth that I desire beside thee." In his rich experience of the goodness and favor of God his soul was transported with love and joy. We can but admire the loving kindness of our heavenly Father in so wonderfully adjusting our personal happiness to our duty to himself and to one another. If we would be happy, as God intended we should be, we must love him, and we must love one another; and we cannot love him and one another without being happy. God hath joined these two together, and it is impossible that they should be put asunder.

Love is the witness of the Spirit. John says: "He that believeth on the Son of God hath the witness in himself." This is plain language, not easily misunderstood. Paul says: "And because ye are sons God hath sent forth the Spirit of his Son into your hearts crying, Abba Father." The Spirit is given to testify to this new relation. He is, in fact, the only competent witness in the universe to testify in the case; "for what man knoweth the things of a man, save the spirit of man that is in him? Even so the things of God knoweth no man, but the Spirit of God." If our sins are pardoned, the act of pardon has passed in the divine mind; and if we are regenerated and adopted into his family, the work is his; and *because* we are sons, the Spirit of his Son is sent into our hearts to communicate to us the gracious intelligence of the new relation, our sonship, our adoption into the family of God. "The Spirit itself beareth witness with our spirit that we are the children of God." Again he says: "If any man have not the Spirit of Christ he is none of his." This is not to be glossed over, as if the apostle had said: if any man have not the *mind* and *temper* of Christ he is none of his, thus denying or ignoring the "Spirit of Christ," "the Spirit of his Son," "the Spirit of adoption," "whereby we cry Abba Father." This witnessing Spirit must be possessed by those who belong to Christ. "Therefore, being justified by faith we have peace with God through our Lord Jesus Christ, by whom also we have access by faith into this grace wherein we stand and rejoice in hope of the glory of God. And not only so, but we glory in tribulations also, knowing that tribulation worketh patience, and patience experience, and experience hope: and hope maketh not ashamed, because the love of God is shed abroad in our hearts by the Holy Ghost which is given unto us." I know of no other agency by which the love of God can get into the human heart but by the Holy Ghost. The Bible tells of no other, but it tells of this. The logic of the apostle is irresistible. If any man have not the Spirit of Christ, he is none of his, because if he have not the Spirit of Christ he has not the love of God shed abroad in his heart by the Holy Ghost; and if he have not the love of God shed abroad in his heart, then is he carnal, sold under sin; but to be carnally minded is death, and they that are carnal are dead in trespasses and in sins. When the soul is adopted into the family of God its vital connections are re-established, and the tide of spiritual life, the love of God, is shed abroad in the heart by the Holy Ghost, the Spirit of adoption. Hence it is that he that believeth on the Son of God—all they who are the children of God by faith in Christ Jesus—"have the witness in themselves."

In spiritual life, as in physical life, there is the consciousness of life as well as the action of life. Others may know that we live by the action of life—"by their fruits ye shall know them;" but we know that we live by the consciousness of life; we know that we have passed from death unto life, because we love the brethren, we love God. Love is a matter of personal consciousness.

"Exults our rising soul,
  Disburdened of her load,
And swells unutterably full
  Of glory and of God.

"His love surpassing far
  The love of all beneath,
We find within our hearts, and dare
  The pointless darts of death.

"Stronger than death or hell
  The sacred power we prove;
And conquerors of the world, we dwell
  In heaven who dwell in love."

My beloved, we cannot afford to dispense with the *consciousness* of spiritual life, as the action of physical life would not long continue without the consciousness of physical life; neither will the action of spiritual life long continue without the consciousness of spiritual life, and while it did remain it would "become as sounding brass or a tinkling cymbal." O let us seek, my brethren, for a deeper, richer experience in the things of God. Let the daily cry of our heart be—

"Nearer to thee, my God, nearer to thee."

But, beloved, let us not for a moment suppose that this consciousness of spiritual life is all that is needful. Its very existence depends upon the action of spiritual life. "As faith without works," in the Christian, "is dead," even so, love will not long continue unless it produce the fruit of holy living. Jesus said to his sorrowing disciples: "If ye love me keep my commandments. He that hath my commandments, and keepeth them, he it is that loveth me: and he that loveth me shall be loved of my Father, and I will love him, and will manifest myself to him. If a man love me he will keep my words: and my Father will love him, and we will come unto him and make our abode with him. Herein is my Father glorified, that ye bear much fruit; so shall ye be my disciples. If ye keep my commandments ye shall abide in my love, even as I have kept my Father's commandments and abide in his love. If a man abide not in me, he is cast forth as a branch, and is withered; and men gather them and cast them into the fire and they are burned." Unless we observe to do all things whatsoever God has commanded us we cannot abide in him; our vital connections will be broken up, and we will be cast forth as a dead branch fit only to be burned.

The commandments of God, however, are not grievous unto us, for the obedience which he requires is a loving obedience. It may be indeed that the pathway of duty may sometimes lie amid trials, but the trial of our faith is more precious than gold that perisheth. Perhaps Daniel was never happier than in the lions' den; nor the Hebrew children, than in the fiery furnace. No other act of obedient faith, in the entire history of Abraham, presents him so grandly as that in which he is offering his son Isaac upon the altar. If we can only hear the voice of the Master, " Lo, I am with you," it is enough.

How intimate the communion and fellowship of God with his children! They dwell in him, and he dwells in them. They repose in the bosom of their Father. They have a blessed consciousness of the warm pulsations of his love in their hearts, permeating their whole spiritual being. They feel that the everlasting arms of the Infinite One are beneath and about them for their protection. Dwelling in God they dwell safely. No weapon that is formed against them shall prosper. While they dwell in God, their adversary the devil, as a roaring lion, may rage in vain; they laugh to scorn his cruel power. He is their stronghold in the day of trouble, their refuge, their hiding place, their covert from the storm. He is the strength of their heart and their portion forever. All the treasuries of his providence, and of his grace, are laid under contribution to supply their wants; no good thing will he withhold from them that walk uprightly. His wisdom and his omnipotence are pledged in their behalf; all things work together for good to them that love God. He is their Father, and they are his children—heirs of his glory and joint heirs with Christ their elder brother.

God dwells in them. How precious, and yet how mysterious and incomprehensible is this truth! The Infinite One, whom the heaven of heavens cannot contain, who filleth immensity with his presence, dwells in each believer's soul. Dwelling in them he is their peace, the peace of God that passeth all understanding dwells richly in their hearts. He is their joy, and the crown of their rejoicing. He is their hope, which, like an anchor, sure and steadfast, enters within the vale and lays hold on Eternal Life. He is their light, to cheer them amid tempest and storm. He is their life and their salvation, their exceeding great reward.

"Beloved, now are we the sons of God." Dwelling in God, and he in us, we dwell in love, and realize that God is love. "And it doth not yet appear what we shall be, but we know that when he shall appear we shall be like him, for we shall see him as he is." There are glories in heaven yet unrevealed to us, splendors about the divine throne yet undiscovered. There are things to be seen and heard in heaven that cannot be symbolized in human speech. The language of earth is too poor to give expression to the things that Paul saw and heard in the third heaven.

Of one thing, my brethren, we may be well assured: when we shall awake in His likeness, amid the splendors of the heavenly world, *we shall be* SATISFIED.

II.

THE CHOICE OF MOSES.

BY REV. C. P. JONES, D. D.,

Of West St. Louis Conference.

" By faith Moses, when he was come to years, refused to be called the son of Pharaoh's daughter; choosing rather to suffer affliction with the people of God than to enjoy the pleasure of sin for a season; esteeming the reproach of Christ greater riches than the treasures in Egypt; for he had respect unto the recompense of the reward."—HEB. xi. 24-5-6.

By one touch of the heavenly limner the few words of the text bring in review before us the life of one who lived nearly thirty-five hundred years ago—a life replete with most extraordinary vicissitudes, and full of lessons of profoundest religious import. Now the helpless babe of a poor bondman, ruthlessly, hopelessly, condemned to die by an absolute, heartless tyrant; now the adopted son of that tyrant's daughter, and a cherished member of the royal family; now in the full vigor of young manhood, amid the splendors of a court, surrounded by wealth, earthly greatness, pleasures; now a voluntary exile, a penniless, houseless, homeless wanderer; now alone in the wilderness watching his flock, or standing awe-struck in the presence of the august Majesty of heaven and earth, who, from the burning bush, commissions him to humble the might of heathen pride, and lead his chosen people to their promised inheritance; now at the court of Pharaoh demanding the enfranchisement of Israel—calling up the dread messenger of death to smite the first-born of him whose sanguinary decrees had carried death and mourning into every dwelling of the poor Israelite, and to smite also the first-born of those who gloried in and executed those sanguinary decrees, till a nation grows pale with fear, and the mightiest monarch of the world trembles on his throne. Now leading redeemed Israel in triumph across the Red Sea, whose waters, as if instinct with life, retire at his approach; now traversing arid wastes, and smiting limpid waters from the flinty rock; now on the mount face to face with the ineffably glorious One, receiving the law; now at the end of his pilgrimage on Pisgah's top exploring each landmark on Canaan's bright shore; and now beyond "the last river," crowned and sceptred with adoring millions, receiving the approbation of Him whose smile is heaven!

The life of Moses abounds also in lessons of deepest religious import. His faith, his choice, his unwavering purpose to serve and glorify God, his moral heroism, his humility, his God-like patience, teach us that man in this corrupt world, in the highest positions, surrounded by wealth and glory, may deny himself all worldly lusts, and live soberly, righteously and godly; may become the architect of a character that shall shine as a beacon light amid the moral gloom of earth, and achieve a victory the glory of which, when compared with the triumphs of earthly heroes, is as the glorious orb of day to a dimly twinkling star! That these lessons may more deeply impress you and lead you to a faith and choice, if you yet halt between two opinions, and to an obedience and holiness like unto the faith and choice, the obedience and holiness of Moses, I propose to examine his choice, and the reasons and motives which influenced him in choosing.

I. First, then, the Choice of Moses.

"Moses, when he was come to years, refused to be called the son of Pharaoh's daughter; choosing rather to suffer affliction with the people of God than to enjoy the pleasures of sin for a season; esteeming the reproach of Christ greater riches than the treasures in Egypt."

As the adopted son of Pharaoh's daughter, and thereby the grandson of the king, Moses may have been heir presumptive to the throne of Egypt. We have no authentic account in sacred or profane history that *that* Pharaoh was blessed with male issue, and as the female issue could not peaceably ascend the throne alone, then Moses might have succeeded to the crown and wealth and glory of the most powerful kingdom then known to the world. A crown glittered before him and challenged his gaze. A sceptre, at the waving of which loyal millions bowed, invited his grasp. The immense wealth of the rich valley of the Nile spread out before him and awaited his pleasure. Countless numbers of noblemen and peasants, of freemen and slaves, of the refined and the great, were expectant to hail him as their rightful sovereign, to obey his commands and bow at his nod. In refusing, therefore, to be called the son of Pharaoh's daughter he refused a kingdom, its power and glory. He gave up, then, earth's greatest prize, in the estimation of her sons—a prize to obtain which heroes have sacrificed upon the gory field millions of the human family; for which hunger and thirst have been gladly endured, stormy seas crossed, sandy deserts traversed, the deadly blast of the sirocco met, rugged mountains scaled and polar snows endured—a prize to obtain and retain which an Alexander, a Cæsar, a Napoleon, tasked and wasted the mightiest energies of body and mind, and sacrificed their all—from that prize Moses turned away to suffer affliction with the people of God. O thou greatest and best of men! what were the struggles that shook thy manly breast as thrones and riches and pleasures passed in tempting review before thee, and must be given up forever?—and as affliction, poverty, reproach, shame, gathered about thee and must be gladly endured? God only knows the war that was waged in thy anxious heart between the powers of light and of darkness, and of the swayings of thy nature to and fro, as an ebbing and flowing tide, and of the light and peace of thy mind, and of the joyous bursts of heavenly music that rolled out from harmonious wires struck by angel hands, when the struggle was over, the choice made and the victory won!

But if the supposition that Moses was heir presumptive to the throne of Egypt be incorrect, still as the adopted son of the king's daughter, and a member of the royal family, the high station and honors of that family were his, their prerogatives and their wealth. Every earthly good, therefore, that heart could desire surrounded him and was within his grasp. Pleasures deep and full crowded his pathway, and lit up with the witchery of their glow the future of his earthly pilgrimage. O, how inviting, how tempting, the prospect spread out before him! Riches, honors, pleasures! Bright laurels, and glittering treasures, and splendid halls flooded with sweet, enchanting music, crowded with merry dancers and genial spirits of sensual pleasure-seekers, and fair arms and loving hearts —*these* tempted, wooed him to stay in the royal palace —hung trembling in the balance, against poverty and reproach and shame. And, as the grandson of the king, his position and opportunities for enjoying worldly pleasures were as great, if not greater, than if he had filled the throne. The duties of a monarch are onerous, his responsibilities great, his cares and anxieties many, perplexing, harassing, and sometimes absolutely destructive of peace and life. He who takes the government of a mighty kingdom or a great nation upon his shoulders takes upon himself a burden that but few can bear. What time, then, has he for indulging in the pleasures of sin, and for pomp and show—what heart for such vanities? But the son, free from the responsibilities and cares of government, in his high position, and with the immense wealth and every opportunity that royalty always affords, can, if he choose, indulge in the pleasures of sin to the full. Moses, therefore, in refusing to be called the son of Pharaoh's daughter, refused wealth, pleasures, honors. He severed the ties that connected him with monarchs and earthly greatness. He turned away from the templed Valley of the Nile and refined society, from loved and loving hearts, to ally himself with the despised Israelites, choosing to suffer reproach and affliction with them.

We are informed by Josephus that Pharaoh elevated Moses to the chief command of the army of Egypt in a war waged against Ethiopia; that he led his army with complete success over a vast, sandy desert infested with venomous serpents, where a hostile force had never before dared to go; that he fell unexpectedly upon the Ethiopians and utterly routed them; stormed and took their capital; successfully and very honorably to Egypt terminated the war, and led in safety his triumphant host back to Egypt to receive the approbation of the king and the plaudits of the admiring multitude. And so popular had he become, so great was his influence with his soldiers, that he could have led them triumphantly, with half the nation at his back, against his sovereign; could have overcome him at a blow and have vaulted to a throne; could have laid the foundation of a new dynasty and bequeathed to his children for unnumbered years the first prize in the world; could have shivered the yoke of bondage that weighed down his kindred after the flesh, and have elevated them to places of trust, honor and profit. In refusing, therefore, to be called the son of Pharaoh's daughter, he threw down his high commission and turned away from the "pomp and circumstance of glorious war," the bright vistas of victorious campaigns, and the conqueror's crown, to suffer affliction with the people of

God, and to bear the reproach of Christ. Examine this subject, therefore, from any stand-point, look at the choice of Moses in all its aspects and bearings, and the conclusion forces itself upon us, that it stands without a parallel; and we are deeply impressed with the strength of his faith, the depth of his humility, the sincerity of his motives, the vigor of his purpose and the elevation of his piety! O! that his mantle may fall on us!

But not only did Moses refuse to be called the son of Pharaoh's daughter, and hence a throne, and power, and pleasures, and choose "to suffer affliction with the people of God, but he esteemed the reproach of Christ greater riches than the treasures in Egypt." Great indeed were the treasures in Egypt. Her pyramids and mighty temples; now glorious in their ruins, her broken shafts and mouldering cities and palace-like tombs, hewn from the rock—mournful mementoes of generations long since passed away—demonstrate to us that she was rich and powerful. Her armies and her commerce, her gold and her silver—who can number them or count their value? Moses gazed upon her pyramids, threaded the streets of her proud cities, walked the aisles of her magnificent temples, marched with and commanded her armies, counted her golden treasures, dwelt in her marble palaces, sat down by her throne, and could have laid his hand upon her crown and her sceptre. But all, *all*, to him were utterly worthless—lighter than the dust of the balance, when viewed in the light of eternity and weighed against the favor of God and eternal life. The reproach of Christ, when endured for his sake and for the hope of heaven, became invested with a value compared with which the immense wealth of the Valley of the Nile was as dross. The glory that gilded the cross of Christ, and thence fell in streams of radiance upon the bar of divine justice, turning away its wrath and re-opening the way to the mercy seat and to the tree of life, and which revealed to his eye of faith the ineffable glories of the final home of the righteous, showed those earthly treasures to be but gilded toys, and that

> "Conqueror's wreaths and monarch's gems
> Shall blend in common dust."

"Esteeming the reproach of Christ greater riches than the treasures in Egypt!" Fabulous, illimitable almost in number and value, were those treasures, but the reproach of Christ is infinitely more valuable. Those treasures—where are they now? Long since they have passed away, but the riches of the reproach of Christ endure still, and will endure, and with new lustre shine after dissolving throes shall have rent the bosom of old earth, and star after star shall have faded from the diadem of night! O that the riches of the reproach of Christ were ours in all their fullness and enduring lustre! O that the far streaming glory which unites its every ray upon the cross of Christ, and thence, as a central sun, floods the universe, were turned full upon our hearts and along our pathways!

II. WHAT WERE THE REASONS AND MOTIVES THAT INFLUENCED MOSES IN CHOOSING?

These are distinctly stated in the text: he could enjoy

the pleasures of sin but for a season, and he had respect unto the recompense of the reward.

"The pleasures of sin"—what are they? All pleasures which God has forbidden—pleasures, however innocent they may seem, which are not to His glory. All others, and they are almost illimitable, are given to us as a part of our rich inheritance here and our glorious reward hereafter. But why are the *pleasures of sin* but for a season?

First of all, because desire is soon gratified, the appetite satiated, and the pleasure-seeker turns away with loathing from the scenes and objects whence he sought and derived pleasure, Hence merry groups go from object to object, half despising each in turn as they pass away; now drinking deep of this fountain, now of that; now threading the mazes of the giddy dance, or quaffing the luscious wine-cup; now trying the excitement of the game of chance; now running after the novel and the strange, and pressing for fields of love and bliss of fancy's painting, but which, alas! when reached are arid wastes; and now, with disappointed hopes and surfeited or hollow, aching hearts, turning and cursing with a bitter curse their own folly, the wine-cup and the dance; and now again going the same rounds of pleasure. Yes, amid the pleasures of sin, while drinking in all their sweets, the keen edge of desire is turned, the appetite palls, and the sickened soul shrinks back with disgust and loathing, and would turn to the fountain of living waters, asserting the divinity of her origin and her high-born destiny! There is not, in short, a single pleasure of sin in which man desires to indulge in which he can indulge *all the time.* He who dances would not dance always. He who is mighty to drink strong drink, must pause some time. Nothing earthly, indeed, meets and satisfies the longing desires of the immortal soul. She turns from all these sordid pleasures, which, ever and anon, when she has tasted, become bitter as the waters of Mara, and pants for her long lost Eden! Such, in fine, are the capacities with which the great Creator has endowed her that the pleasures of sin in their very nature pierce her through and through with a bitter sting; and yet, blinded by the god of this world, she seeks happiness only in them! O, that the thoughtless, pleasure-seeking crowds would pause and read the lessons indellibly written in their own nature, and so often revealed in bitter, burning characters, proclaiming to them and to the world that the pleasures of sin are but for a season!

Again: The pleasures of sin are but for a season, because they are evanescent in their nature. They expire in our embrace, or vanish while we gaze upon them. The springs and streams of which we drink, and at which we would slake our thirst, and the scenes and objects amid which we revel and with whom take delight, pass away ofttimes as the baseless fabric of a vision, and leave not a wreck behind them but our poor, disconsolate, aching hearts.

Go to the halls of merriment. Behold the groups of pleasure-seekers; listen to the swell of enchanting music and the thoughtless laugh. Look again. The merry crowds have disappeared, the exhilarating sound of music is hushed, the thoughtless laugh which rang out on the evening air has died away, and regrets and anguish have succeeded, and the heart deeply feels that the pleasures of sin are but for a season.

Go to the halls of Bacchus. The wine sparkles, the flowing bowl goes round; jolly fellows well met sip and joke and laugh, and laugh and joke and sip again. But soon, ah! soon, the spell is broken, the wine ceases its flow, the joke and the laugh are hushed, and the merry fellows slink away to mourn in loneliness their folly, or to regret that the pleasures of sin were so short-lived.

The rose that blooms by your pathway to-day and throws its sweetness on the passing breeze, ere to-morrow will have withered. The smiling faces and lovely forms with and of whom you now seek pleasures, ere a few hours or days number their brief moments, will have passed away, it may be, never more to return. The rippling streams and flowery landscapes will have ceased the music of their flow or have faded ere the soul realizes the cooling draught or reposes amid their sweets. The golden scenes which imagination paints in the eventful future, and amid which fond hope promises that you shall revel, recede as you approach them, or, alas! when you reach them, are, like the deceptious painting of the mirage, but arid wastes. O! how the soul's fond hopes of sinful pleasure are blighted! The sirocco sweeps the landscape, the fountains are dried up or become bitter, and the loved forms and warm hearts of boon companions are touched by the cold skeleton hand of death, and are dust!

Once more: The pleasures of sin are but for a season, because of the brevity of human life. Few indeed are the days of our pilgrimage; short our stay upon the shores of time. We are as the flower that blooms in the morning and ere noon withers; or, we come and go, as bubbles upon the bosom of the stormy deep. Our days, it is true, may be threescore years and ten, and by reason of strength even fourscore years, yet how soon they fly away, and are but as a moment compared with "the measureless enduring of eternity." But the greater part of our race die ere the noon of life, and countless millions in the full vigor and glow of the bright morning of existence. They but open their eyes to the pleasures of sin, they but hear the songs of revelry, they but taste the sweets of that stream whose surface may be nectar, but whose depths are hell, and see and hear and taste no more forever!

The history of the past is strewed with the wreck of worldly hopes. The devotees of pleasure have chased each other from bower to bower, or have pursued each other along the enchanting ways of sin, and have quickly disappeared, each in his turn, to meet a fiery doom. Solomon and Alexander—where are they? Pharaoh, from the templed Nile, and Belshazzar, from the splendid palaces of Babylon, the voluptuaries of proud Athens, the debauchees of mighty Rome, and the sensual crowds of Pompeii and Herculaneum? And where are the pleasure-seekers of Corinth and Ephesus, of Troy and Carthage, of Cairo and Petra? Echo answers, *where?* Death has hushed in eternal silence their songs of mirth, and many of their proud cities, with their temples of pleasure and chambers of vice, moulder in undistinguishable ruins, and "the voice of harpers and musicians, and of pipers and trumpeters, are heard no more at all in them." The curse of Omnipotence has swept them with the besom of destruction and left them as monuments of avenging wrath to warn the children of men in all ages that the pleasures of sin are an offense to Him, and are but for a season. A few years hence, what and where will be the busy, eager throngs who now seek their happiness and their heaven in the pleasures of sin? Their drinking and reveling will be over; the merry laugh and the charmer's voice will be hushed; the dancer's heels will be still; and noisome worms in the dust will revel then and chime a low requiem by their gnawings in the deserted palace of the soul! O! how brief are the pleasures of sin! How they come and go as the changing scenes of the kaleidoscope, and leave naught behind them but bitter remembrances, sleepless remorse, the curse of God and endless death. Moses felt, aye, by the light of faith knew, that the pleasures of sin are but for a season, that he might wear a crown and sway a sceptre; might revel in halls of feasting and song, and riot upon the lap of pleasure; might expire upon a bed of down, beneath a gilded canopy, surrounded by the great, and lie down in a splendid mausoleum hewn from the imperishable rock, but that in a moment these pleasures and this grandeur would all fade away, and that beyond the wrath of Omnipotence must be met and banishment from His peaceful presence into everlasting punishment would be his doom. And as he sat beside the throne and heard the voice of charmers, and saw merry crowds come and go, and gazed upon the wealth and earthly greatness around him, and saw their waning glory, and then looked up and away to the retributions of the coming judgment and to the imperishable and eternal, I imagine I hear him sing,

> "And am I only born to die,
> And must I suddenly comply
>   With nature's stern decree?
> What after death for me remains—
> Celestial joys or hellish pains,
>   To all eternity?
>
> "No room for mirth or trifling here,
> For worldly hope or worldly fear,
>   If life so soon is gone;
> If now the Judge is at the door,
> And all mankind must stand before
>   The inexorable throne!
>
> "Jesus, vouchsafe a pitying ray;
> Be thou my guide, be thou my way,
>   To glorious happiness!
> Ah! write thy pardon on my heart,
> And whensoe'er I hence depart
>   Let me depart in peace!"

The prayer was heard, the pitying ray vouchsafed, the pardon written on his heart, and he arose and went out from the royal palace and the wealth and pleasures of Egypt, to return no more as the son of Pharaoh's daughter!

"He had respect unto the recompense of the reward." The term reward, in its ordinary import, signifies value received, an equivalent returned. The word recompense is of similar meaning. But as man can merit no favor or blessing of God, we must interpret these terms in an evangelical sense; that is, that the favor of God and endless fruition with Him in heaven are gratuities vouchsafed to the faithful, obedience being the condition upon which they are given.

"The recompense of the reward," which, as a powerful motive, moved Moses to refuse to be called the son of Pharaoh's daughter, and choose to suffer affliction with the people of God, embraces, first of all, peace with Him and joy in the Holy Ghost, and the full light of hope while running the race set before us. An abiding sense of the approbation of God and the indwelling, witnessing Spirit, crying Abba Father, the believer's privilege and realization, make a heaven below and a recompense of reward even in our pilgrimage. Moses realized these in the fullest sense. As he went out from the royal palace, as he journeyed alone in the wilderness, or reposed his weary head at night upon a stone pillow, a still, small voice whispered within, "All is well!" and there welled up from the depths of his glad heart this song:

> "Content with beholding his face,
>   My all to his pleasure resigned;
> No changes of season or place
>   Would make any change in my mind.
> While blessed with a sense of his love,
>   A palace a toy would appear,
> And prisons would palaces prove,
>   If Jesus would dwell with me there."

Yes, surely, he who communed with his Maker face to face; who was hid in the cleft of the rock by the hand of the Almighty, and saw as He passed by all that mortal eye can see of the ineffably glorious One and live; whose face, from the light of joy within and the reflected light of the Shekinah, was too bright upon which for Israel to gaze, so that he was veiled; surely he had a recompense of reward in the wilderness as he toiled on to the promised land—a reward amid the smoke and din of battle. With him, indeed, glory *had* begun below, and

"Celestial fruit on earthly ground
From faith and hope *did* grow."

Again, the recompense of the reward embraces a triumphant, glorious death.

" The chamber where the good man meets his fate
Is privileged above the common walks
Of virtuous life, quite on the verge of heaven."

"And Moses went up from the plains of Moab unto the mountain of Nebo, to the top of Pisgah, and the Lord showed him all the land of Gilead unto Dan; and all Naphthali, and the land of Ephraim and Manasseh, and all the land of Judah, unto the utmost sea; and the South and the plain of the valley of Jericho, the city of palm trees, unto Zoar. And the Lord said unto him, This is the land which I sware unto Abraham, unto Isaac, and unto Jacob, saying, I will give it unto thy seed; I have caused thee to see it with thine eyes, but thou shalt not go over thither. So Moses, the servant of the Lord, died there in the land of Moab, and He buried him in a valley over against Bethpeor." What a death scene! What a happy exit! What a glorious termination of a life, of faith! In triumph he steps across the Jordan of death! No cold wave chills him! No darkness shrouds him! 'Tis but the bright way to endless joy! And now on the eternal shore he receives the crown of life and sits down by the throne of the Great King in his uncreated palace of light!

Finally, the recompense of reward embraces the approbation of God in the judgment and an entrance into and full fruition of His joy forever.

"Well done, good and faithful servant, enter thou into the joy of thy Lord," is the reward that will greet the faithful, and with which they will be crowned beyond this vale of tears.

"Well done, good and faithful servant." How these words, as they shall fall from the lips of the Judge, will thrill the soul with peace and joy! For this we have denied ourselves, and endured the cross, despising the shame; for this run the race set before us, and toiled on amid defeats as well as victories, and hoped, and sometimes feared, and wept and prayed; and now, as we stand before the inflexible bar, time gone, eternity before us, our destiny in the balance, the Judge approves. O! the unutterable bliss of that moment! This was the blessed sound that greeted the ear of Moses, when, having at once ceased to work and live, he stood in the presence of Him who dispenses the awards of eternity. The righteous Judge approved his faith, his choice, his works, and pronounced his eulogy in a sentence that will shine above the brightness of the stars forever!

"Enter thou into the joy of thy Lord"—"the joy of" the ineffably blessed One! What mind can fathom, what tongue reveal it? We know somewhat of his joy, it is true, from the sweet notes of feathered songsters, the gentle lowing of distant herds, the hum of the bee in the flowery vale, the sporting of finny shoals in their watery way, for He is their maker, and imparts to them their happiness. We know somewhat of his joy from the innocent prattle of the dear little child, the ecstatic joy of the new-born soul, the overflowing peace of the pilgrim's heart as he stands upon some Pisgah and sings,

> "We taste a pure drop of his love,
> The life of eternity know;
> Angelical happiness prove,
> And enjoy a heaven below;"

from the seraph's shining face and grateful song, and from the bright host who, in his presence, tremble with fullness of joy, and fall down and in silence adore! We know somewhat of his joy, from the transcendent beauty and loveliness of the city where He dwells; its jasper walls and sapphire gates, its golden streets and crystal streams, its trees of life and thrones of light, its peaceful flow of unending years, forever brightening as they roll! From all these we catch a glimpse of the joy of God, but it is only a glimpse. Beyond the bright cloud that skirts his unseen glory, where angels never tread, could we go and gaze upon that which created eye hath never seen, and hear that which created ear hath never heard, and bow down close by the throbbings of His almighty heart of love, and feel its pulsations of joy, and catch the first warm outgushing from that centre and source of life, and love and bliss—but even then, without an eternity in which to quaff the exhaustless stream, we could know but little of the joy of our Lord. O! it is a theme too high for seraphs to unfold; what then can mortals do? I can only feebly point you to the rills of that infinite ocean, and tell you that in it you may bathe your weary souls forever. Into that joy Moses entered. In that joy he lives and adores to-day, and in that joy he will forever live and forever approximate in intellectual and moral improvement the glorious character and image of Him who sits upon the throne!

These, then, were the reasons and motives that influenced Moses to refuse to be called the son of Pharaoh's daughter, and choose to suffer affliction with the people of God. "The pleasures of sin are but for a season, and he had respect unto the recompense of the reward."

But the Apostle informs us, that it was by *faith* Moses gave up the wealth and pleasures of Egypt, and chose poverty and affliction with the people of God. But *faith* is not a *reason*, a *motive*, but an *instrumentality*. By it the reasons and motives we have reviewed were perceived, understood, appreciated. Faith, "the evidence of things not seen," brings nigh the remote and reveals the invisible; weighs, as in the balance of eternity, the wealth, and pleasures, and glory of earth, against the favor of God and the enduring riches and glories of the heavenly world, and shows their relation, duration, value. Hence, by the light of faith Moses saw as clearly as we now see the emptiness and transitory nature of the riches and pleasures of Egypt on the one hand, and the fullness of joy and pleasures forevermore of the presence and throne of God on the other. And without faith, or had he been a skeptic, the future, the invisible, the recompense of the reward would have been as *nonentities to him*, and the present, the tangible, would have filled his vision, and have engrossed the affections of his heart. In that case, it is more than probable that he would have been a libertine, a conqueror, a haughty, heartless tyrant. In the pleasures of sin he would have lived, and in the darkness of despair have expired. The doctrine, then, which assumes that it matters not what we believe, so our hearts are right, is not only in conflict with the word of God, but unphilosophical and absurd. Without faith, the reasons and motives to self-denial and obedience brought to light in the blessed revealments of heaven can never be perceived, and cannot, therefore, affect the heart. Heaven and hell, to the unbelieving, are as nonentities, the resurrection and the judgment as idle tales. But in the light of faith, they stand out before us as momentous realities, and wealth, and power, and pleasure assume their true character, and dwindle into insignificance. By faith, therefore, the whole current of our feelings is changed, and we walk as seeing Him who is invisible.

By faith Moses peered into the deep abyss of the eternity to which he was hastening. As a mighty panorama, heaven and hell passed before him. The bright plains and mansions of the one, bathed in the light of the glory of God, stretched away, peopled with pure, happy spirits, reposing beneath amaranthine bowers, or beside the bright waters of life, or bowing with wrapt ecstacy before the throne, the melody of whose voices and harps ravished his ear. The fathomless depths, and starless, rayless night of the other, in the dismal distance, came and went, "filled with most miserable beings," "worn and wasted with enormous woe," "forever dying, yet never dead," the wail of whose agony froze his soul with horror. He heard the shriek of its tempests of wrath, and the hiss of its burning waves! Old earth also came up before him. Her charm was broken; as hell threatend and heaven invited, he cast down and trampled under foot, her crowns, and honors, and pleasures, and chose to suffer affliction with the people of God. Wise was his choice, and ineffably glorious his reward!

We learn from this subject that man is a moral agent. Life and death are set before him. Motives and reasons are presented to his enlightened judgment that he may choose life. But in the error of his way he may shut his eyes to the light, reject the proffered good, and choose the pleasures of sin and eternal death. Moses, when he was come to years, *refused* to be called the son of Pharaoh's daughter, *choosing* to suffer affliction with the people of God. These terms certainly imply that he could have acted differently. Man, then, is not a mere automaton or an inert balance, moved only as some impulse moves him, but has in himself a self determining power. "*The spring of the soul's activity is ever within the soul,*" says an able writer of another school. "Man is constituted," says another, "*a voluntary being;* he is endowed with the *faculty of choosing*, instead of taking his place in a succession of antecedents; and, consequently, he is a *free worker*, and consciously governs his inward self independently of foreign antecedents and consequences." "In the fact of voluntariness, the fact of the power of choosing, the Almighty has conferred on man *secondary*, but, nevertheless, *real* independence." "There is nothing but the recognition of such a free agency in man, however mysterious and unaccountable, that can preserve to him *faith in himself*, or the perilous dignity of responsibility among the creatures of earth." You, then, my friends, may *choose life or death*. Nay, you can but choose, for every cherished desire, and every word and act is on the side of God and heaven, and is preparing you, by divine grace, for the inheritance of the saints in light; or is on the side of the enemy of souls, and is fitting you for a place with the damned. God help you choose the better part, and may the foundation on which you build be the Rock of Ages!

III.

PREACHING CHRIST.

BY REV. J. H. PRITCHETT,

Of the Missouri Conference.

"Whom we preach, warning every man, and teaching every man in all wisdom; that we may present every man perfect in Christ Jesus."—COL. i. 28.

True greatness is no accident of fickle fortune, no child of place or circumstance. It is the resultant of God above and the heart within, subordinating time and place and circumstance to the ends of the immortal life that is in us. It is no man's birthright; or, if any man's, under grace, it is every man's. There is no philosophy, no truth, in the threadbare solecism: "Some men are born great." There is still less in that other: "Some have greatness thrust upon them." God's gifts are without partiality, and it is neither honorable nor seemly in any man to boast of these gifts as though he had received them. He is the truly great man who realizes to the Proprietor of the universe the highest possible return for the investment made in him. Greatness, then, is the achievement of consecrated labor. Simple place has nothing to do with it; the manner of filling the place, everything. The number or character of the talents is of little consequence; the manner of using what we have, all we have, is of infinite moment. "Act well your part," solves the whole problem.

> "If done to obey God's laws,
> E'en servile labors shine;
> Hallowed is toil if this the cause,
> The meanest work divine."

On the other hand, there is an infinite littleness about the grandest human achievements when they are prompted by motives of selfishness and unholy ambition, that the philosophy of this world has never undertaken to estimate. Hence, the greatness of men is littleness with God, just as the wisdom of men is foolishness with God; and, just because these things are so, "God has chosen the foolish things of this world to confound the wise, and the weak things to confound the mighty, that no flesh should glory in his presence."

If this theory holds good as applied to men at large, it is pre-eminently true as it affects those who minister in holy things. Here there can be no mistake touching the law under which greatness is evolved. "If any man will be great among you, let him be your minister, and whosoever will be chiefest shall be servant of all:' for even the Son of Man came not to be ministered unto, but to minister."

These remarks are pertinent to the matter introduced in the text, as they furnish us with a standard by which to measure the character of its author.

If Saul of Tarsus was a very "chief of sinners," by this measure Paul the Apostle was a very prince among great men—a very Gabriel among the "angels of the churches."

Under Jesus Christ no other man's influence has been so profound, so intense, so far-reaching. If infidelity were to-day competent to disprove his divine inspiration, it would still be subjected to the severer task of accounting upon any other hypothesis for the impress which he has left upon Christianity, and, through Christianity, upon the world.

His birth, which was that of a freeman among political slaves; his natural endowments, which were second to those of no contemporary; his education, which was thoroughly Jewish, though liberally Grecian; his conversion, which is without a parallel in any age; his supernatural gifts, which were wholly peculiar to himself, have all been frequently instanced as indicative, not only of a remarkable personage, but also of a remarkable relation to the system of philosophy with which he became so suddenly, so unexpectedly, so strongly identified. His field of operations, too, covering, as it did, Western Asia, Northern Africa and Southern Europe, embracing, as it did, almost every possible variety of faith and practice, religion and government, caste and color, language and learning, has been noticed as furnishing the most ample opportunities for the right investment of his gifts, the most useful employment of his powers. The things which God thus gave to Paul, the place in which he put him, and the work which he gave him to do, certainly evidence in no small degree his infinite wisdom in adapting means to ends. But the thing which signals Paul as the great man and the model preacher of his age is that his extraordinary sphere was filled, and his heaven-tempered weapons were wielded so as to yield the largest possible revenue of honor to God, of blessing to men. In his utter abandonment of self, in the entire absorption of his powers by the cause of Him who had called him to his apostleship, he became, next to the Great Head of the Church, the embodiment of its spirit, the exponent of its doctrines, the founder of its government. As a wise master-builder he laid broad and deep the foundations of the whole Christian system; witnessing in the Spirit, " Other foundation can no man lay." And, having so well performed his own part, for the warning and instruction of each succeeding "craftsman" who might come to labor upon the walls of his beloved temple, over the main portal, in bold relief, he inscribed these startling memoranda: " Let every man take heed how he buildeth hereon; for every man's work shall be made manifest; and the fire shall try every man's work, of what sort it is. If any man's work abide which he hath built hereon he shall receive a reward. If any man's work shall be burned, he shall suffer loss." To follow the designs, then, which this spiritual Hiram has left upon the gospel "trestle-board" is always safe for those who are engaged in the glorious work of " polishing " and fitting stones for that "house eternal in the heavens." But, in whole or in part, to substitute other degrees for these is, under any circumstances, to say the least, both impertinent and presumptuous. Surely all who would be characterized by the apostle's " we " of the text, must walk according to his rule, and preach after the model which he furnishes.

In the light of the text, we proceed to examine that model now.

The language under consideration is pre-eminently Pauline. It is chockful of seed-thoughts, each of which is more precious to the true "man of God" than all the

"Gems from the mountan, and pearls from the ocean,
Myrrh from the forest, and gold from the mine."

From this rich vein I adduce, first of all, the truth, of which the whole life of our apostle, from the hour the scales fell from his eyes in Damascus to the day of his martyrdom in Rome, was but a beautiful and striking illustration, that God, in consummating a plan for saving sinners, has made it the business of some men to preach. "We preach," says the grand old missionary for the Roman empire, and his declaration was no idle boast. He did preach. With what effect, let the fallen fortunes of Diana of Ephesus, the confusion of the supreme court of Athens, the trembling slave-governor of Judea, and the almost persuaded King of Chalcis, testify. Paul believed in preaching, and showed his faith by his works. He was emphatically and pre-eminently a preacher. His faith in the world's subjugation to the authority of the Nazarene rested neither in the policy and cohorts of Ceasar, nor in the mock ministrations of an effete priesthood at an obsolete altar; but in the fulminations of the pulpit, filled with a living preacher made eloquent by the "tongue office," and baptized with the Holy Ghost sent down from heaven.

His faith knew and his practice made no compromise with the world, the flesh, or the devil. His preaching gave him the mastery of every situation — the victory in every conflict. Said he to the Corinthians, "Christ sent me to preach." As a reason for his commission to this work exclusively, he says futher: "For after that, in the wisdom of God, the world by wisdom knew not God: it pleased God by the foolishness of preaching to save them that believe."

Paul evidently expected that his successors in the Gospel ministry would, as exclusively as himself, be devoted to preaching. Said he to Timothy, "I charge thee, therefore, before God, and our Lord Jesus Christ, ... preach the word."

The world, the Church, even the ministry of to-day, have no adequate conception of the power that God has lodged in, and the results that God has ordained shall flow from, earnest, simple, faithful preaching.

Preaching, as a means, wrought all the wonders of Pentecost, and of the days that immediately succeeded in Jerusalem. Incident to the persecutions that followed the martyrdom of Stephen, the disciples went everywhere "preaching." The Church was first planted in Syria, Asia Minor, Greece, Rome, and indeed in every place by preaching; and only as faith in the eternal word, as the only means of human enlightenment and salvation, was dimmed by the glare and glitter of pride and power; only as the Church exchanged the arm of her "beloved" for an arm of flesh; only as her pulpits were substituted by altars (falsely so-called), and her preachers affected to be priests, did her glory depart, and she became the apostate, the corrupt, the abominable thing of the middle ages.

Furthermore, every prominently successful reform in the Church (instance that in Germany under Luther, that in Scotland under Knox, and that in England under Wesley,) has been effected under the auspices of bold, uncompromising, soul-searching preaching. Happy the Church whose ministers preach with an unction from God! Happy the preachers who belong to the Pauline "succession." But woe to the Church when her demand is that of the ritualistic Jew, or the rationalistic Greek. Woe to the ministry when the bold, sin-reproving, God-honoring utterances of the Gospel are displaced by the popular secularisms and morbid sentimentalisms of the age. The world to-day, east, west, north and south, needs, sadly needs, just what Paul's mission-field needed—preaching; and nothing but this will ever witness the gospel to "every creature," and gloriously usher in the "acceptable year of the Lord."

God help his servants to preach, until the apocalyptic angel, flying through the midst of heaven, shall supplement our mission and proclaim the fall of Babylon!

Another weighty truth gathered from the text is, that the Alpha and Omega of every Gospel sermon is Jesus Christ, "whom we preach." Him first, him last, him midst, him only. Says our model preacher, "I am not ashamed of the Gospel of Christ, for it is the power of God," etc. Again, "I determined to know nothing among you save Jesus Christ and him crucified." Still again, "We preach not ourselves, but Christ Jesus the

Lord." Finally, "Though we or an angel from heaven preach any other gospel unto you than that we have preached unto you, let him be accursed."

With Paul Christ was the central figure of the world's history, in fact as well as in theory. With him he was emphatically " Head over all things to the Church." Hence, the cause of Christ was to him the summation of all human interests; and the preaching of the Cross in his esteem furnished the only antidote for all the personal, domestic, social and political ills that curse the world. A few extracts, taken almost at random from his Epistles, will at once confirm and illustrate this view:

"If any man be in Christ he is a new creature. Whatsoever ye do, do all in the name of the Lord Jesus. Wives, submit yourselves to your husbands as unto the Lord; husbands, love your wives, even as Christ also loved the Church and gave himself for it; children, obey your parents in the Lord; fathers, provoke not your children to wrath, but bring them up in the nurture and admonition of the Lord; servants, be obedient to them that are your masters, according to the flesh, ... not with eye service as men-pleasers, but as the servants of Christ. Now, therefore, there is utterly a fault among you, because ye go to law one with another; why do ye not rather take wrong? Why do ye not rather suffer yourselves to be defrauded? The servant of the Lord must not strive. The weapons of our warfare are not carnal. Be not overcome of evil, but overcome evil with good. If any man have not the spirit of Christ he is none of his. If any man will live godly in Christ Jesus, he shall suffer persecution. If we suffer with him, we shall also be glorified together."

But I forbear. Be it known, however, that Paul himself never once swerved from the true philosophy of life's relations herein enunciated. Hence he soon found himself antagonized, like his divine Master, by every dominant system of earth, religious, scientific and governmental. Nor did his own personal inoffensiveness, nor did the conservative nature of his philosophy, protect him from any one of them. To the bigoted ecclesiatic his theory and practice constituted a "stumbling block." To the proud rationalist they personate "foolishness." While to the arrogant representatives of the "beast," his body became a fit subject for stripes, imprisonment and death. But to the scorn and malice of the Jew, to the sophistry and worldly wisdom of the Greek, to the scourge and sword of the Roman, Paul made but one answer: "None of these things move me; neither count I my life dear to myself, so that I might finish my course with joy and the ministry which I have received of the Lord Jesus, to testify the gospel of the grace of God. . . . God forbid that I should glory save in the cross of our Lord Jesus Christ, by whom the world is crucified unto me, and I unto the world. Let no man trouble me; I bear in my body the works of the Lord Jesus." And, whether confronting the ferocious mob in Jerusalem, or disputing with the wily disciples of Plato and Aristotle in Athens, or answering for himself before Agrippa in the court of Festus, or awaiting within his prison walls in Rome the pleasure of the bloodthirsty Nero, there was never the semblance of a compromise of his high principles. The only defense he ever made before any tribunal was to preach Jesus. Against profane and vain babblings and oppositions of science, (falsely so-called), the only argument he ever employed was, " Christ Jesus of God is made unto us wisdom, and righteousness, and sanctification, and redemption." He had no party sympathies, he made no political harangues, he glorified no human governmental system, he rode no sensational hobbies merely to lead the mob. But always, everywhere, for all ends, he preached Christ; himself the servant of all for Christ's sake: proving and alleging that he only is "Lord of lords and King of kings," and that before his judgment bar every one must appear, to be judged in the body for the things done.

Indeed, the "whom we preach" of the text but epitomizes the whole life and labors of this man of God. Here was the secret of his power. Hence sprang those ever-widening waves of influence which, continuing to bless the Church and the world throughout the history of both, will break only upon the shores of eternity.

My brethren, where are the Pauls of the nineteenth century? Where are the builders who are utilizing the foundation which he laid by heaping thereon gold and silver and precious stones? I have no fear for our foundation. The gates of hell cannot move that. I have neither time nor disposition to mind those who, in their vain pretense at building, discard, theoretically or practically, that foundation. They cannot be answered according to their folly, else we become like to them;

they cannot be answered otherwise, else they become wise in their own conceits. Too much time has thus been wasted by good men, only in making fools of themselves, or in consummating the supreme folly of others. But, oh! I do fear that much of the building that is being done to-day in the name of our great "Corner-Stone," and that, too, with the greatest possible amount of parade and self-gratulation, is nothing more than a miserable combination of wood and hay and stubble, which, at best, but serves to feed personal vanity here, and will in the end kindle the holocaust of a fruitless ministerial life. God deliver us from the insinuating strategy of the devil, already too successful, by which he persuades the church and the ministry that the ends of redemption, in whole or in part, are to be secured by compacts with human systems of philosophy and polity. In the name of the "Holy One" of Israel, and by the authority of his great apostle, I protest that there is no similarity, no congenialty, between any of these systems and our beloved Christianity. The sap that feeds the one is a deadly poison to the other. There is, there can be, no fellowship between light and darkness, no concord between Christ and Belial; religiously Christ is everything, else he is nothing. The preaching of Christ must subdue all things to him, else faith to him is vanity and labor for him is naught. The process of converting one soul is, in miniature, the process of converting the world. What these witty inventions of men cannot do in restoring one woe-blasted, sin-wrecked mariner to a haven of peace, they can never do in bringing back the race to its long-lost moorings. Christ in us "the hope of glory," in our preaching "the power of God and the wisdom of God," alone puts ministerial success beyond contingency. We but deceive ourselves and lead others astray, mistaking both the genius of our mission and the weapons of our warfare, while we predicate success of the mere accidents of personal ability, learning and the so-called helps of the age. The want of these, in a large class of our ministry, is to-day being earnestly and extensively deprecated by both preachers and people, and a large and increasing share of public attention is being constantly turned in this direction. I could not hope to divert that attention if I would—I certainly would not if I could; but I am profoundly impressed that we are suffering a thousandfold more from another want, and that the share of attention turned in that direction is neither great nor increasing. Our faith in a personal, present, reigning Christ is too weak, our zeal for that Christ is too politic, our knowledge of that Christ is too partial and superficial, to inspire us with the courage necessary to make, at all times, a square issue with the world, the flesh and the devil. We mince the truth, mingle it with soporific draughts of pleasing error, and play the part of contemptible caterers to miserably morbid appetites.

We study more, and make more strenuous efforts to be "approved" as "learned" by self-constituted savants, as "eloquent" by the proprietors of "itching ears," as "liberal" and "progressive" by gaping, ignorant, fluctuating mobs, as "loyal" by the votaries of that particular form of the "beast" that happens to be dominant, than of God, as "workmen that need not be ashamed." Oh! to see, to hear, to feel, the power of the Paul, the Luther, the Knox, the Wesley of the nineteenth century!

I notice but for a moment Paul's conception of the scope of gospel preaching, "warning every man, and teaching every man in all wisdom."

Sin best beseems itself and best bespeaks its diabolical paternity, in that it appears other than it is, both in character and fruits, to its blinded votaries. God's ministers are especially entrusted with two items of warning: 1st. All have sinned, and come short of the glory of God. 2d. The soul that sinneth shall die; thus concluding in every man's consciousness his own condemnation and death. The final and full success of every gospel ministration depends largely upon its power to develop, with God's blessing, clearly and forcibly, this consciousness. Until this is done the teachings of the gospel go for naught. They are but as pearls before swine, hence no part of ministerial duty is more important, more imperative than this; yet no part is more undesirable to himself personally, no part faithfully performed so unwelcome to his auditors, and no part, I grieve to say, upon which compromise is so often made between preacher and people.

Few men love to be reproved, rebuked, warned; and, though the wise man tells us that "open rebuke is better than secret love; that faithful are the wounds of a friend, but the kisses of an enemy are deceitful;" still, for the time being, men generally prefer the latter to the former; and there is no surer way to incur most men's displeasure, to make them your enemies, than by telling them the truth concerning themselves. Notwithstanding this, he who has a care of souls has no option; he must declare the whole counsel of God, he must warn every man, he must hear the words at God's mouth, and speak them to warn the people, otherwise blood will be upon his head. Moreover, men are ready to be taught the things of God only when they have accepted God's warning. Then, too, we find they are always anxious to be taught the things which make for peace. It is a provision of infinite mercy that man is a creature of education, that his powers are flexible, and yield to influences from without; that he may unlearn what he has learned amiss, and learn what is transformingly opposite in its nature.

This age is not deficient in knowledge, nor is it a stranger to the experience expressed in the proverb, "knowledge is power;" but, like the early, so the later " fruit of that forbidden tree, whose mortal taste brought death into the world, and all our woe," bears all the marks of illegitimacy, and is far more potent for evil than for good. Man's self-assumed knowledge of religion is evil. Better be an ignorant Hottentot than a conceited, atheistic Comte. Man's pretended knowledge of science is evil. Better be as stupid as a Chinaman—as ignorant of the laws of matter as a South Sea Islander, than to pretentiously affect a wisdom concerning any of God's works contrary to and contradictory of what he has revealed.

Man's knowledge of political economy is primarily and essentially full of evil. Better live the life of a Russian serf, or die as ignorant of the science of government as a Congo slave, than assert and undertake to maintain the "divine right" of the "Beast" under any of his multiplied forms, thus putting loyalty to "Cæsar" upon a par with loyalty to Christ, and making that virtue which Christ denounces as crime.

Human knowledge, as such, I repeat, is full of evil. It could not be otherwise, while the immutable law holds good, "An evil tree cannot bring forth good fruit; the stream cannot rise above the fountain; the effect must be like the cause." Truth, divine truth, such as the gospel alone contains, such as the true man of God alone preaches, can cure this evil; nothing else can. It is the duty and privilege of the preacher of the cross to teach truth, to teach it in "all wisdom." "Wisdom," says the apostle, not such as the world teacheth, "but which the Holy Ghost teacheth." Such teaching is best accomplished, not by affecting the metaphysician and hastening to meet such dreamers as Kant and Comte, Hegel and John Stewart Mill, "upon their own ground;" not by following the tortuous trail of Darwin and Huxley, Tyndall and Thomson, that their fond conceits may be exposed in detail; not by dabbling in the muddy waters of political strife, championing this set of government notions or that; nay, verily, but by inculcating the precepts and example of Jesus of Nazareth. "The wisdom that is from above," the wisdom which is not a libel upon its own name, "is first pure, then peaceable, gentle, easy to be entreated, full of mercy and good fruits, without partiality and without hypocrisy. "Let the potsherds of earth strive with earth's potsherds." The gospel furnishes its humblest minister with a higher plane of thought, a more direct path to all truth, and a more general, practical and efficient system of political economy. The teaching that becomes the pulpit, that will correct all human errors, that will never grow obsolete, and of which Paul's is the model, is on this wise:

"Repentance toward God, and faith in our Lord Jesus Christ. Seek first the kingdom of God and his righteousness. All things whatsoever ye would that men should do to you, do ye even so to them. Let not the wise man glory in his wisdom; neither let the mighty man glory in his might; let not the rich man glory in his riches; but let him that glorieth glory in this, that he understandeth and knoweth me, sayeth the Lord.' When the pulpit everywhere becomes the radiator, and the Church everywhere becomes the practical expositor of this teaching, then, and not till then, may we hope to at least approximate those results so long prayed for by both.

I shall conclude with a brief notice of the end of gospel preaching: "That we may present every man perfect in Christ Jesus." An end truly worthy of the means employed to reach it.

What a wonderful history, what a glorious consummation has the gospel! "Jesus Christ, by the grace of God, tasted death for every man." The Holy Spirit convinces every man of sin, of righteousness and of judgment. The word teaches every man how to flee the wrath to come.

What a comment is here upon the worth and possibilities of an immortal soul!

> "God, to reclaim it, did not spare
> His well-beloved Son;
> Jesus, to save it, deigned to bear
> The sins of all in one.
>
> "The Holy Spirit sealed the plan,
> And pledged the blood divine
> To ransom every soul of man—
> That price was paid for mine.
>
> "And is this treasure borne below
> In earthen vessels frail?
> Can none its utmost value know,
> Till flesh and spirit fail?
>
> "Then let us gather round the cross,
> That knowledge to obtain;
> Not by the soul's eternal loss,
> But everlasting gain."

The blood, the spirit, the word of Christ can make every man perfect. "Thanks be to God for his unspeakable gift;" and "Blessed be the God and Father of our Lord Jesus Christ," that he has ever counted any "worm of the dust" worthy the high privilege of presenting this gift to his fellow sinners, with the glad hope of finally presenting them, and of being presented with them, before the throne of the Father, "perfect in Christ Jesus."

My brethren; it is true—I feel it, I know it—the humblest preacher of the gospel is greater than the mightiest monarch of earth. Because He whose word is the immutable law of heaven and earth has said, " he that converteth a sinner from the error of his ways shall save a soul from death and shall hide a multitude of sins." Earth's mightiest achievement is as child's play to this. It may not seem so now, but, my hearers, the dawn of the day is hastening, in the light of which God will fully vindicate the wisdom of those who count all things loss for the excellency of the knowledge of Christ—when " they that be teachers shall shine as the brightness of the firmament, and they that turn many to righteousness as the stars forever and ever." And now, " unto him that loved us and washed us from our sins in his own blood, and hath made us kings and priests unto God and his Father, to him be glory and dominion forever and ever. Amen."

IV.
THE TRIAL OF CHRIST, THEN AND NOW; BEFORE PILATE AND YOU.

BY REV. W. M. PROTTSMAN,

Of the West St. Louis Conference.

"Knowest thou not that I have power to crucify thee, and have power to release thee?"—JOHN xix. 10.

One of the most remarkable features of the trial of Jesus Christ was the five points of his defence by Pilate himself. We may well pause and examine ourselves when we find in the very crucifier of Jesus his own advocate.

What is our relation to Christ? is the question of most importance. Are we his advocates? Ah! and are we also his crucifiers? Do we gather with him? Do we scatter abroad, or do we both? True, indeed, we cannot serve God and mammon, but we think we can. A careful review of the trial of Christ will reveal the fact that it is still going on; that Pilate has his representative in every one to whom Christ Jesus is preached; that, like Pilate, all who hear the words of salvation virtually preside at the trial and sit in judgment, and render their decision for or against the Savior. In short, all, like Pilate, must hang their sins or their Savior on the cross. These important facts we learn from certain laws of our nature and from the history of the trial. We can but only glance at these certain laws of our nature, which seem to necessitate a decision on the important question of salvation by Jesus Christ. Wherever there is authority there is a corresponding responsibility. Office, whether municipal or otherwise, confers authority, and this includes responsibility; and as is the degree of authority so is the responsibility. The accident of office enters not into the law of man's life, except as it may increase the degree of his obligations to his fellow-man—obligations which are based upon relations and principles not quite as uncertain as office.

The highest authority on earth is the breath of life: "And the Lord God formed man of the dust of the ground, and breathed into his nostrils the breath of life, and man became a living soul." All office, whether in Church or State, is simply when he takes the servant's place. On his individuality hangs his responsibility; and in regard to his salvation this includes the necessity of decision. So perfect is the great plan of human redemption in its adaptation to all the wants of man, and to all the laws of his moral constitution, that he may reject it, he may despise it, but accept or reject it he must—on the cross he must hang his sins or his Savior. This necessity of decision is plainly seen in the repeated attempts of Pilate to evade the trial of Christ and throw off his responsibility in the matter. "A double-minded man" he was, "unstable in all his ways," constantly alternating between hope and fear, duty and self-interest. But, notwithstanding his evasions, the unseen hand of necessity would press the case upon him, as if determined to coerce the decision for or against. That trial has not ceased, and will not till the last man for whom Christ died shall have accepted or rejected him. Every hour men are receiving or rejecting him; and we fear many are "crucifying to themselves the Son of God afresh, and putting him to an open shame." Bringing Christ, the prisoner, unto Pilate's judgment hall, it is said "they themselves went not into the hall, lest they should be defiled." They were already defiled with the blood of innocence, for they had pronounced the sentence of death upon him. The high-priest had said to the council, "what further need have we of witnesses: what think ye? And they answered, He is guilty of death." The malignant piety of these self-righteous members of the Sanhedrim, which feared pollution from the touch of a heathen, may well suggest in us an examination for that true humility wherein Christ is glorified on earth. This standing aloof through fear of contamination has become so common that it is claiming divine right from its age and respectability. It were certainly more to its credit to claim respectability from divine right.

Ye are the salt of the earth; and should the salt stand aloof from the flesh lest it be corrupted? Ye are the light of the world; and shall the light stand aloof from darkness lest it be obscured?

These chief priests and elders, it would seem, had one virtue left—that of decision, and this they used speedily, and that to condemn. So far, however, as the execution of their own sentence is concerned, they seem to hesitate, or, perhaps, seek to involve the Roman government in their guilt. They said, "It is not lawful for us to put any man to death." But they had the power of life and death, and made use of it about a year afterward in the case of Stephen. But they desired the concurrence of the Roman governor that they might make our Savior undergo a more severe and ignominious punishment than they could have inflicted upon him by their own power, because crucifixion was a death unknown to their law. For this purpose, and to induce the governor to comply with their demand, the accusation which they brought against him was of a civil nature, and such as would consign him to the punishment they desired: "We found this fellow perverting the nation, and forbidding to give tribute to Cæsar." Pilate's previous bad character led them to presume on the immediate fulfillment of their desires. But how surprised must they have been when the stern judge demanded, "*What accusation do you bring against this man?*" Could an advocate of Christ put his claims, his gospel, or any part of the great plan of salvation before an unbelieving world in a more proper form than this question of Pilate? What accusation do you bring against his religion, against his doctrines, against his principles of human government, against the only condition of salvation—faith in him as the Son of the living God and your Savior? Are you silent? Do you bring no accusation, not even against his divinity? Then why not embrace him? If you have one interest paramount to all others, it is the salvation of your soul, and this is surely the last thing that should remain undetermined. Whatever else may be undecided, this should be settled, and must be. You have power to crucify and power to release him; sooner or later the choice must be made. If it involve sacrifice, better your health suffer than your soul die; better be bankrupt than be damned; better suffer with him here than reign with his enemies hereafter; better let men kill the body than fall unprepared into the hands of that God who can destroy both soul and body in hell.

The answer of Christ's accusers to the inquiry of the judge is the expression of infidelity everywhere: "If he were not a malefactor we would not have delivered him unto thee." Men who will not take upon themselves the trouble of searching diligently for the truth amidst the various contending claims, jump to their conclusions, and often find that hasty conclusions are enduring errors. From the well-known character of Pilate no one supposed he would hesitate in giving judgment against the prisoner; therefore, his accusers were wholly unprepared, and even confounded, when he manifested a disposition to deal justly, and called for evidence of the guilt of the accused. In their confusion they manufacture testimony, and, as is often the case, overreach themselves in the matter. They charge the prisoner with "sedition," beginning at Galilee. They are snared in their own falsehood, in that Galilee was not in the jurisdiction of Pilate, but in that of Herod. Pilate now saw his opportunity, as he supposed, to evade the trial and escape a decision that might involve serious consequences. He at once dismissed the whole matter from his court by sending all to Herod. Whatever his convictions of duty, justice, and his responsibities in the matter, he now felt that he was relieved of them all. Whatever should be the fate of the prisoner, or of the cause of truth in his case, were of little consequence compared with his own safety.

Pilate has never wanted for representatives in this watchful care of himself and manifest disposition to evade a decision on the trial of Christ. When the claims of the religion of Jesus Christ have been before you, his name offered you as the only plea under heaven whereby you can be saved, his blood the only means of being cleansed from all sin, like Pilate, you send the cause of Christ away. When the gospel points to your ambition endangering your soul, your love of gain estranging you from God, your pride lifting you above God, your strong passions, your unholy companions, your loose and unsettled principles, your skeptical thoughts, your love of self, your exposure to death, and all endangering your salvation, and you are urged to a decision in favor of Jesus Christ, you turn the whole matter over to your neighbor. Be not deceived; you have not found rest when you expected it; an evasion is not a decision; the case will come back to you as it came to Pilate. How exceedingly cautious we should be in guarding against the insinuations of self in religious matters. Pilate had mingled the blood of some Galileans with the sacrifices at the time of the Passover at Jerusalem, which act Herod had resented as an indignity put upon him and an invasion of his authority. As a question of state, this act was operating to the prejudice of Pilate, and at the mention of Galilee he saw not only, as he supposed, an opportunity to evade a troublesome case, but a chance to restore himself to favor with Herod, and immediately turned Jesus Christ to his own personal account by sending him to Herod.

Herod's examination was only a personal affair, for he feared that Jesus Christ was John the Baptist risen from the dead. His fears quieted on the subject of his murder of John, he sends the prisoner back to Pilate. Pilate said he had power to crucify him and power to release him. So he had, and he must use it. What is all power but a name, if it be not exercised. His subterfuge failed; the case is before him again. Pilate now addressed himself to the priests and rulers of the people, telling them that, though they had brought this man before him as a seditious person and a seducer of the people, yet, upon examination, he could not find him guilty of any of the crimes. In short, he told them that he "found no fault in him," and bade them take him and judge him according to their own law. They cried out that it was not lawful for them to put any man to death, and that Jesus ought to die because he made himself the Son of God.

This effort of Pilate to rid himself of the case by proposing to send it to an ecclesiastical court having failed, he addressed himself more seriously to the consideration of the matter. These last words, " he made himself the Son of God," no doubt gave Pilate great uneasiness, for, taking them in such a sense as a heathen might well put upon them, he feared that if he gave sentence against him, he might destroy not only an innocent person, but possibly some hero or mighty demi-god, and so at once commit both an act of injustice and impiety. Therefore, taking Jesus to the judgment seat he inquired, "Whence art thou?" It being no part of our Saviour's intention to escape death, he said nothing in his own justification. When Pilate inquired of Christ concerning his title as king of the Jews, he informed him that "his kingdom was not of this world," therefore it had nothing to do with men's temporal interests or privileges; it left rulers and subjects in the same condition it found them, and, therefore, no object of jealousy to any government. In short, his kingdom was not of a secular nature, but related wholly to spiritual and heavenly things, and would be supported entirely by spiritual sanctions and authority.

Perceiving a disposition in the govenor to release the prisoner, the Jews made a direct appeal to his fears by crying out, "*If thou let this man go thou art not Cæsar's friend.*" A powerful menace, indeed, for one who knew the jealous temper of his master Tiberius, and how a wrong representation of the proceedings might prove his ruin. Observe how seriously Pilate comes to the judgment seat when this cry from Satan's kingdom falls on his ear. His office and his salvation both confront him now. And never did he see anything clearer than he now saw his power to crucify and to release. And these powers became conflicting claims that pressed upon him like the hand of necessity.

You are no stranger to his situation. The kingdom of Christ has been unfolded to you; its nature explained; its government set forth; the conditions of salvation presented; and pardon offered on the plain and easy terms of faith in the Lord Jesus Christ. You have been admonished of the allurements of the world; of the arts of a cunning and subtle foe; of the deceitfulness of your own hearts, and of the propensity to delay—all endangering your salvation. The shortness of time, the certainty of death, the error of procrastination and the danger of delay have been faithfully presented to you. The fullness and the freeness of the grace of God have been shown you, and all offered you on the easy terms of acceptance. Jesus Christ has been presented to you as your Saviour, who suffered death upon the cross for your redemption—who made then full satisfaction for the sins of the whole world. And you have been urged, begged, pleaded by all the interests of your immortal soul to accept him as your Redeemer. In the matter of conscious convictions your case and that of Pilate are similar. The sense of right, of justice, of duty, by the silent force of conviction, pressed heavily upon him. And your own consciousness now carries the impressions of your convictions of the same character. But "if thou let this man go thou art not Cæsar's friend." If you acquit Jesus Christ of the charges which infidelity brings against him you are no friend of the world. The world now puts in its claims. All that can please the ear, the fancy, the passions, the lust of the heart or the pride of life, now pass in inviting review. Ambition, avarice, worldly honor and fame, all appeal to the depraved feelings and desires of a nature always bent on ruin. The restraints which virtue and true religion impose are now held up to view in most unfavorable light. Religion is presented to you as a most unreasonable restraint upon the pleasures of life. Burdens to be borne, crosses to be taken up, and uneasy yokes to be worn, are held up as the sum and substance of Christianity. Sin is clad in her beautiful robes, and all that is fascinating on earth is presented to you; and then the generous offer made, "All these things will I give thee if thou wilt fall down and worship me."

Such was the pressure now brought to bear upon Pilate that his weak nature would, perhaps, have immediately yielded, and his power to crucify been exercised in his decision. Surely the moral government of God shall be fully vindicated at his judgment bar. It will then appear that not only are all men endowed with power to crucify and power to release, but that God, in his infinite goodness and mercy, bestows all needed grace and truth to bring us to the knowledge of salvation. When the pressure of the menace, "thou art not Cæsar's friend," was about to compel Pilate to condemn the prisoner, against his convictions of justice, a most powerful reminder of the momentous consequences of an unjust decision, and of his sworn obligation to do right, confronted him in the message of his wife, "Have thou nothing to do with that just man, for I have suffered many things this day in a dream because of him." Strong indeed must be the power of resistance to the truth when the unmistakable force of inspiration alone can bring conviction. This dream, which was providentially sent upon Pilate's wife for the clearer manifestation of our Lord's innocence, must have removed every remaining doubt from Pilate's mind.

To know the right is not always to do it. The truth alone is not sufficient to lead the heart from sin to holiness. Nothing is more common than for the human mind to turn its back upon a truth, firmly believed to be from God, deeply felt to carry eternal hopes, but demanding the sacrifice of present gratifications, or of the friendship of the world. Mere conviction never carries a point of practical moral conduct. With every evidence given of the innocence of the prisoner that the skeptical mind could ask, and given in a manner not even admitting of doubt, by inspiration, by the hand of a wife, Pilate still sees self, and self only. Having the power to release, and the full, clear and distinct conviction that he ought to release, he sets himself to work to find another expedient to evade a decision, save the prisoner from death, and, what was of far more importance to him, save himself in the eye of Cæsar.

How true it is that all men seek first their worldly prosperity. They know nothing equal to that. Everything is made to give way to it. The cause of Christ must wait for that and is only held secondary to it. This desire to subordinate all things to self is a pit into which those who dig it often fall themselves. It was sadly and fatally so in the case of Pilate. For popular favor he himself instituted the custom of pardoning one condemned criminal at every Passover, whom the Jews should nominate. The feast of the Passover was celebrated by the Jews in memory of their deliverance from Egyptian bondage. So shrewd a politician as Pontius Pilate soon saw how very agreeable to the nature of that feast would be the deliverance from bondage of a criminal at the time of its celebration. But however much of favor or compliment he pretended to the Jews, he meant it only as a matter of popularity for himself; and now, when the clear conviction of the iniquity of the persecutors of Jesus came upon him, and the innocence of the accused was made manifest to him, and truth, justice and conscience all demanded the release of the prisoner, but self-interest cried, "If thou let this man go thou art not Cæsar's friend," he thought of the "custom," and seized upon it as a subterfuge to save himself and carry his prisoner away with him. Here was Pilate's fatal error. At every stage of the trial some strong and sure conviction would seize him of the innocence of his prisoner, but every conviction was immediately met by some appeal to his pride, lusts or worldly desires. And thus his self-interest, leading his indecision, kept him vacillating between a clear conviction of duty and the hope of safety by a course of conduct manifestly wrong. The unseen danger is often the most fatal danger. Pilate's fall was just before him, and yet he saw it not. The Jews asked only condemnation at the hands of Pilate; the execution of the sentence was an easy matter. The very offer of Pilate to release the prisoner by pardon presupposed condemnation. Who ever heard of pardon for one on trial and uncondemned? This was but adding insult to injury. The Jews saw Pilate's mistake, saw their opportunity, seized upon it and cried, "Not this man, but Barabbas." Pilate now saw his error, but saw it too late—saw that in his weak, time-serving effort to save the prisoner he had condemned him.

The cry of the mob, "crucify him! crucify him!" startled him to a consciousness of his fatal error. When Pilate saw that he could prevail nothing, but that rather a tumult was made, he took water and washed his hands before the multitude, saying, "I am innocent of the blood of this just person." A basin of water to wash the blood of innocence from his guilty hands! Not all the waters of Neptune's great oceans or Noah's greater flood could wash that blood from his guilty soul!

Look now at the result of indecision—of trifling with the most sacred truths, and stifling the deepest convictions. With you this trial must end. You are invested with a responsibility that absolutely necessitates the decision to crucify or release the Lord of life. You have been hesitating and doubting; undetermined whether to acknowledge Jesus Christ as Lord of all and Savior of the world, or whether to bow down to the god of this world. You hold to the world because it imposes no restraints; the way to office, fame and wealth depends upon conformity to it, and great license is given to the indulgence of corrupt passions. On the other hand, you have the evidence of the truth of the religion of Jesus Christ, the conviction of conscience that his religion is pure and holy. Vacillating between these conflicting claims, you present the sad spectacle of patronizing all systems and embracing none—looking with equal complacency on antagonistic religions, professing liberality to all, and manifesting preference for none. You look at the cross of Christ and see around it all the happy effects which it produces. You hear all the arguments from miracle and prophecy in its favor, and all the offers which it makes of an eternal heaven; you are thrilled with the hope of the joys it offers, and yet you will not let go of the world long enough to embrace it. And, on the other hand, all the influence of pride of heart and the love of fancied liberty, all the power of corrupting passion and the desire of indulgence in sin, prompting you to cast off the restraints of religion, crowd upon you, fill your mind and consume your time, and yet you will not entirely close your eye to the cross of Christ. Standing on what you term neutral ground, you are in reality at the farthest point from Jesus Christ. There is no art which Satan practices that evinces more skill and cunning than in retaining such persons on what is deemed neutral ground, and in preventing, by a thousand pleas, their giving their names and their influence to the cause of true religion.

Now, what is before you? Your sins, your Savior and the cross. You have the power to crucify, and you have the power to release. *On the cross you must hang your sins or your Savior!* Thus far you follow the track and example of Pilate with great precision. Shall his error and final decision be yours? There is nothing in the question which you are called upon to decide to warrant your indecision. It is simply *for* or *against;*

but between the two there is no place to rest the sole of your foot or the soul of your immortal being. The simple question is, whether you will depend on Jesus Christ for salvation or not, for you cannot depend on him and on yourself. Whether you will forsake your sins or not, for you cannot be saved while you cleave to them. Whether you will live to God or to yourself, for you cannot do both. Whether you shall love Christ or crucify him! Even to entertain this question is deeply sinful; and on such a question as this you hesitate and are in doubt. Truly a most alarming state. You hesitate not in your heart to crucify; you hesitate only in the act. By every principle of the law of God you are already condemned.

The law of God does not rest the offence in the degree, but in the spirit; and establishes it not by evidence of fact, but by evidence of conscience anterior to fact. It is in the state of vindictiveness in the soul, and not in the thousand vindictive acts, that God sees the sins; and in the state of wantonness in the soul, and not in the thousand impure acts — in these first conceptions of evil God finds the criminality. In the sight of heaven crime is perpetrated long ere it proclaims itself in the act. The law is, therefore, addressed to the spirit, from which nothing is hid of its own designs or transactions, of which designs not the thousandth part ever sees the light. So that God's laws, though a thousand times less numerous, apply to a thousand times more cases than the laws of man. Seeing, then, that into the secret place of the heart nothing penetrates but conscience and the eye of God, these two alone can arbitrate the matter.

In conclusion, we ask, will you ever be in circumstances more favorable for a decision than the present time? Have you the least ground of hope that if you evade a decision just now, the case will not soon come back to you again? You have all the revelation that can ever shed light on your path, all that will ever be given you to aid you in coming to a decision. On every question of this character raised by Pilate, Jesus Christ was silent. The evidence before him was as full and complete as the wants of Pilate and the full vindication of the moral government of God could demand. The word of life is in your dwellings and in your hands; the lamp of salvation shines on your way. There will be no new prophet sent into the world; no Pilate's wife more potent than the "still small voice" that has so often said, " have thou nothing to do with that just man." The present is the only time which you may have to decide this matter. To-morrow may find you in another world. Your long delay, your hesitancy and your indecision may provoke the Almighty to come forth in judgment, and cut you down as a cumberer of the ground.

And now we bring our closing appeal to your decision, in behalf of the Divine clothed in the raiment of the flesh. He puts on your own nature that he may be touched with the feeling of your infirmities. He opens up the heart of God, and shows its boundless tenderness to his fallen creatures. He opens up his own heart, and shows it devoted to death for your life. He opens his lips, and loving-kindness drops upon your bitter hatred. He stills the elements above your head and makes your stormy heart a calm. Your mourning he turns to joy, and brings you hope from beyond the grave.

"This is the stone which was set at naught of you builders, which is become the head of the corner. Neither is there salvation in any other; for there is none other name under heaven given among men whereby we must be saved."

> There is a time, you know not when,
>   A point, you know not where,
> That marks the destiny of men
>   To glory or despair.
>
> There is a time, by you unseen,
>   That crosses every path—
> The hidden boundary between,
>   God's patience and his wrath.
>
> O, where is this mysterious bourne
>   By which your path is crossed,
> Beyond which God himself hath sworn
>   That he who goes is lost?
>
> An answer from the skies is sent —
>   Ye that from God depart,
> While it is called to-day, repent,
>   And harden not your heart!

V.
THE GLORY OF THE CHURCH.

BY REV. H. A. BOURLAND,

Of the Missouri Conference.

"The king's daughter is all glorious within: her clothing is of wrought gold. She shall be brought unto the king in raiment of needlework: the virgins, her companions that follow her, shall be brought unto thee."—PSALM xlv. 13, 14.

This prophetic song celebrates the relation between Christ and his Church. There is a magnificence of diction and wealth of poetic imagery befitting so high a theme. The King of Glory is the royal bridegroom who is portrayed as leading the Church, the chaste bride, to the sacred nuptials. The dignity of Godhood is blended with the condescension of the man, Christ Jesus, in these epithalmic strains: "Gird thy sword upon thy thigh, O most mighty, with thy glory and thy majesty. And in thy majesty ride prosperously, because of truth and meekness and righteousness, and thy right hand shall teach thee terrible things." As the glory of the Church is so associated with the glory of her Lord, the supreme deity of Christ is stated in the strongest terms. "Thy throne, O God, is forever and ever. The sceptre of thy kingdom is a right sceptre." The Elohim here seated upon a throne to endure forever, and swaying a sceptre of universal dominion, is the same who in the beginning created the heavens and the earth. If there could be any doubt of the Messianic character of this psalm, it would be set at rest by the use made of this verse by the Apostle, (Heb. i. 8,) who applies it to Christ.

Heaven had but one purpose in view in the incarnation, teachings, death and resurrection of the Son of God. That sublime purpose, pre-arranged in the counsels of eternity, foreshadowed in the sacrifices of slain victims, and typified in the purifications of the temple, was to wash away the stains of sin. Christ came to earth to seek and espouse a pure Church—"a glorious Church, not having spot or wrinkle or any such thing, but that it should be holy and without blemish." The text is a prophecy which is but partially fulfilled. The full realization of the ideal Church is still reserved for the future, when there shall be one fold and one shepherd, and a pure language shall be turned upon Zion. The Church is coeval with the fall, and has gradually expanded with the lapse of ages. The world has never been without a divine revelation, and to make this revelation of the will of God known to all there have always been some divinely called and commissioned. Thus, from Abel to Noah, and from Noah to Moses, and onward through the prophets, God has at sundry times and in divers manners spoken to his people, and through them to the world. Every true believer, in whose heart is set up the kingdom of God, whether he be Papist or Protestant, bond or free, is a member of Christ's body, which is the Church. Every congregation of such true believers in which the pure word of God is preached, and the sacraments duly administered according to Christ's ordinance, is a Gospel Church.

The glory of the Church consisteth not in outward circumstances, neither in numbers nor wealth, the patronage of the great, the glitter of her temples nor the decorations of her altars. The true glory of the Church consisteth:

I. IN FIDELITY TO TRUTH. During nearly six thousand years there has been a relentless strife between truth and falsehood. The conflict began when the woman yielded her belief in the truth of God, and credited the gilded lie of the serpent. The divine Logos entered the lists as the champion of truth, and has been waging war upon error ever since. Take this key and go abroad, and unlock the mystery which shrouds the dealings of heaven with man. The Mohammedanism of the East and the Mormonism of our own Continent, the pretensions of Zoroaster and Confucius, the charlatanry of "science," falsely so-called, and the lying pomp and vanities of the world opposed to God, are all founded in a fierce antagonism to truth. Truth, like the treasured ores hid away from common sight, must be dug up at the expense of labor; but toil will be richly compensated, and the earnest seeker will become the joyful finder in due time. The Church is entrusted with objective truth, and is successful in the highest sense only as her creed agrees therewith; therefore, we have the injunction, " earnestly contend for the faith once delivered to the saints " — not the saints canonized by ecclesiastical courts of the post-apostolic ages, but the faith delivered by the "sent of God" and inspired writers. St. Paul would let a burning curse fall upon the head of an angel should he preach any other gospel than that he had received of the Lord Jesus. Every system, whether of philosophy or religion, has a few cardinal principles which give it character. Out of these flow sequences which are more or less tinged with the character of the fountain. The chalybeate spring may divide into many minor streams, and mingle with other waters, but the iron is there, and exerts its influence in the new combination. No high development of Christian life can be reached without sound beliefs as the basis. The Synod of Dort, which announced its five points of doctrine, sowed the seed of an immense harvest of exclusiveness and bigotry, and has led many into such contracted views of the atonement and the operations of divine grace, which have proven alike dishonoring to God and damaging to the hopes and interests of immortal souls. Superficial views of sin lead to the wildest vagaries of doctrine, and the greatest laxity of morals. If sin be a *state of the heart* which is enmity itself against God, then it must be eradicated, or the soul forever banished from his presence and the glory of his power; and around this doctrine cluster all the precious truths of the word of God. But if sin be a *disease*, as we are gravely told, revelation is a fiction, and the glory of the cross is obscured. The Bible is the religion of Protestant Christianity, and the Church has only to publish it in full confidence that it is *the truth*, with an emphasis that will make it felt, and it will work out its own demonstration.

Never before was error more rife than in this restless age, and against the whelming floods of materialistic ideas the Church is to oppose a breakwater, saying to these angry waters, in the name of our God: "Hitherto shalt thou come but no further, and here shall thy proud waves be stayed." The doctrines of revelation are being subjected to the severest tests, and the words of the Psalmist are being gloriously vindicated: "The words of the Lord are pure words—as silver tried in a furnace of earth, purified seven times." The Church is to be as true to truth as the needle to the pole, otherwise disaster will come upon her, and she shall be brought in deepest humiliation to bewail her unfaithfulness; but God will have his witnesses, and will work by whom he chooses. It was a Latin maxim, "Truth, by whomsoever spoken, comes from God. It is, in short, a divine essence." But the truth, in its unmixed purity, came through Jesus Christ. For this purpose was he born, and spent three years in the ministry of his own everlasting gospel, that he might bear witness to the truth. It is not only the duty of the Church to proclaim the truth, but it is imperative upon *her alone*, since no other institution proposes to discharge so comprehensive a work as teaching "the whole counsel of God." The school professes to educate the mind in the useful and ornamental arts of life, and induct the intellect into the temple of science, and cultivate the æsthetical susceptibilities of our being. The social and benevolent institutions teach truth of a certain kind, veiled in allegory and illustrated in expressive symbols; but these do not pretend to adjust man's relations to

God, and impart a kind of information that will survive the umbrage of death, and be of service in the higher range of thought that awaits the soul beyond the Lethean waters of death. The Church is the pillar and the ground of truth, not by the publication of formulated dogmas of comparative theology, or the multiplication of articles of religion, or proclaiming ever and anon, as Romanism has done, some new tenet, but by holding fast that form of sound doctrine which the canon of Divine Revelation contains.

> "Within this awful volume lies
> The mystery of mysteries.
> O! happiest they of human race
> To whom our God has given grace
> To read, to watch, to fear, to pray,
> To lift the latch, and force the way;
> But better had they ne'er been born
> Who read to doubt, or read to scorn."

II. THE GLORY OF THE CHURCH IS IN HER INWARD PURITY AND POWER. "The king's daughter is all glorious within." Nothing in the eyes of an honorable man can substitute purity in woman, above all, in that one whom he has promised to love and cherish. The Church as a chaste virgin is espoused to Christ, and it is only as the Church is pure that it is lovely in his sight. Not the elegant millinery of her priesthood, nor the intoned service, nor chasuble, nor surplice, nor dim religious lights delight the God who looks upon the inner man, and reads the thoughts, and to whom the most acceptable sacrifices are broken hearts and contrite spirits. When the Church has lost its heart-purity it has ever sought to hide its deformity by these outward trappings. In vain does Israel carry out the ark of God to the battle unless the Lord is between the cherubim. "The kingdom of God is not in word, but in power." As in nature the most potent influences are the most quiet and unobserved; as heat, which sends the juices through vegetation, and robes the forest, and clothes the plains in vernal loveliness; as electricity, which vitalizes the decaying forces in matter; as gravitation, which binds atom to atom, and links star to star and system to system, and sends them circling around their respective centres: all these, silently working, are God's greatest agents in nature. The Church is glorious when clothed with power. There can be no argument against a holy life; the good man's influence is like a caravan bearing sweet spices; the very atmosphere where he moves is fragrant with perfumes, and when he goes to his reward his memory and name is like ointment poured forth. Like the lign aloe which dies at an advanced age amidst clusters of blossoms, which it took years to mature, the good die amidst the praises of souls led to Christ through their instrumentality. Upon the subject of inward holiness it behooveth all to know what is taught, for the full measure of usefulness can never be reached by the Church until the people of God are holy in heart and life and all manner of conversation. Some place this state so high it is unattainable by the dwellers on earth, who are compassed with infirmities. It is not angelic, much less is it absolute; but it is, in brief epitome, the

THE GLORY OF THE CHURCH.

supreme love of God, and the love of man as ourself. To reach such a state requires "the gift of power." "The love of God is shed abroad in the heart by the Holy Ghost." It is "the fruit of the Spirit." The same power that can sanctify a soul wholly, can preserve it blameless until the coming of Christ. Whatever of prejudice there may be arrayed against this experience, it should yield before the majesty of the word of God.

Does this inspired volume teach anything upon this subject? If it does not, it is most remarkable that a large denomination should have had its birth in the promulgation of this very doctrine, and feel itself especially charged with its advocacy in all lands. If it is taught it behooves us to know the truth, and the truth will make us free. It avails nothing to object to any truth that unworthy persons have held it, or it has been the occasion of fanaticism. Such an objection would hold with equal force against any doctrine of the Scriptures. Almost every book of the inspired canon teaches something upon this subject, either by precept, promise or example. Enoch, among the patriarchs, by faith walked with God three centuries, and had meanwhile this testimony, that he pleased God. Job was a perfect man. Moses, by inspiration, makes this glowing promise to Israel: "The Lord thy God will circumcise thine heart, and the heart of thy seed, to love the Lord thy God with all thine heart, and with all thy soul, that thou mayest live."

Ezekiel, among the prophets, utters the same language in the name of the Lord: "Then will I sprinkle clean water upon you and ye shall be clean; from all your filthiness and from all your idols will I cleanse you."

But what says Christ? "Blessed are the poor in spirit; for theirs is the kingom of heaven." Is, this promise true? "Blessed are they that mourn; for they shall be comforted." Will the mourner be comforted? "Blessed are the meek; for they shall inherit the earth." Shall the meek thus inherit the earth? "Blessed are they which do hunger and thirst after righteousness; for they shall be filled." "Blessed are the pure in heart; for they shall see (enjoy) God." If the other beatitudes hold good, will not these also? Then if the soul is filled with righteousness it is not filled with sin, and if the heart is pure it cannot at the same time be impure. The unscripturalness hence appears of those who earnestly contend that the hearts of sincere believers are necessarily full of sin; that it cleaves like leprosy to every word and act, and extends down to all the thoughts. All distinction is thus broken down between the believer in Christ and the sinner; righteousness is a myth; virtue is no more virtue, but vice.

The heart is the battle-ground of a fearful conflict between heaven and the powers of darkness. Is it possible in this strife that Satan is generally victorious? Then is the power of the vanquished serpent greater than the omnipotence of the Son of God. Did not our Lord rest his claims of divinity on his superior power over Satan? "If I cast out devils by the Spirit of God, then the kingdom of God is come unto you; or else how can one enter a strong man's house and spoil his goods except he first bind the strong man." This was the purpose that brought him to earth and led to the battle of Calvary, that he might destroy the works of the devil. Does he look with admiration upon his bride guilty of dalliance with his own eternal, irreconcilable enemy, or rather does he not delight to see her arrayed in pure garments and adorned with the chaste jewelry of grace? God requires truth in the inward parts, and makes no compromise with sin in any sense whatever. His law is perfect, and any departure from it in the heart or intention forfeits to that extent his favor, and persisted in, unfits for heaven. It is not necessary for us to sin in anything; but the soul may bear the image of the heavenly, its every lineament fair and lovely. This purity is real and personal, and hence the absurdity of the antinomian plea, that one's acts are contaminated with corruption, but Christ has woven a robe of righteousness spotless and pure, and in this righteousness of Christ's personal acts we are clothed, and are to thus appear before the throne of his glory. In the visions of the heavenly world given to John we read of the saints who had washed *their* robes and made *them* white in the blood of the Lamb. They did not wash Christ's robes, but their own, for it would be a strange mixture of metaphor, and contradictory of all reason, to affirm that we wash *his* robes in his own blood. In the same book we read of the clean linen which is the righteouness of the saints; and we hear a voice from heaven proclaiming the blessedness of the dead who die in the Lord, for their works do follow them.

Nor in this do we undervalue the merit of Christ; for while the creature is responsible for all the acts done, and thoughts conceived, and words uttered, these are acceptable to God only as they are made so by his gracious assistance. None so magnify the grace of God and are such debtors to his boundless love as that one who walks by faith.

> "Jesus, thy blood and righteousness
> My beauty are, my glorious dress:
> 'Midst flaming worlds in these arrayed
> With joy shall I lift up my head."

God does no imperfect work either in nature or grace. Sin blasts much that he does, and modifies all his works on earth. Consider his work in the renewal of the soul. A babe in Christ is a perfect babe, but not a perfect man— there is an imperfect development of mind and heart and body; but this babe, observing the conditions of growth, may, in due time, reach a robust manhood in Christ Jesus. "Whosoever is born of God doth not commit sin; for his seed remaineth in him: and he cannot sin, because he is born of God." What words could be stronger? The soul born of God cannot sin, because the seed of purity dropped in this soil, prepared by justifying and regenerating grace, remains; but temptation will come, and in most instances this purity is yielded; but until such compliance there is no actual sin. Can an honest man steal? We answer unhesitatingly, no! for the moment he yields to the temptation to take what belongs to another his integrity is gone. Perhaps we describe the experience of every Christian when we say, they were very careful to walk before the Lord with pure hearts when first brought to know him as a pardoning Savior. With some this lasted but a short time; with others for weeks or months. At last came the enemy in some artful form; then arose the struggle; there the battle of life should have been fought out and decided. Sanctification, so far as it may be considered a distinct blessing, is this consecration which follows conversion; it is complete.

> "Take my soul and body's powers,
> Take my memory, mind and will,
> All my goods, and all my hours,
> All I know and all I feel,
> All I think or speak or do,
> Take my heart, but make it new."

Such a state must come of sore travail. Our deepest and tenderest feelings are born of sorrow, our purest and strongest friendships are cemented by the tears of sympathy in times of grief. Charcoal is carbon, and so is a diamond; but one is tested, tried in the fire. There is no perfection that does not admit of growth, an endless progression. Through the vast ages of eternity the watchword will be, " Let us go on unto perfection." Perfection is with us a relative term; no one is absolutely perfect on earth. The Scriptures may appear somewhat paradoxical. The patient Job was a perfect man—not a perfect angel, much less a perfect God—and yet Job sinned at one time. St. Paul was a perfect Christian, yet he was tempted, and still he reached forward, not as perfect, to the richer things before him. The tree is a perfect shrub as a shrub, when born into the vegetable world, but it must grow; the storms of winter must shake it, that its roots may strike down deeper and throw its boughs more widely, and sunshine must attract the sap upward and push out the buds and form new wood—*it must grow*. If it is a fruit-bearing tree, God will look for fruit thereon, and, alas! if he finds "nothing but leaves" he will wither it from its loftiest bough to its deepest root. It is not so much the profession of holiness that is called for, as the living it. Let no one hide his light by refusing to own his Lord before men, but as no true painter or poet is heard to speak of his own work, the work speaking for itself, so the true saint is known and read of all men.

III. THE CHURCH IS GLORIOUS IN HER SOLEMN ASSEMBLIES AND ORDINANCES OF DIVINE SERVICE.

God has ever shown a peculiar respect for sacred places where he has recorded his name and blessed his people. He showed to Moses a pattern in the Mount, according to which he was to build his tabernacle and order the services. The temple was an enlargement of these ideas, and made glorious with God's presence: "Here have I placed my name, and here will I dwell, for I have a delight therein." "How goodly are thy tents, O Jacob, and thy tabernacle, O Israel! As the valleys are they spread forth, as gardens by the river's side." The order of the house of God should be preserved, and nothing added or taken away. At various eras sacraments have been appointed which Christ never ordered, and performances have taken place which marred the fair beauty of the Church. The order of God is three-fold—devotion, rites, temporal economy. The first division comprehends prayer, preaching, praise. The second, baptism and the eucharist. The last, benevolence. These we are taught of God to observe, and only them. The tendency is to more form and less spirit, but the palladium of the Church is in this sublime proposition of Christ: "God is a spirit, and they that worship him must worship him in spirit and in truth."

1. How glorious is the king's daughter in the solemn assembly. There stands the man of God, not as man simply, but as an ambassador for God, speaking in the stead of Christ, as though the Master himself spoke, beseeching sinners to be reconciled to God.

> "By him the violated law speaks out
> Its thunders; and by him in strains as sweet
> As angels use, the Gospel whispers peace."

A redeemed world is to be led to the knowledge of salvation through the preaching of the Gospel; Christ has given commission to disciple the world. This means of heavenly appointment is the most important of all the services of religion.

The Church is glorious in prayer. Moses in audience with God was glorious—such a radiance lingered upon his face that human eyes could not endure it; but the whole congregation may now come to God and commune with him. The Church is a royal priesthood, and every believer is his own priest, to offer sacrifices acceptable to God. The prototype of the Church was not the Temple, with its slaughtered lambs, but the Tabernacle on Mount Zion, with the sacred ark in the midst of the people. Draw nigh *to God*—not to priests and altars, nor to interceding angels, but to the *living God*. His eyes are over the righteous, and his ears are open to their prayers.

Not less glorious is the service of praise. Every season of spiritual declension has been marked by the decadence of song.

2. The Church is glorious in her rites. There are two simple shafts standing before her, like the two pillars of Perfection and Beauty before the Temple of Solomon, monumental of the two leading truths which she holds most sacred. Baptism is the expressive type of purification, not putting away, in itself, the corruption of the flesh, but the answer of a good conscience toward God, and a symbol to the world of the distance which separates between it and the Church. It is the sign of regeneration effected by the Holy Ghost. The Holy Supper is a family ordinance, expressing to the beholder the fellowship which Christians hold with each other, and with their living Head, and keeps alive the death of Christ in the conscience, and shadows the coming feast to be celebrated in the Father's House, underneath the radiant arches of that temple whose light is God and the Lamb. Who can look upon these scenes without the desire to be better, and enter into them, and realize their significance. How eloquent these ordinances are of a dead and buried past, when the sainted mother and honored father kept them in our sight. But these ordinances may be abused by a too superstitious observance, and instead of becoming the means to an end, the chan-

nels through which we receive grace, they may be rested in as sufficient to save the soul.

3. The activities of the king's daughter are to be employed in the relief of the poor: these are her Lord's representatives on earth. The tears of widowhood and orphanage are to be wiped away by her pure and loving hands. She is to scatter smiles, but food and clothing as well; and by weeping with those who weep, and visiting the fatherless and the widow in their distress, she weaves for herself a robe of wrought gold, more valuable than the purple with which kings adorn their persons, and raiment of needlework such as the most delicate handiwork cannot equal.

IV. THE GLORY OF THE CHURCH IS MANIFESTED IN HER WORKS. Her clothing is of wrought gold; she shall be brought to the king in raiment of needlework. In this the Church is not peculiar, for God is only manifested by his works. "The heavens declare the glory of God;" and "the invisible things of him from the creation of the world are clearly seen, being understood by the things that are made, even his eternal power and Godhead." Everything in nature reflects his wisdom and power.

> "All are but parts of one stupendous whole,
> Whose body nature is, and God the soul;
> That changed through all and yet in all the same,
> Great in the earth as in the ethereal frame;
> Warms in the sun, refreshes in the breeze;
> Glows in the stars, and blossoms in the trees."

We say his wisdom and power, but not his grace, is manifested in nature. In the Theophanies of the early dispensations we have manifestations in the bush of Horeb, which burned with fire and was not consumed, and in the cloudy pillar in the wilderness, and in the Shekinah in the tabernacle, we have God manifesting himself in providence; but the only-begotten Son in the bosom of the Father from all eternity hath declared him. Being the brightness of his glory and the express image of his person, he revealed the fatherhood of God. How often was it upon Christ's lips, and how he proclaimed the new evangel, God's fatherhood bending in yearning pity over his erring offspring.

1. To the individual consciousness the knowledge of forgiveness is ultimate, and is a well of water springing up into everlasting life; but this experience is not transferable to another; by no words can it be made intelligible to others; but we manifest the interior life by our exterior conduct. It is a test as natural as reasonable, and is demanded with the greatest exactitude. "By their fruits ye shall know them." As the tree is, so will be the fruits. Does the Holy Spirit live in the heart? The fruit is "love, joy, peace, long-suffering, gentleness, goodness, faith, meekness, temperance."

The juices of the tree are hidden, and as the tree stands out barren against the wintry blasts it seems to the eye dead, but the elements of life are within, and the leaves and fruitage will in their season appear. The fruit which is acceptable to God is that which is borne by us in our connection with Christ. "As the branch cannot bear fruit of itself except it abide in the vine, no more can ye except ye abide in me."

2. The Church shall, in accord with the truths of Revelation, the commands of the Lord, bind and unloose, and unloose and bind men in the various obligations which the gospel imposes. The forgiveness of sins is a divine work, the prerogative of God alone, but what the Church does, as directed of her Lord, is ratified in heaven. The Church cannot make a Christian any more than it can make a world, but she can clothe the Christian in the badges of forgiveness, and at her altars are vows plighted which it would be mockery to violate. The Church is the repository of rights in the appointment of laborers in the moral vineyard, the solemn authorization of ministers, and no Church is in a healthful state which does not raise up and send forth men to publish the gospel. When the Church ceases to save souls from the errors of their sinful ways, and nurse her converts with the sincere milk of the word from her only maternal breast, the curse of the Lord will rest upon her. Nor is it enough to adopt the children of others, and act as a step-mother to them; but the evangelical denomination, scorning the sophistries of proselytism and the sectarianism of the bigot, addresses herself to the more noble emulation of bringing many sons and daughters to glory. It has long become a golden maxim: "In things essential, unity; in things not essential, liberty; in all things, charity." If God honors some who accompany not with us, shall we refuse to honor them? Shall any ban those whom God blesses, or forbid any to gather for the Lord? Is not the world in need of all the good that can be wrought? God will smile if men frown, and his

bannered hosts will achieve success. Therefore, we labor in this great harvest-field, being assured that God will not forget our labor of love. If we cannot go into the heaviest standing corn and gather the weightiest sheaves for God, each one may glean after the reapers. It is not the great work that is productive of the largest aggregate of good. Christ praised what the world in its haughtiness overlooked—the widow's mite, the cup of cold water given to a disciple, Magdalene's tears washing his feet. What a crown will the king's daughter weave for the brow of her Lord gathering the souls of men and women and little children, made clean by her labors in the various departments of Christian enterprise, and this he will wear as his peculiar honor through all eternity. Go forth then, beloved of the Lord, sheltered by the broad, protecting ægis of the God of love, "always abounding in the word of the Lord, for as much as ye know that your labor is not in vain in the Lord." When Christ comes to lead his bride to the home he has gone to prepare for her reception, clad in her pure robes, she shall accompany him through the starry pathway, and the whole universe shall resound with the loud choral, "Praise our God, all ye his servants, and ye that fear him, both small and great. And I heard as it were the voice of a great multitude, and as the voice of many waters, and as the voice of mighty thunderings, saying Alleluia: for the Lord God omnipotent reigneth. Let us be glad and rejoice, and give honor to him, for the marriage of the Lamb is come, and his wife hath made herself ready."

VI.
THE LAWS OF SPIRITUAL DEATH AND LIFE.

BY REV. F. X. FORSTER,

Prof. in Central College.

"The law of the Spirit of life in Christ Jesus hath made me free from the law of sin and death.—ROMANS viii. 2.

There is in man a law of sin and death—of sin working death.

There are means provided for deliverance from this law—these means themselves a law—the law of the Spirit of life in Christ Jesus.

Such are the two great facts presented prominently in the text—facts interwoven with the history of our race through all the ages past, through all the ages yet to come. The first tells us what we are; the second, what we may be. The first finds expression in the heart-shriek, "O, wretched man that I am!" the second, in the shout, "I thank God through Jesus Christ our Lord." The first puts us in the valley of the shadow of death, with a future of ever-deepening gloom, ever-augmenting woe; the second sheds around us the beams of the Sun of Righteousness, and maps out the eternal progression "from glory to glory." Let us for awhile earnestly study these facts.

All creation exists under law; it must so exist, else creation would be but chaos. The object of law is to secure order, and thus to enable each subject thereof, in the best possible manner, to work out the end of its creation—namely, the *highest possible good* of which its nature is capable. There may be two subdivisions: namely, the law for or *over* the creature, holding it to its right place; and the law *in* the creature, in accordance with which development and destiny are wrought out.

No divine law is the arbitrary enactment of the divine will, but the expression of the nature and character of both Creator and creature. To law is necessarily attached penalty; and this penalty, like the law, is not arbitrary, but a necessary consequence of the nature of the offender and the offence. Not being arbitrarily appointed, it cannot be arbitrarily set aside—cannot be set aside at all; it must be met.

The two laws mentioned in the text, the "law of sin and death," and the "law of the Spirit of life in Christ Jesus," entered into the original scheme of creation: the one as a statement of a possible contingency; the other as a timely provision for that contingency when it should arise. In order that the creature might develop character, he must be endowed with moral and intellectual faculties; in order that he might attain to the highest possible good, he must be endowed with free will; the good must be wrought out by the intelligent, voluntary exercise of his own powers. In unfallen beings, holiness, which is a positive state, is higher than purity, which is a negative state. God could create man pure, and by arbitrary control keep him so; he could not create him holy, much less keep him so; for holiness, whether in God or man, results from the voluntary exercise of his own powers in doing right. But freedom in electing and doing the right necessarily involves the power to do wrong; and in the creature, imperfect in his powers, a liability to the wrong. The omniscience of Deity foreknew the doing of the wrong; the same divine benevolence which dictated the freedom, must either forego the creation, and thus the highest good, or provide along with the creation the remedy for the wrong—the means of Atonement and Restoration. This means, called in the text "the law of the Spirit of life in Christ Jesus," was, therefore, no after-thought, but really, in the purposes of Deity, antedated the sin. While sin formed no part of the original purpose in the creation, as some have vainly taught, God, foreknowing the sin, did incorporate the Atonement as an integral part of the plan.

The contingency foreseen occurred. Man, in the exercise of free will, chose to sin. In this act were involved not only the transgression of the divine command, but also *the inversion of his whole nature*.

Man was material as well as immaterial, physical as well as spiritual, of the earth, earthy, as well as of heaven, heavenly; and in this compound nature was to work out character and destiny. By the proper exercise of all the powers of this mixed nature he was to attain to his highest possible good. The senses, the appetites and desires, all kept to their proper place and work by unclouded intellect and pure affections, and, above all, by conscience, that upward and Godward impulse urging to the right, were all to do their part in attaining the proposed end. But man, fully forewarned, chose to subvert this beautiful arrangement, and taking the control from the higher to give it to the lower powers, chose to take a shorter and easier road to the desired end—to deny the truth, "in the day thou eatest thereof thou shalt die," and to believe the lie, "ye shall be as gods;" chose to eat of the fruit because it "was good for food," was "pleasant to the eyes," and "to be desired to make one wise;" chose to give control to an appetite, a desire, and thus to develop these into a lust. Lust speedily conceived; and sin became, not a contingency, but a tremendous fact; sin was finished, and it brought forth death. No new powers were acquired, none were lost; but the more noble and God-like were dethroned, and the lower, the sensual, were enthroned. Man had voluntarily placed the sceptre within their grasp, and these, now uncontrolled, ran beyond their appointed sphere, and wrought ruin. The "law of sin and death," thus, by the concurrence of his own will, became the law of man's moral constitution. He was cursed, for he used his own powers to curse himself; he died, for he used sin to kill himself—a spiritual, immortal suicide.

But "like produces like" is the great primal law of development—the only law of normal, righteous development that we at least can recognize. Designed to carry man upward, this law, acting on his now inverted nature, carried him downward with a terrible gravitation. Indulgence produced increased lust; increasing lust produced increased sin; increasing sin produced an ever-dying death; and the "law of sin and death" became the law of man's development.

Again, "like produces like." Those springing from these parents must inherit, not the sin and guilt, but the nature now inclined to sin. The inversion of the powers, the enthroned self and sensualism, the blurred and misled intellect, the affections inclined to earthly, sensual objects, the dethroned conscience, all are transmitted by the law of "like produces like." No child of Adam comes into the world a sinner; there is neither in him nor imputed to him any sin, for this must be his own voluntary act. There is no guilt, and, therefore, no condemnation, for "the free gift hath come upon all men unto justification of life." All of his activities, both physical and spiritual, have been touched and depraved by sin; and his tendency is necessarily downward in an ever-spreading, ever-deepening depravity.* His intellect remains, but it has been weakened, and is misled by passion. His conscience remains intact, but it is guided by this weakened, misled intellect, or is overruled by those lower powers to which its imperial sway has been transferred. "To will is present" with him; but "how to perform that which is good," how to combat the stronger inclinations, and hold the will to that performance, he finds not. There

* Depravity is total in the sense that it reaches all the faculties; "spreading and deepening," in the fact that these faculties are continually brought more and more under the dominion of sin.

is a law in him that when he "would do good, evil is present with him." He yields a willing obedience to the lower powers of his nature, although he feels them to be such, because they *are* the stronger; and these no longer restrained, overleap their legitimate bounds, and there is sin. The "law in his members warring against the law of his mind, and bringing him into captivity," is the "law of sin and death." He is "dead in trespasses and in sins."

Further still; sin could not destroy his immortality, though it might debase and ruin the entire nature. Sin brought forth death; but physical death cannot annul the law of spiritual being, which is not annihilation, but development; and the law of development is, that "like produces like." There must be an eternal progression in sin, under the "law of sin and death." The same facts continue, the same law governs, the same state exists, all expanded and developed, expanding and developing so "long as immortality endures." And as sin, by its violation of order and right, necessarily introduced misery, so with the ever-increasing sinfulness must there be an ever-increasing misery. Eternal misery is the same misery eternally continued and developed; eternal death is the same spiritual death eternally perpetuated—the foliage, the flower, the fruit of the one deadly Upas. Neither is the will or act of God; each is the result, the one ever-developing result under the "law of sin and death."

And now, standing in the midst of the wreck which sin has made; conscious of all its deep degradation and misery; looking out into the future and beholding that immortality designed by the wise and good Creator as the grand field of an eternal progression toward Himself, converted into a vast lazar-house, for an eternally increasing, eating, spreading corruption, and degradation and misery; beholding, feeling all this, I cry out in agony, "O, wretched man that I am! who shall deliver me from the body of this death?" I am bound—I have bound myself—to this festering corpse; I am myself a festering, rotting corpse! The "law of sin and death" drives relentlessly the rot and the woe into every part, every fibre of my nature. It spreads, it tortures, it kills. Onward, downward I am going, eternally going—gone, hopelessly gone. Terrible, O terrible is the fact, that in each one of us there is a "law of sin and death!"

How does the Creator meet this fallen, lost condition? Curse his creature, his child, because he had sinned? Had he even been so disposed, it would have been a useless work, for sin had already cursed its victim—a deep, a withering curse. Leave him alone under the dominion of the "law of sin and death," to work out a horrible character and a terrible destiny? That would have been as unlike the great and good Father as would the useless curse. Turn from such unworthy thought to the Revelation which He has made, and there view God, on the one hand subsidizing His own eternal "power and wisdom"[*] to the work of restoration; and on the other, coming down and searching amidst the very ruins which sin had made for helps in this work.

[*] 1 Cor. i. 24.

The contingency foreseen had occurred, and at once the remedy provided was put into operation; coeval and coextensive with the "law of sin and death" began the restoring energy of the "law of the spirit of life in Christ Jesus." Atonement—penalty endured by another that the offender might escape—is prepared, in order that a worse thing might not be introduced into creation by the pardon than had already been by the sin—namely, the destruction of the sanction and authority of all law. In the "determinate counsel and foreknowledge of God" Deity assumes a nature that could suffer, that in this nature and by this suffering he might "magnify the law and make it honorable;" thus giving to it eternal sanction, by himself enduring its penalty. The promise of this Savior is given as a stimulus to exertion and an object of faith. Sacrifices are appointed as helps to this faith; the ground is cursed for man's benefit, that in conquering its barrenness, its thorns and thistles, he might learn to hold will and energy to worthy ends, to conquer and control himself; the very suffering which sin had brought is made to point to the One able to save; "he gives his angels charge concerning him, to bear him up in their hands, lest he should dash his foot against a stone;" all secondary agencies, material and spiritual, are employed to aid in the grand result. And when "the fullness of the times" had come, God in Redemption binding again to Himself the severed humanity in the person of Jesus of Nazareth, ascends the altar of sacrifice, and makes "his soul an offering for sin." He dies; and the death-cry, "It is finished!"—the grandest words that ever fell upon human ears—proclaims the coming deliverance from the bondage to the "law of sin and death," and the full inauguration of that mightier "law of the spirit of life in Christ Jesus."

The Atonement by itself could not break the power of the "law of sin and death;" for this is a law of development *within* the individual nature; and in order to restore, Deity must enter the same field, and the divine energy be brought into immediate coöperation with the human. Without the Atonement preceding, this could not be; it was "needful that Christ should go away that the Comforter might come." With the Atonement it might be; and God the Spirit—God in direct contact with the creature—enters the disputed field, and, by the consent of the individual will, becomes an actor in the contest. The power must be of God. God works in man "both to will and to do;" but the man himself, thus supplemented by divine power, must "work out his own salvation." The Spirit gives power to the truth to reach the intellect, and to the intellect to perceive and apply the truth; so that it is no longer an abstraction, but a conviction. It gives energy to the will, not only "to will," but also "to do" the good thus allowed; not simply a spasmodic volition and effort, but a persistent holding of the activities to the good: and there is reformation, repentance. He points the soul thus made conscious of sin, and of its own inability, to the Atonement in Christ, and enables the affections to grasp that Atonement; and thus "with the heart man believes unto righteousness." The Spirit "helping our infirmities," the man puts himself in alliance with Christ as his Savior; sin is pardoned; he is "renewed in the spirit of his mind;" conscience is restored to its rightful supremacy; there is now no condemnation, for he "is in Christ Jesus;" and the "righteousness of the law is fulfilled in him, for he walks not after the flesh, but after the Spirit."

Thus, by the union of these two forces, the human and the divine—the one to work, the other to help in that work—the order which sin had inverted is restored, the "law of sin and death" is broken, and the soul moves forward toward holiness and God. "Raised by the power of God" into "newness of life," in this new and free life its activities go forth joyfully in search for their proper objects; and walking in this "perfect law of liberty," "like producing like," the man progresses toward his highest good. He lives—all his powers and activities are in free and full exercise; he lives—'tis the man himself in all his individuality and entireness; yet not he, but Christ liveth in him; he has so infolded and inwarped the divine with the human, that the very warp and woof of that life is CHRIST; the energies of Redemption are a living power within him, operating along with his own energies; and the life which he "lives in the flesh" he "lives by the faith of the Son of God." He no longer cries, "Who shall deliver me?" for he has found a deliverer—"the law of the Spirit of life;" and in the bounding joy of that deliverance he shouts aloud, "I thank God through Jesus Christ our Lord!"

And thus all along we have traced the co-existence and co-operation of divine law and human freedom in the work of Redemption. In the fall is human freedom *without* God; in the restoration is human freedom *with* God. There is bondage; yet is it not the ordinance of God, but the result of sin voluntarily indulged. In his original state man could have stood firm, remained pure, developed into holiness, by his own powers freely acting in accordance with the laws and arrangements of his Creator. -He chose to do otherwise; and thus he introduced a new law into his nature which inverted the direction of his development, and brought all his powers and activities into subjection to itself; and *here is the only bondage*. There is the deepest philosophy as well as the largest promise in those words of Jesus, "If the Son shall make you free, ye shall be free indeed." Man has sold himself under sin; and the new master thus chosen, converting the law of "like producing like" to its own purpose, perpetuates its own dominion. The plan of salvation is designed to atone for the offence by the vicarious death of Christ; and by the direct operation of the Holy Spirit, to supply to each individual thus enslaved the power to break the bondage and maintain the original freedom. The election in this case, as in that of the sin, must be made by the individual man; it is a *personal* election, but it is human, not divine—made by the man, not by God.

So also this liberty is perpetuated in its true form, only by a life of holiness. True liberty is freedom to pursue voluntarily the proper ends of being, the highest good, by the best means. There can be no such thing. as "liberty to sin;" it is not liberty, but license; that is, an abuse of power or privilege, and, like every other abuse, must end in either despotism or destruction. To sin is to enslave one's self, to degrade and destroy the true manhood. A sinner is a degraded, enslaved man. Redemption proposes to destroy the sin, and, therefore, the slavery; to assist the slave to recover his freedom— the sinner to become again in very deed a man; and the "law of the Spirit of life in Christ Jesus" is none other than the divinely-appointed means whereby the sinner may work himself up to true manhood by voluntarily seeking after the best development and the highest good to which his nature may attain. So soon as sentient being dawns into existence, so soon these two laws begin their action—the one downward toward slavery and destruction; the other upward toward freedom and God. And this action continues, the one or the other in the ascendency, according to the election of the individual will, until at length one is overpowered, the contest ceases, and the man is either left to "work all uncleanness with greediness," to "believe a lie," to "glory in his shame," to develop eternally into a yet more sinful nature and a yet deeper suffering; or else he is "made free from sin, has his fruit unto holiness, and in the end eternal life"—an eternal progression, in his own character and history, "from glory to glory, even as by the Spirit of the Lord."

May we not be permitted, before concluding, to enlarge upon the thought presented awhile back? Terrible as is the fact of sin—a foul leprosy eating into the vitals of the universe, a dark, sad eclipse upon the powers of man and the glory of God—yet even out of it Redemption brings a blessing. The labor and suffering which sin, and which the "law of sin and death" developes and perpetuates; the barrenness, the thorns and thistles of the ground; the sorrow and anguish of the woman; the mind and heart struggles of the man; all are converted, by the "law of the Spirit of life in Christ Jesus," into aids and ministries whereby men may subdue self, break the bondage of sense, and " by patient continuance in well-doing," rise to a higher life, and seek after "glory, honor and immortality." Man must "eat bread by the sweat of his face;" but this will help him to recover that original fact in his constitution, that "man shall not live by bread alone, but by every word that proceedeth from the mouth of God." Even physical death, itself the terrible result of sin and a mighty woe in the path of every one, becomes changed into a merciful means of escape from the temptation and struggle and agony which the presence of evil must ever induce, to a state where evil does not exist. Earth is made a sepulchre for bodies, that it may not be an eternal battle-field and charnel house for both bodies and souls; a sepulchre that shall quietly hold these bodies until the "law of the Spirit of life in Christ Jesus" shall bring them also to share in the completed triumph, when "death shall be swallowed up in victory." Here I find, not a reason for sorrow and pain and death, for this is found only in sin, but a use of these that sheds a light and glory over earth and heaven. That glory is the glory of the Cross; that light is from Him whose " life is the light of men."

And still a step farther; I see not why the great subjective result of all these agencies may not, aye, must not, continue so long as man himself continues. I find no power in death to change the essential laws of being; and the law of mind is progression, development. I read, too, that " if patience have her perfect work, ye shall be perfect and entire, wanting nothing;" and I may not limit such an exceeding great and precious promise to the narrow possibilities of the earth-life, but rather to the higher capacities and grander attainments of the heavenly. I read that " the trial of your faith might be found unto praise and honor and glory at the appearing of the Lord Jesus;" that " these light afflictions shall work out for us a far more exceeding and eternal weight of glory;" and I learn, not simply that I am by these to be assisted in the work of restoration, not simply that heaven is a far higher and happier place than earth, but also that the height and happiness *there* shall be greater because of the labor and suffering *here*. The struggle developed the muscle and the strength; the very ardor of the conflict gave energy to the will; and these together held the powers to yet more arduous struggle and more perfect development. The heroes whose memories we reverence would, perhaps, have been good and great men wherever placed, but without the fierce conflict, the protracted agony, the glorious victory, and even the unmerited defeat, they would never have developed into those grand proportions that have won for them the homage of the nations. So man would have found a heaven, and heaven would have been a high and happy home, had sin never entered the world; but now it is all the grander and the happier for the labor and the suffering which sin brought and saints conquered. There ever was and ever will be a " glory yet to be revealed;" yet it is a "far more exceeding and eternal weight of glory" because of the afflictions of earth. On those high mountain-tops of glory stand prophets and apostles, and the company of those who " have come through great tribulation," all scarred over with the sorrows and conflicts of earth— each scar the focal-point of a far more exceeding glory— shouting back to earth, " I thank God through Jesus Christ our Lord!"

And there may you and I, fellow-laborers and fellow-sufferers " in the kingdom and patience of Jesus," at last stand—on a lower height it may be, yet oh, how high !— with a lesser glory, yet "a far more exceeding and eternal weight of glory;" and catching up the shout, send it echoing down the ages of eternity, " I thank God through Jesus Christ our Lord. The law of the Spirit of life in Christ Jesus hath made me free, and I am free indeed!" Heaven re-echoes the shouts of earth, and eternity repeats the triumphs of time.

VII.

AMAZING LOVE.

BY REV. W. C. GODBEY,

Of the West St. Louis Conference.

"God so loved the world that he gave his only begotten Son, that whosoever believeth on him should not perish, but have everlasting life."—JOHN iii. 16.

What if God is more like man than we have thought him? Man loves, hates, sorrows and rejoices; the Scriptures affirm the same of God. The terms, when applied to Him, are used in their ordinary signification, or in some other; but if in some other, then, to me, they mean nothing at all, since their import is absolutely past conjecture.

The Scriptures say that the feelings of God are sometimes wrought upon in the liveliest manner—that he is moved by love, indignation, grief, etc. Yet we say these expressions are only employed to adapt to our understanding things otherwise hard to be understood. Language, I believe, is not generally very comprehensible that says one thing and means another. If love is not love, if indignation is not indignation, if pity and grief are not pity and grief in God as well as in me, then tell me, if you can, what they are. But, again, I am told that the Holy Spirit, by attributing to God these passions, only aims to adapt himself to my understanding. I verily believe it, and I shall understand him to mean just what he says.

Now, then, I shall believe that God is a being capable of suffering, and that he does suffer. What reason will you urge against it? Must I be told that God is a perfect being, and that suffering cannot be a quality of perfection? The conclusion is by no means clear from the premise, while observation wants but little to demonstrate it false. The nearer a being approaches to perfection the greater its capacity for suffering. It is not possible for a swine to suffer as a man. Ascending from the lowest to the highest in the scale of animal existence, we find the capacity of suffering evidently increasing exactly in proportion as progress has been made toward perfection. Among men there is also a difference of capacity, and the highest and most perfect organization of mind and body is that which can suffer most. Will I be told that goodness excludes suffering, and that, therefore, to perfect holiness suffering is impossible? The best beings that we know are those that can suffer most, and for some causes do suffer. A bad man will not grieve much over his prodigal son; a good one will grieve, and, other things being equal, the grief will be in proportion to the goodness. The purest souls are susceptible to the intensest pain at the sight of moral wrong, and the pain is in strict relation to the purity. But this is only mental suffering, you say. My answer is, that the mind can suffer more than the body. A physical nature is by no means essential to a capacity for suffering. So far as the facts of constant observation can teach us, the highest and purest spiritual organization is that which can suffer intenser pain than anything else whatever. If these inductions may be trusted, then God can suffer more than any other being.

This conclusion is borne out by one other consideration. Capacity of happiness involves capacity of suffering. The one is the exact measure of the other. You love your child: precisely in proportion to your affection, which is an occasion of happiness, is your anxiety for him when he is sick; your pain when he disobeys you; your agony when he dies. It would be easy to give a thousand illustrations, but this is sufficient. Whatever under some conditions is a source of pleasure, is equally, under opposite conditions, a source of pain, and the measure of power to enjoy, in every being that we know, is exactly the measure of power to suffer. If this be not true of the Highest of Beings, then nature has herein failed to interpret her great Author.

As for the Scriptures, they tell us that God is our Father; that "we are his offspring;" that man was created "in the image of God." "Yes, in his moral image," says the theologian. I grant it; but the assertion is broader; the limitation is purely human. The image extended to all the faculties and capacities of the soul, so that in his spiritual organization the child was an exact reproduction of his father. It may be that I have not every faculty of the Divine Being, but such as I possess are copies of his own; only mine are finite and his are infinite. To make my meaning clearer, I will assume that I am a perfectly good man. And now I will say that I know, but in the same sense of the word God knows more perfectly; I hate, but the things I hate he hates more intensely; I love, but his loves are stronger; I sorrow, but his sorrows are deeper. The passions and emotions I feel belong to God also, but his are more powerful every way—as much more powerful as his nature is greater than mine. Is all this denied? Then what is the alternative but a Hindoo god, passionless and impassive, untouched by any sentiment or concern for his creatures; or a god like that of Herbert Spencer, perhaps equally impassive and unconcerned, and besides, absolutely unknown and unknowable.

These preliminary reflections I felt were necessary to prepare us to explore the meaning of our text. In so doing we shall see, perhaps, that what thus far may seem to be little more than philosophy, is well sustained by that which is revealed. And now, praying to be taught of God, let us endeavor to search the meaning of the words, " God so loved the world that he gave his only-begotten Son."

My imagination carries me back to the time when the world was not, and man was yet but an unaccomplished idea of the divine mind. I see in God a being of infinite benevolence. I see in life a blessing—if well improved, an unspeakable blessing—a happinesss no arithmetic can sum, and sin only can make it a curse. The benevolence of the Divine Being prompts him to impart life. The highest benevolence produces the highest life, and man is created in the image of God. An essential part of that image is freedom, therefore man was created free. I speak it with reverence; the Almighty had no choice except between an agent and a mere machine. The highest possibilities of happiness were on the side of agency; infinite benevolence, therefore, compelled that man be created free. A being that had no choice was not capable of exalted bliss. Yet if the will were free, there was a possibility that the being would choose evil. Were it not that Infinite Wisdom leaps at once to the right conclusion, I should picture to myself the great eternal Three as counseling long ere it was at last announced, " Let us make man *in our image and after our likeness.*" The work was done; and now I behold the infinite Father watching over this offspring of his love with a solicitude of which our tenderest fatherly affection is but a poor interpreter. He gives him an abode worthy to be the dwelling-place of angels, and himself often comes to his children in the cool of the day. In sublime and holy converse he teaches them the lessons it is needful for them to learn. He spreads no snare for their feet—far otherwise; but there is danger, and he graciously points it out and bids them beware. He made them, and is, therefore, thoroughly acquainted with the conditions of their happiness. They must ever abide in loving relation to him as he will to them. Love must be the chord fastening them to him as to a centre. Within the circle to be described by such a radius they may exercise all their powers and be blest. Obedience will be the test of this love, and when obedience fails it will show that the chord is broken; that the centrifugal forces of passion have overcome the centripetal power of love, and man has gone off at a tangent from his Maker. To prove obedience, the Father lays upon them a single command; and for this why not as well say, "Ye shall not eat of the fruit of that tree?" The impulse to violate that command will indicate the danger of the heart's defection; the struggle with the tempter will proclaim it nearer; disobedience will demonstrate its completion—demonstrate it not to God, for he knew it the moment the volition was formed; but demonstrate it to other intelligences and to man himself; compel him to plead guilty at the tribunal of his own conscience, and convict him without a trial. Who can object to an arrangement like this? Who that will pause and candidly consider will not admit that here were wisdom and goodness in their highest exercise?

The essential condition of happiness—I mean loving obedience—was despised, sacrificed to baser appetite, which now, by a law that increases its force with exercise, began to assert supreme control. What should the Almighty Father do? Should he destroy this creature of his goodness and create again? A second creation must involve all the conditions of the first—be subject to the same dangers, and to it, sooner or later, the same event would come. Should he then refuse to create at all, dwell alone in the midst of a silent universe, look in eternal solitude from his throne upon upper, nether and surrounding space, or build for himself a universe devoid of moral life, and, therefore, of his own image, the habitation of brutes alone? Benevolence forbade it. Benevolence said, "Go, rescue the child of the fall." "But how do this?" said Justice, "for his life is forfeit to me, and he must die." Everlasting Love said, "Spare him, for he is my offspring." Justice cried again, "It must not be; wouldst thou stain the throne of God, and by denying to me that which is rightfully mine, make the Ever-Blessed himself a sinner by consenting unto sin?" Eternal Wisdom spake and said, "Hear me, and I will end the strife. Justice shall have her own, and Mercy too. Justice, that Mercy may have her way, let thy stroke, glancing athwart from man, fall on me that made him." Justice and Mercy kissed each other. Heaven smiled through tears. God came down to earth to say to man that he was no longer a fit inhabitant of Eden, and kindly to clothe him with skins against his departure to a more inclement clime. Justice led him forth, but Mercy wept upon his steps, and whispered to him in going, "'The seed of the woman shall bruise the serpent's head." Justice and Mercy together closed the gate behind him

> "Till one greater Man
> Restore us and regain the blissful seat"

And now,

> "To their fixed station, all in bright array,
> The Cherubim descended on the ground,
> Gliding meteorous as evening mist
> Risen from a river o'er the marish glides,
> And gathers ground fast at the laborer's heel,
> Homeward returning."

But Adam and his spouse,

> "Some natural tears they dropped, but wiped them soon;
> The world was all before them where to choose
> Their place of rest, and *Providence* their guide.
> They, hand in hand, with wandering steps and slow,
> Through Eden took their solitary way."

Ere long God looked down upon a world that was full of wickedness. He saw men as children that had learned to hate their Father. He saw in them his own image, divinity, dishonored, sullied and eclipsed, and it grieved him at his heart. Yes, my brethren; I have but quoted to you his own confession—"*it grieved him at his heart.*" I suspect that these are no empty words; that he felt a thousand times more than you or I could feel if our children should dishonor our authority, curse us to our face, do whatever we had forbidden them, and delight themselves in all that we abhor the most. I say God felt; if you understand it better, that divinity suffered—suffered ten thousand times more than you or I could suffer, because its capacities are ten thousand times greater than yours or mine; that when God regarded the depths of man's iniquity from the lofty height of his own purity; when he regarded the mental anguish and bodily pain his children had entailed upon themselves, and which his eye could take in from the beginning of time to its close with one wide sweep; when he regarded the consequences of sin, not as transient, but lasting as eternity, a duration which his infinite mind alone could comprehend—I repeat it, he suffered as only a God could suffer. I accept, therefore, with a meaning that to me is boundless, his own declaration, that it grieved him at his heart.

Do you ask for further demonstration of a thought so bold? I answer, that what God has done for men indicates a deep concern—more than a father's solicitude for his children. You are a father, and your child, dishonoring and despising you, has entered upon the paths of vice. Your eye never rests upon him now without your fatherly heart being pierced with an unspeakable sorrow. For him you have endured mental suffering, anxiety and solicitude, more distressing than bodily pain. This may be to you a dim and distant intimation of what the Almighty Father suffered when he saw all his children armed against him. This may serve to indicate to you something of the meaning of some of his utterances and expostulations with men. With fatherly anxiety he superintended the passage of Israel through the wilderness, and the prophet, referring to this, says. "In all their afflictions *he* was *afflicted;* the angel of his presence saved them; in his love and in his pity he redeemed them." Hear him amid the darkness of Mount Sinai talking to himself, and bemoaning the hardness of his children, saying: "O that there were such an heart in them that they would fear me and keep all my commandments always, that it might be well with them and with their children forever!" Again, with weeping voice he cries after them, "Turn ye, turn ye, for why will ye die!" And again, "Is Ephraim my dear son, is he a pleasant child? for since I spake against him I do earnestly remember him still. How shall I give thee up, Ephraim? how shall I make thee as Admah? how shall I set thee as Zeboim? mine heart is turned within me, my repentings are kindled together. I will not execute the fierceness of mine anger." What fatherly tenderness when he says, "Come now, and let us reason together; though your sins be as scarlet, they shall be white as snow, and though they be red like crimson, they shall be as wool." Such expressions as these indicate to me that the great ocean of Divinity is heaving beneath the tempest; that the heart of God is shaken with an unutterable sorrow. If they mean less than this, how shall I understand that they mean anything at all.

I seem now to see God struggling with human wickedness from age to age, and striving to remove it. I see evil existing still, not because God permits it, but only because he cannot prevent it—cannot prevent it, I mean, without doing something inconsistent with the final and greatest good. He cannot prevent it without taking away from man the power to do good as well as evil, without reducing him, in fact, to the condition of a brute, and depriving him of moral responsibility. But this would make the moral universe a solitude, and destroy the possibility of happiness to the many who will attain it. I see his hand uplifted to strike the blow that would leave the earth without an inhabitant, and I hear him say, "It repenteth me that I have made man upon the earth;" but his fatherly affection prevails, and the stroke is deferred a hundred and twenty years; and during this time he pleads with his rebellious children.

And when, at last, they will not repent, he drowns them, less by a flood of waters than by the tempest of his sorrow for their sin. It is not resentment that takes them away; it is the last desperate resort of that love which amputates the limb to save life. Afterward I see him rain fire and brimstone upon the guilty cities of the plain, not for their destruction, but that he may save, by the sad example, from eternal fire the millions that shall come after them. I see him talking with Abraham, and anon calling the Israelites his chosen people; and yet his love is not exclusive, it is only working through these for the recovery of all his children. It is not partiality that impels him; it is necessity imposed by the constitution of human nature and its relations to the divine nature. A little reflection will suffice to convince us that there was no other way—at least, no other open to so few objections. If God had spoken to all men, what is supernatural in such a communication would have become common, and all men would have rejected it as lacking the evidence of miracle; had he taught more rapidly than he did, he would have outrun the slow processes of minds that were learning against their will. I see clearly there was no other way, and I acknowledge further, that as often as he applied the scourge, it was; but the desperate resort of love that had no other resource. I am not astonished now that such love should go its utmost length and immolate itself, although it should result in the recovery of but a portion of his children. I wonder no more that God so loved the world that he gave his only begotten Son.

Great was the mystery of God manifest in the flesh, no doubt, but the love that prompted it is to me more a mystery than the fact. Could we understand the one we should cease to view with surprise the other. And, now that we have familiarized ourselves somewhat with the real meaning of all that went before, we gaze with somewhat abated wonder at the Babe of Bethlehem. Indeed, we can almost say it was what we expected to see. Yet it was an event which took the world by surprise. Men saw in the scourgings and rebukes of a former age only the demonstrations of divine wrath. Spiteful and obstinate children were agreed that their Father smote them but in anger, and they only seemed to grow harder under the rod. They looked, indeed, for the promised seed of the woman, but they thought he would arm his hand with thunderbolts, and mounting his war-chariot hurl them flaming on every side and ride victorious over the necks of prostrate nations. Such a victory, if achieved, would not be lasting. Man would have done so, but Divine Wisdom knew that "he who wins by force hath overcome but half his foe." He must break the hearts of his children by the condescension of his love if he would gain to himself the allegiance of their hearts forever. He took them by surprise; they had not dreamed that he was about to stoop so low. The difficulty from henceforth would be to believe their senses, when they saw divinity veiling itself in the poor shrine of an infant's body and reclining in a stall. The Great Teacher had, in his anxiety, well nigh overreached the capacity of his pupils. The star, the angels, and the wise men were not enough. It wanted the labor of years to convince— years fraught with deeds such as none but God could do, and marked by utterances such as never fell from the lips of man. But it was not till the life of Jesus on the earth was ended that its full significance, flashing upon the understanding, broke the hearts of men. Nay, it was not until his resurrection from the dead. They saw then and believed that the child of the manger was the Son of God. They saw then that the insulted and agonized Father had, to win back his children, given his only begotten and well-beloved Son; not, indeed, with a certainty that by so doing he would save all, but only that "whosoever believeth on him should not perish, but have everlasting life."

Let us pause a moment now and consider this stupendous fact. God gave his only begotten Son. The words imply a sacrifice, and there can be no sacrifice without suffering. We constantly speak of the act as one of the greatest sacrifice, and yet we as constantly ignore the fact that it cost real suffering on the part of God. Who gave us liberty so to interpret the Scriptures I cannot tell. That God should really suffer to win back erring men is, I know, such an astounding demonstration of love that the world has ever staggered to receive it. Even good men have generally disbelieved and said that nothing suffered but humanity. Many have found even this too much for their faith, and have said that humanity suffered but in appearance only; while others, more doubting still, have claimed that Jesus Christ was not a real person, but only a shadow, a divinely-sent illusion to soften the hearts of men. The great majority of Christians have contended that the sufferings of humanity were real, but they have confined them to humanity alone. But, O my brethren! I can but think that, by such a conclusion, we still do injustice to the love that redeemed us. The Scriptures tell us that God gave his only begotten and well-beloved Son. If the words have meaning, then by that act his fatherly heart was wrung with an infinite sorrow. Did God then, indeed, suffer to rescue his fallen children ? It must be true if he indeed pitieth as we pity our children. Need I ask if you, my brother, would suffer to see that loving and obedient child of yours degraded to the lowest condition, made the servant of the meanest, despised by all, the victim of unknown sorrows, and then nailed to a cross full before your eyes, there to agonize and die ? If a little nature like yours would feel thus to give up one son among many, how did the great heart of God then resolve itself into an ocean of sorrow when he gave his only begotten and well-beloved Son?

The Scriptures declare that Jesus was God not less than man, and they tell us that he suffered. He suffered in his entire being. At the grave of Lazarus God wept as well as man. When they said, " Thou hast a devil," God felt the insult as well as man. When he said, " O Jerusalem! Jerusalem! thou that killest the prophets and stonest them that are sent unto thee, how oft would I have gathered thee as a hen gathereth her brood under her wings, and ye would not!" divinity no less than humanity felt all that was meant by the bitter, burning tears that fell.

And who can look upon the closing scene and believe that it was humanity alone that suffered then? He had often spoken of his hour as still in the future; what unspeakable sorrow when at last he announced, "The hour is come!" And then his intercessory prayer, that "escaped from his heart like a long sigh of sorrowing love!" And then Gethsemane! O the length, and breadth, and depth, and heighth of the love that was manifested there! One has eloquently said, "It was love that had failed in life, determined to succeed in death." You know the rest, my brethren. Before your eyes now are buffetings, and mockings, and revilings, insulting priests, mock robes, false disciples, the dreadful scourge, a crown of thorns, and one staggering under the weight of a cross he is not able to bear. Humanity alone felt the scourge, the smiting, and the nails, but the insult went to the heart of divinity. The agony of that father's heart is not to be imagined who should receive such things at the hands of his children; the anguish of that son is not to be surmized who should receive such things at the hands of his brethren. To be seized by ruffian soldiers and spiked to the fatal wood—this implies a suffering that can only be divinely understood. But it was not this, I believe, that killed the blessed Jesus. He died, *literally*, of a broken heart. Two or three days at least must have been required to end his existence on the cross, but in six hours he was dead. For what I speak now I can give the highest medical and scientific authority—that the excess, not of bodily but of mental anguish, ruptured the walls of his heart. The proof I cannot give in this place, but the fact is highly probable. It is known that grief may be so intense as in some instances to occasion the rupture of that vital organ and the instant extinction of life. It must have been so with the world's Redeemer. There is no other rational account of the blood and water that followed the soldier's spear. He went to the cross sustaining himself with the assurance that if earth frowned heaven would smile, and that hereafter he should see the travail of his soul and be satisfied. But it was the hour and power of darkness. When the nails were already in his hands and in his feet, and his soul was pressed by the sins of the world like a cart under many sheaves, Heaven, that the sacrifice might be complete, turned away his eye of compassion and refused to behold the unutterable sorrow; or it may be that the sight of such agony in one so beloved was too much for the Divine Father. He blotted out the sun and withdrew his presence. Under that awful sense of the hiding of his Father's face which forced from the Man of Sorrow the only complaint that ever broke from his lips, " My God! my God! why hast thou forsaken me!" his heart burst asunder in the midst of his bowels, and instantly he ceased to live. If it cost the Son thus much to endure, imagine what it must have cost the Father to conceal his face. O my brethren! unless bewildered by false lights of Scripture rather than of reason, we are now adrift upon a silent sea of sorrow, boundless, fathomless, vast as the infinite God. Words could not be more expressive, and yet we but mock our feelings when we say that " God so loved the world that he gave his only begotten Son."

Two or three brief reflections and we resign this oppressive theme, too vast, too mysterious, too deeply solemn for an angel's thought or a seraph's tongue. I see now better than I ever did what must be the meaning of the words, "The Son of Man is come to seek and to save that which was lost." I understand better than I ever did what joy there must be in the presence of the angels of God over one sinner that repenteth. Nor did I ever comprehend so well before what Jesus meant when he told of a father who ran and fell on the neck of his prodigal son and kissed him. My soul stands amazed at the length, and breadth, and depth, and height of the love of God, and owns it past finding out.

I am drawn into sympathy with God. I bear his image, intellectual as well as moral. I am a feeble transcript of the divine mind. God thinks, and feels, and suffers for my sake; then, wherefore should not I for him. He is one of my kind, only infinitely above myself. I am overwhelmed with the thought that when I do wrong God suffers—suffers as only a father can suffer for his child. What suffering is like wounded love? and what love can suffer like that which gave an only begotten Son? My heart is touched, and I say, "O thou blessed God, was not the cross, then, all, but dost thou even now look down and sorrow after me that I so often disobey thy commandments? I desire to do thy will, and from henceforth with all my heart I will strive to do it. I suffer, and I feel that thou sufferest in sympathy with me, and wilt ever suffer while I sin." The Father will not cease to sorrow till the sins and sorrows of the children shall have an end. But now comes a thought that makes me sing, Alleluia! The vast universe is struggling on through sin and pain up to perfection. The grand result of God's suffering love will be to destroy the works of the devil, and remove the curse and make all things new. Then the sufferings of the Father and the children shall end together. That will be the bridal day of creation, the beginning both for the Creator and the creature of perfect and everlasting joy. "Fly swiftly round, ye wheels of time, and bring the promised day," when the sins and sufferings of the children being ended, grief shall vex no more the Father's heart, but the Father and the children rejoice together that the ages of perfect happiness are now at last begun, henceforth to roll on without pause or close.

My conception of humanity is vastly augmented. That surely is worth something which is in the image of God and for which God is concerned so much. Man is but an inferior God and fallen. "Upon the wrecks of his being there lingers still a strange light of divinity." What man can tell the worth of his immortal nature? Let us infer it from what God has done to save it. Shall such labor and such love be lost? He gave his only begotten Son that "whosoever believeth on him should not perish, but have everlasting life." Though he had promised no reward, yet who could long hold out against such love? O thou blessed God, make all thy goodness to pass before us now, and "fill our hearts with sacred grief and penitential pain." "Love so amazing, so divine, demands our souls, our life, our all." To withhold it longer is to cause the heart of God to grieve. O then, impenitent man, at last relent! Fall at his feet and say, "I yield, I yield, by dying love compelled." End thy Father's grief and thine by coming back to him. No doubt he waits thy coming, and will receive thee with open arms. His house will resound with merriment, and he will say: "This, my son, was dead, and is alive again; was lost and is found."

VIII.
THE LAW OF SACRIFICES.
BY REV. M. B. CHAPMAN,
Of the Missouri Conference.

"Behold the Lamb of God, which taketh away the sin of the world!"—JOHN i. 29.

"I beseech you therefore, brethren, by the mercies of God, that ye present your bodies a living sacrifice, holy, acceptable, unto God, which is your reasonable service."—ROM. xii. 1.

Sacrifices and oblations are as old as the human race. As we travel through the nations, our feet can nowhere reach a region where offerings of some character are not found. We hear the cry constantly coming from the great heart of humanity, "What is the acceptable sacrifice?" The most beautiful flowers of the earth and the choicest fruits of the field; strange divinations and streaming altars; hecatombs of slaughtered animals and rivers of human blood flowing through the temples of heathen idolatry; cakes for the queen of heaven and prostrations before the brazen image; children passing through the fire for the insatiable Moloch, and the "fruit of the body given for the sin of the soul"—these are the responses from classical and pagan nations. The altars of blood in the dark forests of America, Indian self-torture and mutilation, African fetichism, Hindoo immolations, and the atrocities of savage cannibalism—these are the hollow answers from the untutored consciences of heathens. Then the voice of a Divine Revelation is heard, and its authoritative commands are, " Behold the Lamb of God, which taketh away the sin of the world!" "Present your bodies a living sacrifice, holy, acceptable unto God."

These declarations unfold to us two great principles which form the foundation of God's revelation to man, and give the true idea of sacrifices. They constitute a divine answer to the great question of all ages and all nations. By a sacrifice of blood, atonement for sin must be made; and then the accepted man must give himself to God. The law called the one a burnt-offering, and the other a meat-offering; the Gospel calls the one faith in the death of the Lamb of God for the sins of the world, and the other a dedication of self in acts of love to the service of God.

The entire system of Revelation is harmonious, and hence we find these two forms of sacrifice reaching back to the very gate of Eden. The altar of blood, whereon lay the burnt-offering, was doubtless erected ere yet the flaming sword had ceased to flash its sheet of fire on every side, thus showing in type that that barred-up way of access to the Tree of Life was to be opened by the blood of the bruised seed of the woman. And to another altar the first pardoned sinner brought the first fruits of that bread won from the ground by the sweat of his brow, as a dedicatory offering typifying his entire surrender of himself to the service of his Maker.

These principles formed the ground of the distinction between the sacrifices of Cain and Abel. Abel was an humble believer in the Atonement to be made by the future "Seed of the woman," and hence, confessing himself a sinner, he first brings a lamb as a type of the Redeemer, and slays it as a burnt-offering. Afterward, having become justified through this act of faith, he doubtless made a meat-offering to God.* But Cain was a rejecter of the Atonement, and sought to present himself to God as if he was under no curse that needed blood to wash his sins away. He brought *only* the meat-offering, and sought to be accepted through his holiness or good works. There was no confession of sin, no acknowledgment of guilt deserving death, no plea for forgiveness through the shedding of blood, no exercise of faith in a Divine antitype. And because his offering of first fruits was not thus founded upon a slain lamb previously offered, God did not accept his sacrifice.

The adumbrations of antediluvian worship become the

---

* "God testifying of his *gifts*."—HEB. xi. 4.

well-defined shadows of the Levitical ritual. Under the law of Moses there were two great classes of sacrifices—those with, and those without blood. The burnt-offering was the most important and significant of the one, the meat-offering of the other. Imagine yourself with the host of Israel as these two important sacrifices are offered, and you will be able to form a lively appreciation of all that was intended and typified by them. The whole congregation is assembled within that vast enclosure, while in the midst is the smoking altar, beside which stand the priests in their official garb. An offerer approaches with his victim, a young lamb, carefully selected from a select portion of a select kind. He solemnly lays his hand upon its head, thus showing the transfer to it of his own sins; leans upon it, thus figuring trust or reliance, and then the animal is slain in his stead—the innocent for the guilty. The priest then takes the blood and sprinkles it around the altar, as a sign of the bestowal of pardon. The whole transaction means confession of sin, faith in the merits of vicarious suffering and death, and pardon through an atonement.

And now that he has offered his burnt-sacrifice, and obtained forgiveness through faith in the promised Redeemer, typified by the lamb, he is prepared to make his meat-offering, and thus dedicate himself to God. This consists of fine flour, frankincense and oil, which represent his person and property—all that he is and all that he has. He brings it to the altar and gives it to the priest, thus acknowledging himself to be the Lord's, and it is burnt as "an offering made by fire, of a sweet savor unto the Lord."

We are now prepared to see the significance of the two passages before us. When John said to his Jewish audience, "Behold the Lamb of God which taketh away the sin of the world!" the image of a smoking altar, a bleeding victim, sprinkled blood, and guilt thus expiated, rose before them, and knowing what all that typified, they beheld in Jesus the promised Messiah—the Lamb slain from the foundation of the world. But when Paul said to the church at Rome, " I beseech you, therefore, brethren, by the mercies of God, that ye present your bodies a living sacrifice, holy, acceptable unto God," considering them already justified by faith in that Lamb who was manifested to take away their sins, he had in his mind the Jewish meat-offering, and was urging them to an entire consecration to the service of God.

From these two passages thus collocated we arrive at two great fundamental truths of our religion: (1.) The burnt-offering, faith in Christ, must always precede the meat-offering, consecration of self in words or works, or the latter will be utterly worthless and unacceptable to God. (2.) When the first has been accomplished, God commands the second.

I. The shadow has now given way to the substance, the type to the antitype. The altar, the sacrificial flames, the slain lamb, the officiating priest, have disappeared before the Cross, the picture of the suffering Just One, " the Lamb of God which taketh away the sin of the world." The smoke of the morning and evening sacrifice no longer ascends from the midst of

THE LAW OF SACRIFICES. 139

the camp of Israel, for "This man after he had offered one sacrifice for sins forever, sat down at the right hand of God."

The grand truth, the greatest the world has ever known, cannot be too often reiterated, that there is salvation only by Christ. The only road to heaven leads by the Cross; there is no escape from hell save by the blood-besprinkled way. Those who attempt to travel to heaven over a road strewn with the palm-branches of good feelings and deeds of self-denial, though it may be watered with tears, will, like Cain, be rejected as despisers of the great sacrifice made for sin. Faith is the only absolute condition of justification, and those who substitute for it morality, good works, penance, church ordinances, or aught else, however good or necessary in itself, are bringing to God their meat-offering before their hearts have been cleansed by the blood of the great burnt-offering.

There is a system of morals abroad in the world at the present day, called by some religion, which consists only in meat-offerings. It tramples the blood of Christ under foot as an unworthy thing, and virtually denies the efficacy of the Atonement. It has reared again the altar where the hand of God planted the Cross; it listens to the thunder of Sinai rather than to the voice of love that comes from Calvary; it turns from "the Lamb of God which taketh away the sin of the world," and looks to outward ceremonies and ordinances to purify the heart and save the soul. Oh, that the words which stirred the soul of the poor Augustinian monk, as he was climbing Pilate's stairway on his knees, might again be reverberated through the world, and the church learn afresh the truth, that "the just shall live by faith."

Krummacher gives us an incident which well illustrates this important subject. A certain minister, noted for his zeal and earnestness, but who had never been very successful in winning souls, was on one occasion preaching from this subject, " A new creature in Christ or eternal condemnation." During the sermon this question forced itself upon the conscience of one of his hearers, " How is it with myself? Does this man declare the real truth? If he does, what must inevitably follow from it?" This thought took such hold upon him that he could not shake it off, and day after day it became more and more troublesome, until finally he determined to go to the preacher himself and ask him, upon his conscience, if he really believed what he had lately preached? He carried out his intention, and the preacher, much astonished, assured him with great earnestness that he had spoken the Word of God, and consequently infallible truth. " What then is to become of *us ?* " replied the visitor. His last word, *us*, startled the preacher; but he rallied his thoughts and began to explain the plan of salvation to the inquirer, and to exhort him to repent and believe. But the latter, as though he had not heard one syllable of what the preacher said, repeated with increasing emotion the anxious exclamation, " If it be *truth*, sir, I beseech you, what are *we* to do ?" Terrified, the preacher staggered back. " *We*," thought he. "What means this *we ?* "

And endeavoring to stifle his inward uneasiness and embarrassment, he resumed his exhortations and advice. Tears came into the eyes of the visitor; he smote his hands together like one in despair, and exclaimed in an accent which might have moved a heart of stone, "Sir, if it be truth, we are lost and undone!" The preacher stood for a moment, pale, trembling and speechless. Then, overwhelmed with emotion, with downcast eyes and convulsive sobbing, he cried, "Friend, down on your knees; let us pray and cry for mercy!" They knelt down and prayed, and shortly afterward the visitor took his leave. The preacher shut himself up in his closet. Next Sunday word was sent that the preacher was not well, and could not appear. The same thing happened the Sunday following. But on the third Sabbath he made his appearance before his congregation, worn and pale with his recent conflict, but his eyes beaming with joy, and commenced his discourse with the surprising and affecting declaration, that he had now for the first time passed through the strait gate. And his new experience gave him a power which he had never before possessed, for now God, accepting his labors and prayers, granted him many seals to his ministry.

There are many men in the Church of God to-day, serving at her altar and worshiping in her temples, who have never felt the power of the Holy Ghost, and who are depending for salvation wholly on the fact that their lives are in conformity with certain church regulations, and that there is a semblance of good works in some of their actions. Herein lies the secret of an unfruitful ministry and a lifeless church. Brethren, examine yourselves and see whether or not you are in the faith. Have you a rich Christian experience? Have you found peace in believing? Has your heart been purified by the sprinkled blood of the slain Lamb? If not, leave your gifts before the altar, and rest not day nor night until you realize that "the blood of Jesus Christ cleanseth us from all sin."

II. When the burnt sacrifice has been offered, then a meat-offering must be made.

The Jewish meat-offering was presented daily, along with the morning and evening sacrifice, teaching us that we are to consecrate all that we have to the Lord's use, not at irregular intervals, as impulse or expediency would dictate, but *daily*. When the soul has been accepted in Christ, and the pardon of sins experienced through the Holy Ghost, then we are to bring our bodies—all that we have and all that we are—"a living sacrifice, holy, acceptable unto God."

The Church of God needs to-day, more than ever before, a consecrated membership to worship at her altars, a consecrated ministry to stand in her holy places. The powers of darkness are being marshalled for a conflict severe beyond precedence. A bold and irreverent materialism would rob Christianity of her holiest and most precious truths. Infidelity, wise above that which is written, is seeking to array the creature against the Creator, nature against nature's God, science against the Bible. Crime no longer waits for the midnight hour to steal forth covertly from her hiding place, but in the broad glare of the sun she flaunts herself before the eyes of all men. Wickedness and corruption in high places have ceased to be exceptional. It is an age of compromises, which seeks to obliterate the old landmarks, to bend creed to practice, to bring the Church into conformity with the world. If these be some of the characteristics of the times upon which we have fallen, how all-important it is that a spirit of deeper consecration should come upon the entire Church!

It was a custom of the Middle Ages for a page, before he was dubbed a knight, to enter a temple dedicated to the Most High, and, reverently approaching the altar, to lay thereon his sword and his shield. Then a white-robed priest came forward, and solemnly consecrating the weapons to the cause of truth, of innocence, and of virtue, invoked the blessing of God upon them and upon him who should bear them. The Middle Ages, with their knights, their chivalry, their Damascus blades, and their shields, have gone, but a similar duty devolves upon every one. Let Christian hearts bow before the altar of God, and, with solemn vows, consecrate all they have and are to his service and glory. And then a thousand attendant angels, clad in the garments of immortality, shall surround us, as Christ, our great High Priest, blesses us, and dedicates us by the influx of new powers, new wisdom, and new strength, to the grander, the holier, and the sublimer purposes of human life.

Has God blessed you with high intellectual endowments, with commanding mental powers, so that at your talismanic touch nature opens her arcana and reveals her secret treasures; so that your soul exults in discovering "those immemorial truths which wander through the ages," in traversing the vast empyrean of thought, ever rising to loftier heights and fairer scenes? God commands you to dedicate all these rich and glorious gifts to him, to consecrate to his service these powers of mind. Let your thought exult in discovering the infinite things of God, and as it rises to the magnificent conception of an eternal and omnipotent Being, administering the affairs of a universe, and views the vast exhibitions of divine wisdom and love, and comprehends the stupendous sweep of the spiritual and the material, let the world be blessed, and humanity exalted, and God glorified through your imperial mind.

Has God given you influence and power in the world, and do men vow fealty to you? Is it as though a thousand telegraphic wires met where you could touch them, and with each volition you could send abroad an influence that would reach thousands of beings, while every pulsation of your heart or movement of your mind modified the pulsations of other hearts and the movements of other intellects? Use all this for God, and let that magnetic influence draw immortal souls toward heaven. That power, if exerted for good, is a mighty weapon which may prove effectual in tearing down the strongholds of Satan and leading the armies of God on to victory. It was a mighty power that was latent in steam until Watt evoked its spirit from the waters and set the giant to turning the iron arms of machinery. It was a mighty power that was latent in the skies until science climbed their heights, and seizing the spirit of the thunder, chained it to our surface, abolishing distance, outstripping the wind, and flashing our thoughts across rolling seas to distant continents. But a far mightier power than these is the power of a life devoted to good and great purposes—moral power consecrated to God and used for heaven.

Has God given you wealth? Is there a Midas touch conferred upon you, and are the guardian genii who preside over the hidden treasures of this world the servants of your pleasure? Are your storehouses full, your coffers overflowing, your homes filled with luxury and surrounded by elegance? You have been invested with weighty responsibilities, and God has but made you his steward in the proper disbursement of these riches. Lay your wealth upon his altar, and let earthly accumulation buy heavenly treasures, that you may not only be rich in this world's treasures, but also rich toward God.

But it may be that none of these gifts are yours; that you have but the one small talent, for God has left none of us utterly bankrupt. It is as much our duty to bring the single talent as though we had ten. God will not despise the day of small things. The eye that notes the falling sparrow and numbers the hairs of your head will not overlook the smallest offering of his weakest creature.

Being then "sanctified through the offering of the body of Jesus Christ, once for all," let us, brethren, "present our bodies a living sacrifice, holy, acceptable unto God." Come, Lord, and accept the offering!

IX.
MORE LABORERS IN THE HARVEST.

BY REV. J. P. NOLAN,

Of the Missouri Conference.

"But when He saw the multitudes, He was moved with compassion on them, because they fainted, and were scattered abroad, as having no shepherd.

"Then saith He unto His disciples, The harvest truly is plenteous, but the laborers are few; pray ye, therefore, the Lord of the harvest, that He will send forth laborers into His harvest."—MATT. ix. 36–38.

This passage, that tells how Jesus was moved with compassion when he saw the multitudes fainting and scattered abroad, as sheep having no shepherd, while it leads us at once to the idea of his mission, it also reveals *the place which preaching has* in connection with the Church and the religious life of the world.

The ministry of Christ, in its lower form, shows him to have been the first of philanthropists. While preaching the Gospel of the kingdom in all the cities and villages whithersoever he went, the number who received healing at his hands is indicated by the statement, that " they brought unto him all sick people that were taken with divers diseases and torments, and those which were possessed with devils, and those which were lunatic, and those that had the palsy, and he healed them all." So that we are not surprised that St. Matthew says in the next verse (iv. 25), "And there followed him great multitudes of people from Decapolis, and from Jerusalem, and from Judea, and from beyond Jordan." And now in the text we are told that with these multitudes before him, whose bodies and minds, too, had shared so largely in his beneficence, he turns to his disciples and says (for such is the *spiritual import* of the occasion): "You all see the pitiable condition of these poor people—many of them diseased and maimed in body, others possessed with devils and demented, all of them distressed with faintness, and scattered abroad without teachers, and with none to bless and take care of them. And you also see how I have had compassion on them and healed them all. Now here are two lessons I would have you learn—*First*, the bodily and temporal condition of these multitudes is a sensible illustration to you of their far greater spiritual infirmities and wretchedness. *Second*, as I have had compassion and have cured them of whatsoever disease they had, so do I propose, by giving my life for the people, to save them eternally in the kingdom of heaven; and you are also to turn toward your fellow-men in compassion, as you have seen me do, and be my witnesses of these things, to the intent that all may come to the knowledge of the truth and be saved from their sins."

Such was the mission of Jesus. And through the whole of his public ministry he sanctified preaching by making it the method of publishing to us sinners that "he came to seek and to save that which was lost." From the Mount of Ascension he gave, as his last commission to his disciples to establish and consolidate his kingdom, the well-known injunction, "Go ye into all the world, and preach the Gospel to every creature." That was to be the lever by which the world should be turned upside down. No instrument is so powerful as the "foolishness of preaching;" and the Master himself has ordained this institution to the end of time as the chief agency in the world's conversion.

However powerful the press, through good books, the religious periodical, and the weekly Church paper, preaching doth far surpass it as a means of "calling sinners to repentance." St. Paul's dispensation of the Gospel was not so much to administer the sacraments, nor to bear rule in the Church, but the rather "to preach." (1 Cor. i. 17.) His labors and epistles show in how wide a sense he understood that commission.

The great times of restoring doctrine, and of renewing the life of the Church—the times of the outpouring of the Spirit of God when many "turn unto the Lord"—have been distinguished as times of preaching. And who does not see the highest wisdom in the ordinance on the simple principle of the power begotten in the sympathy of kindred natures, when brought into contact through the living voice proclaiming the riches of God's mercy toward them that believe?

Thankful should we be that "we have this treasure in earthen vessels," and not by "the ministration of angels," or by the rising of "one from the dead."

And it is the *Gospel* which is to be the great subject of their preaching—not science, not politics, not "preaching to the day." Moreover, this Gospel—of facts that never grow old, of truths that abide with an eternal power—coming to every man of this age, and of all ages, as "a savor of life unto life," is to be preached, not in the words which man's wisdom teacheth, but which the Holy Ghost teacheth. (1 Cor. ii. 13.)

In the light of these thoughts we can easily discover,

I. THE OBJECT OF THE MINISTRY. — *To stand in Christ's stead with a heart of love and pity for poor sinners, and show them " the ways of life."*

The sacred heart of Jesus is that blessed fountain of mercy which would fain send out its crimson current until the souls of men, touched by the life-giving stream, should feel the inspiration of renewed virtue, and shout with conscious joy : " In that day there shall be a fountain opened to the house of David, and to the inhabitants of Jerusalem, for sin and for uncleanness." (Zech. xiii. 1.) " Unto him that loved us and washed us from our sins in his own blood," etc. (Rev. v. 1.) " Feed the Church of God which he hath purchased with his own blood." (Acts xx. 28.) Since " Christ loved the Church and gave himself for it, that he might sanctify and cleanse it" (Eph. v. 25–26), so ought the souls of men, all of whom are conditionally saved, and by construction are or may be the Church of God, the Lord's harvest—so ought these souls, I say, to be precious in the sight of God's ministers, and receive such loving care and attention as Christ himself would give them if he were again on the earth.

The sympathy of our Lord for the miseries of mankind was so sincere an affection that he performed the office of relieving their distresses in a way that clearly showed how sensibly he entered into the sorrows of others. And among the great number of miracles he wrought it is instructive to see how many were *miracles of healing.* But Jesus, approached by a woman "which was a sinner," while he sat at meat in Simon the Pharisee's house, and receiving her tears and kisses on his feet, opens his tender, gracious heart to our sinful humanity when he says to her, "Thy sins are forgiven," (St. Luke vii. 36,) as scarcely any one of his miracles can do.

Thus when, in imitation of Christ, his ministers manifest compassion for the wants of men, it is a lovely grace, even when it has respect only to the temporal needs of mankind. But it is of a much higher stamp when produced by a deep sense of their spiritual wants, and seeks to administer relief by pointing them to the cross of Christ. Such was the compassion our blessed Lord was moved with on the occasion before us, and which he sought to inspire in the hearts of his disciples.

The special end of the ministry, then, is not the creation of a hierarchy (1 Pet. v. 3), as that in the Roman Church; nor that the office should be made subservient to the purposes of human ambition, with high-sounding titles and princely revenues (St. John xiii. 16), as is seen in Churches established by the State; but, in the simple words of the history of its origin, it appears as a *vocation of men by Christ to the holy work of rescuing their fellowmen from the guilt and consequences of sin.* The single and Christly aim of the minister lies right on the face of his commission : " Go ye into all the world, and preach the Gospel to every creature." From this commission it is plain that before the Master was the spread of his saving truth by chosen agents and suitable means. And equally evident is his view of the *character of the agents* and the *nature of the means* to be employed.

The minister must be self-denying, holy, and a lover of the souls of men. And the real power of the Gospel will appear, as in the olden time, the closer we get to the apostolic way of preaching it.

St. Paul took as his subject the central truths of the Gospel, "Jesus and the Resurrection." His spirit was that of a heroic self-abnegation : " Neither count I my life dear unto myself." (Acts xx. 24.) His love for his Jewish brethren (Rom. ix. 1–3), was a type of the passion he had for all men, and it was near akin to that of the Savior. How great was his sense of the sinner's unhappy condition. (Rom. ii. 9.) What an instance of ministerial solicitude in the words, " I would that ye knew what great conflict I have for you, and for them at Laodicea, and for as many as have not seen my face in the flesh." (Col. ii. 1 ; see 2 Cor. xi. 1–3.) If ministers would only keep in view the *original design* of their sacred calling—to have compassion on sinners, and go to them, as Paul did, in loving sympathy (1 Cor. ix. 22), and " warn every one night and day, with tears " (Acts xx. 31), to be reconciled to God—what mighty results would follow ! How soon we should behold the beginning of the end, " the promised day of Israel ! "

But the passage requires that we consider in the next place,

II. THE NEED OF MORE MINISTERS.—"*The harvest is plenteous, but the laborers are few.*"

The harvest plenteous—the laborers few! This was the infallible judgment of the Savior "in the days of his flesh." More truly and impressively can the same declaration be made to-day, though eighteen hundred years and more have come and gone.

In the roll of these centuries what mighty changes have occurred among nations and peoples!

The Roman Empire, then so vast and dominant, fell into "decline," was overrun and dismembered limb by limb, and has utterly perished as a nation. The Jewish people, rejecting the Christ of their own Scriptures, were peeled and scattered over all the earth, and live as a striking and perpetual illustration of the truth of prophesy and the sin of unbelief. Mohammed, the false prophet, of wonderful genius and character for conquest and organization, with sword and torch, founded an empire, political and religious, embracing portions of Europe, Africa and Asia, that has continued to this day. The Czar of Russia governs a realm long reckoned among the Great Powers. Great Britain, on whose territorial expanse the sun never sets, and which may still be regarded as the bulwark of our Protestant Christianity, was a Roman province of barbarians when Jesus delivered the Sermon on the Mount. The mighty empire of free government and Christian civilization in this Western world, stretching from ocean to ocean, the gathering place of the nations, now rapidly becoming the centre of the strongest moral and spiritual forces, and which, under God, we trust, shall be made to our common humanity the hope of Freedom and Religion from the rising to the setting sun, was a land unpopulated and unknown while the disciples tarried in Jerusalem " to be endued with power from on high." The man who sits, as he says, in the chair of St. Peter, whom a Council in 1870 voted to be infallible! and who erst was a temporal prince, governing " The States of the Church," and not long ago was wont to make kings and potentates tremble when he hurled his anathemas at them from the Vatican, has been despoiled of " The States" (the poor remains of his temporal sway), sees his windy bulls laughed at in every land, and is now in this year of grace, thank God, a much altered Pope from what he was. Prussia, through the happy results of two recent wars, has widened the limits of her rule; and Fatherland rejoices to see Kaiser William reigning in peace (and cheering hope for our Protestant faith) over the States of Germany, united and freer than ever they were before. Want of space will not allow me to pursue this line of thought further, nor is it important. Amid all these changes of national limits and conditions, of the falling of old governments and the rising of new ones—sometimes where none had ever existed—the population of the world has been steadily increasing. It is *vastly larger* now than at the time when Jesus uttered the words of the text. I could wish for proper statistics at hand to make the truth of my statement sufficiently impressive. But is the disproportion between the extent of the harvest and the number of the laborers as great now as when the Master spoke of the need of more laborers? Certainly not. That was the day of the beginning of the Gospel dispensation.

Will it not be argued that if the Church, with a ministry more or less faithful for these long ages, has reached only about a fourth of the world's population, and a large part of that but nominally, there is slight hope that Christianity will ever become the religion of all mankind? This cannot be said if the real facts are considered—as these: (1.) The Church is made the agent, though a voluntary one, in the diffusion of the Gospel. (2.) None but moral and spiritual means can or should be employed in bringing men to Christ. (3.) Those to whom we tell the story of the Savior's love may despise the riches of his mercy, as many have done and continue to do.

Greater fidelity, perhaps, among Christians, a profounder conviction in the Church as to the value of "the foolishness of preaching," a trustful looking to Christ for the continued fulfillment of his promise to send the Holy Ghost, "who would reprove the world of sin, and of righteousness, and of judgment," would have preached the gospel long before now, and preached it successfully, to the very ends of the earth.

Much of the great work the Church has in hand *has been already accomplished*. She is learning better how to do what remains to be done. The problem of the world's regeneration is not so complex as it used to be.

The means to be employed, while remaining the same in kind, have been multiplied a thousandfold. If men need teachers yet—and they do and will—I think they are more willing to be instructed. Difficulties once in the way have been removed. Many wrong prejudices have been successfully combated. Superstitions, that once degraded men to the level of brutes, have disappeared before the advancing light. It cannot be doubted, too, that among Christians generally the true, essential spirit of our holy religion is much better understood. We have had a development of the doctrine, as well as an unfolding of the spirit of Christianity. Albeit there is nothing among us materially different from, or more than, the perceptions and experience of a few of the wisest and best living in the first ages of the New Testament Church. But as Christian belief, as also the Christian life that it begets, is a growth, when we look at the entire body of believers, there has been growth—growth in knowledge, in zeal, in charity; growth in the conviction that this world belongs to Christ, and shall have the gospel of Christ, and be saved by that gospel if it will.

The last century has witnessed the flaming up of a missionary zeal like that of Apostolic times, which carried the gospel into all the world known at that day. With the revival of the spirit of evangelism in the Church there is a painful discovery of the *insufficiency* of the present number of laborers to do the work. The harvest is plenteous: whether we look at the domestic field, or lift our eyes to distant lands, the harvest is *abundant*. (*Vide* St. John iv. 35.)

From one cause or another, the peoples heretofore inaccessible can now be approached.

The East India Company, like a wedge, by the providence of God, has opened all India to British rule and British civilization; and along with commerce and the love of gain went the Gospel more than fifty years ago, and Christian converts to-day in that country are counted by thousands, and the laborers, both foreign and native, are hopefully harvesting in the valley of the Indus, on the table-lands of Rohilcund, and at the foot of the Himalayas. The population of India is about 240,000,000. China, a colossal empire, ancient, peculiar, self-contained, bigoted and peaceful, from time immemorial was quite closely shut up against all efforts by Christian missionaries, but within the present generation has thrown open its principal inlets, and Christianity, by treaty stipulations, is recognized, and the liberty of preaching its doctrines guaranteed by the government. What a magnificent harvest-field for the Church! With what holy ardor should the heralds of the Cross long to enter that land where *one-third* of the earth's inhabitants are perishing for lack of knowledge! What an army of laborers will be required to gather so vast a harvest!

A beginning has been made. Sixty years ago Dr. Morrison translated the Bible into the Chinese language. To say nothing of what the Papists are doing, Protestant missionaries of nearly every name have kindled a light here and there at a few of the chief centres, that shines with an increasing blaze upon the darkness of teeming millions.

Japan, with a population of forty millions, ingenious, imitative, and now strangely tolerant, has become dissatisfied with its ancient civilization, turns to Europe and America, willing to receive the improvements of Western art and science, and the whole country is *literally open* to the advances and work of Christian charity.

These three—India, China and Japan—are the great objective points of missionary enterprise. They furnish fully one-half of the population of the entire globe. We know unbelief will shake its head and doubt of ever seeing them become the "inheritance" of our Christ. They are covered with such gross darkness—are so given up to vile affections, "being filled with all unrighteousness, fornication, and wickedness." But, dear Christian reader, who and what were *your ancestors* at the remove of only a few generations back? *Idolaters* they were—benighted, sensual and devilish. No better than these heathen. No more prepared to receive the Gospel. Somehow *you* have been *won to Christ.* Nor is the Lord's arm shortened that it cannot lift up the poor and needy as of old.

Look at the Sandwich Islands! In the beginning of this century the American Board sent out its first installment of Christian laborers. Two years ago the missionaries were withdrawn—the people, once so lowly and brutal, having received a written language, established schools and founded a constitutional government; and the churches, supplied with a native ministry, able to take care of the mental and spiritual wants of the population.

Turn your eye to the South Pacific, and you see a multitude of Islands, like stars in the midnight sky, dotting the bosom of the ocean. There our brethren of the Wesleyan Missionary Society have been harvesting, for two score years. What are the results? Cannibals have been turned into Christians—naked savages have clothed themselves with the garments and ways of Christian society—schools, churches, agriculture, regulated government, are now the blessings of the people. Lying to the east of Africa is the large and beautiful Island of Madagascar, with three million souls, which in the last decade has been decisively won to the Cross, and now shines as a permanent star in the diadem of the Savior.

Is our holy religion true? Let it be judged by its fruits in Europe and America. Does it give sufficient promise of universal extension and final triumph? O yes! we are fully persuaded of this when we consider the pledges of its Author, the nature of its doctrines, and their relation to the wants of us sinful men. *No other religion can be universal*, for it alone has power of God to be for the salvation of men.

St. Paul, rehearsing the story of his conversion in the presence of King Agrippa, declared how Jesus had said to him, "I have appeared unto thee for this purpose, to make thee a minister," and "now I send thee unto the Gentiles, to open their eyes, and to turn them from darkness to light, and from the power of Satan unto God, that they may receive forgiveness of sins, and nheritance among them which are sanctified by faith that is in me." (Acts xxvi. 16–18.) Every minister of the Lord Jesus going forth to the harvest of the world, is divinely assured that these blessed signs shall follow in them that believe.

We now come to the last division of our subject.

III. HOW MORE MINISTERS ARE TO BE OBTAINED.— *"Pray ye therefore the Lord of the harvest, that he would send forth laborers into his harvest."*

Most happily for us, the question, How may a needful supply of ministers be obtained? has been answered by the Lord himself, and, like all questions of deepest import to our spiritual life, has been answered *plainly*.

Here and there in the progress of his ministry, as without design, in an easy, natural way, Christ asserts his *divinity*. Abraham, Moses, David, Elijah, think of themselves as *only men*. Paul and Barnabas (Acts xiv. 8–19), when the Lystrans "would have done sacrifice" unto them for healing "a cripple who never had walked, rent their clothes and ran in among the people, crying out, Sirs, why do ye these things? *We also are men* of like passions with you." But Jesus of Nazareth quietly receives the *worship* of the disciples and many others as though it were *all right*. He works divers miracles in their presence, but with no more effort or pretension than they would have shown in moving their hands or eating their evening meal. He had already spoken of himself as Lord, and as having authority to open or shut "the kingdom of heaven" to men (Matt. vii. 21–24); and consequently in the text he calls the harvest of souls "*his harvest.*" Whose harvest but his could it be? Creator of our souls (John i. 1), and Savior of our souls (Eph. i. 17), he, and he alone, is "the Lord of the harvest." If the harvest is his will he not save it? Will he not provide the necessary laborers? Who does this in any case but the owner of the harvest?

1. *A call to the sacred work of the ministry is from the Lord.* He reserves to himself the right of choosing those who are "to preach unto the people," and "to feed the church." "No man taketh this honor to himself, but he that is called of God as was Aaron. (Heb. v. 4.)

So the apostle testifies as to himself, "It pleased God, who separated me from my mother's womb, and called me by his grace, to reveal his Son in me, that I might preach him among the Gentiles." (Gal. i. 15, 16.)

Men will sometimes mistake duty and intrude themselves into this ministry. To such how irksome is the toil of the harvest! How few the sheaves they bring in with them! If consciously unsent they go into the harvest, it is a great presumption, a daring adventure, partaking of the nature of a crime. (See Numb. xvi. 1–36, and 2 Chron. xxvi. 16–22.) But the Lord makes no mistakes, whatever we may think about it, although all his laborers are not careful to follow the wholesome advice St. Paul gave his "son in the gospel" (2 Tim. ii. 15), for preachers may lose the testimony of a good conscience, and fail to teach themselves while they teach others. Some of those, however, that we think unlearned, and whose "bodily presence is weak and their speech contemptible," are chosen instruments, and precious to "the Lord of the harvest." God has a very sovereign way in this matter of calling men to be preachers. But we should mistake greatly if we supposed it a way without reason and without a plan, a part of which he has shown us.

2. *Very consistently the good Lord promises to be with the laborers while harvesting*, for the Great Commission closes with the words, " Lo, I am with you always, to the end of the world." This means : (*a*) He will grant his comforting and guiding presence to the ministers of the gospel. A difficult and arduous work is theirs. The wisest cannot meet the responsibility alone—*this care of souls*. And when temptations arise, when unlooked for troubles come, when perplexity, sickness, want, distress, are encountered, what shall the servant do without the Master? *He does guide and comfort the harvesters.* Ministerial biography, from the letters of the apostle to the journal of the humblest itinerant, is full of touching proofs of the dear Savior's presence. (*b*) It also means that the Holy Spirit will give success to the word. " Not by might, nor by power, but by my Spirit, saith the Lord, shall ye prevail." (Zech. iv. 6.) " Our word came in power and in the Holy Ghost." (1 Thess. i. 5.) Also in Phil. ii. 13, " It is God who worketh in you both to will and to do of his good pleasure."

" The Lord opened the heart of Lydia," by which she was enabled to attend to the apostle's message, and understand and receive it. Unless the Holy Spirit breathe *life* into the sermon, and apply the word to the sinner's heart, most certainly he will continue to sleep and be as one dead. But while the preacher's dependence on the working of the Spirit is thus absolute, he has definite assurance that God will not withhold "the increase."

This success may not always be in the quickening of the hearer to the life of faith. There *is* a success of the word in testimony against sin—a vindication of it in the punishment of evil doers. In both ways—in the justice and in the grace—our Thrice Holy Lord reveals himself to angels and to men. Dear reader, may we behold his milder face in the Son of his love!

> " O Spirit of redeeming love,
>   Help preach the reconciling word;
> Give power and unction from above,
>   Whene'er the joyful sound is heard."

3. *The rate of ministerial supply is conditioned upon our prayers.* Two things embarrass me just here—the importance of this article, and that I am so near the end of the sermon. Many no doubt have wondered at the words, "Pray ye the Lord of the harvest that he would send forth laborers into his harvest." If he understands the wants of the church and the world, if none can or should go forth without his commission, if he exercises the right of choosing who shall be ministers, why concern ourselves about the matter at all? This is the old objection of blind unbelief and foolish reasoning against prayer for *any* object. Prayer to God for pardoning mercy, and for all other things promotive of our well-being and happiness, can be easily vindicated by reason and the Scriptures. In God's goodness, no less than in his wisdom and sovereign pleasure, prayer and blessing, and their opposites as well, stand connected, like cause and effect, by his un-

changeable counsel and decree. This arrangement is in the interest of *his glory* and *our happiness*. Who should complain if all richest gifts in the hands of our Heavenly Father *wait* upon our *asking* for them? Unprayerfulness explains (and justifies as to God) everything in the sinner's condition. A backslidden, unworking, ineffective church at any time results from not having continued to look to God in prayer. It is the same remark to say that the apparently slow subjugation of the world to Christ is largely explained in the too great want of prayer among the people of God, and especially in respect of this very question of ministerial supply. How deeply should it affect our minds and hearts to remember that the *lack of ministers* in number, character, and efficiency, is made dependent on our prayers? O let us consider our great responsibility in the premises! At this very hour the openings of opportunity for preaching the gospel are such as the Church never witnessed. In almost all the world, go where you will, the ministers of Jesus may preach him without hindrance. And with the opportunity there is abundance of means in the hands of the Church—everything in fact but men, and the Lord of the harvest says, " Pray for these and I will send them forth." Shall we not betake ourselves to prayer as he directs—prayer in the congregation, in the family circle, and in the closet?

> " On thee, O Lord, we wait,
>   Our wants are in thy view;
> The harvest truly yet is great,
>   The laborers are few.

> "Convert and send forth more
> Into thy Church abroad,
> And let them speak thy word of power,
> As workers with their God."

A thought or two will close the discussion. Faith and works are intimately connected. In the effort sometimes to answer our own petitions we receive the blessing we have prayed for. We pray for health, friends, success in business, and we try to shape our life to these ends. We seek by earnest appeal to bring some one to Christ, but the effort presupposes prayer. You pray that God would raise up more ministers. Why not try to answer the prayer by offering him *your* son? I know the pay is poor as the world looks at it, and the work hard, and much of it right against the grain of all our natural inclinations; but if your son has good parts and promises well, the Lord has need of such and may like to use him. The consecration of our children, *both sons and daughters*, to God to be employed in his harvest, if he pleases, is a *part* of the prayer we make for the spread of the gospel. Some pious mother is drawn out in prayer for the same object, and her little Samuel is taken to the temple. St. Paul must have received an *early* consecration by prayer for the service of the Church, and his *education was directed* accordingly. A noble-hearted layman, or an individual church, seeing the greatness of the harvest, prays for an increase of laborers, but the prayer is followed by the aid which helps a young licentiate through the college and the seminary. Ministerial aid societies, and *all bequests* to assist young men to prepare for the ministry, are endeavors with a view of answering our prayers. May we not expect, too, that God will always look chiefly among *the children of his people* for the laborers he wants? What I *insist upon* is, that we shall humbly *ask* the Lord to use *any* of our children, *all of them* if he will, in the holy service of the Church.

The *noble uses* of ministerial service, and the *sweetness* of ministerial life, are eloquently referred to in the following extract from a late address of the most widely known of American preachers:

"Men say that the pulpit has run its career, and that it is but a little time before it will come to an end. Not so long as men continue to be weak, and sinful, and tearful, and expectant, without any help near; not until men are transformed and the earth empty—not until then will the work of the Christian ministry cease; and there never was an epoch, from the time of the apostles to our day, when the servants of Christ had such a field, and there was such need of them and such hope and cheer in the work, and when it was so certain that a real man in the spirit of his calling would reap so abundantly as to-day. And if I were to choose again, having before me the possibilities of profits and emoluments of merchant life, and the honors to be gained through law, the science and love that come from the medical profession, and the honorable ranks of teachers, I still again would choose the Christian ministry. It is the sweetest in its substance, the most enduring in its choice, the most content in its poverty and limits (if your lot is cast in places of scarcity), more full of crowned hopes, more full of whispering messages from those gone before, nearer to the threshold, nearer to the throne, nearer to the brain, to the heart that was pierced, but that lives forever and says, 'BECAUSE I LIVE YE SHALL LIVE ALSO.'"

X.

DOING THE SAYINGS OF CHRIST.

BY REV. C. C. WOODS,

Of West St. Louis Conference.

"Therefore, whosoever heareth these sayings of mine, and doeth them, I will liken him unto a wise man, which built his house upon a rock."—MATTHEW vii. 24.

That wisdom which received the approbation of the Master must insure to man the highest results, both in this world and in that which is to come. No end less than this was, in his estimation, worth the effort of man, nor can he now approve anything the tendency of which is contrary to this. He "commended" the dishonest steward because he exhibited craftiness and foresight in turning his dishonesty to account, but he did not endorse the course pursued by him, nor pronounce him wise. He might declare the "children of this world wiser *in their generation* than the children of light," but it is easy to see in this a criticism upon the sluggishness and want of zeal characterizing many who profess to labor for eternity, rather than an approval of the eager pursuit of pleasure and gain manifest in those who look not beyond the present life. He could unqualifiedly endorse nothing save that which tended directly to the higher interests of man as a citizen of eternity. And he who in his way of life meets the approval of the Savior, the favor of God, certainly occupies the highest position humanity can secure, and has nothing to fear in the time to come.

Whatever the character of his creed or the soundness of his *faith* in the estimation of the theological world, if he only consciously rests in God and follows the path of his appointment in singleness of heart, all is secure.

Our Lord, from the standpoint of his divinity, teaches us that this wisdom, which means so much to man, has two essential manifestations, and only two—" the *hearing* and the *doing* his sayings." And if any object that these are *only* manifestations of a hidden principle, we answer that the Savior here approves the first alone, saying nothing whatever of the last. And if the principle were *all*, and its manifestation nothing, it is yet unquestionably true that this wisdom cannot live in the soul without outward indication; neither is faith known to others nor recognized by our Lord under favorable conditions except by the fruit it bears. It is true, therefore, that whosoever fulfills the conditions mentioned by the Savior, whosover *hears* and *does* his commandments, is saved from sin in the present, and from pain in the future life. And man must possess the power to do this, either inherent in self or supplied from above, else is our Gospel a delusion and a cheat, and Jesus Christ mocks the sin-bound children of earth by offering to them a salvation he well knows they have no power to secure.

The hearing the declarations of the Son of God is a matter of primary importance. Without this, in fact, while we would not abridge the mercies of God, we can truly say that salvation *by faith in Christ* is an impossibility. It is not necessary, of course, that man should receive the word in the usual way. Circumstances may forbid his attendance upon the sanctuary, ignorance or poverty may prevent a personal use of the Bible; but the great truths embodied in the sayings of Christ must in some way reach the mind and touch the heart before there is a reasonable probability of any action resulting from the revelation of the Master's will. And it is not only a matter of grave importance that enough of the truth be garnered to change the current of the life, but it is likewise necessary, in order to *intelligent* Christianity, that man should imbibe as much as possible of the divine wisdom.

That which is called a conviction of sin is the legitimate *result* of giving attention to the truths of the Gospel—of hearing "these sayings" of the Savior. And it is an *invarible* result in that mind which receives the Bible as a revelation from God. This, of course, necessitates the conclusion that all those who acknowledge the divinity of Christ, and yet do not obey him, are convicted of sin. And is it not true? What is conviction more than a knowledge of sin as resident in the soul? How many of this class will deny it as a fact revealed in consciousness that they are sinners in the sight of God? Few indeed! Of course, there are times in the life of every man when this knowledge of personal sin becomes agonizing. But it is equally true, that there may often be the strongest outward indication of conviction—even amounting to physical convulsion—when the soul has not, and does not, clearly receive the fact of its guilt in the sight of God. And as the stronger influences of conviction generally exhibit themselves with decreasing force from time to time, it ought to be conceded that it is as unnecessary as it is unsafe for the sinner to *wait* until the floodtide of his emotions may bear him over the shallows of hesitation. And it can certainly be clearly established from the Word of God, that he expects man to wait for nothing, save a knowledge of his ruin and the remedy provided. The sinner should be taught from every pulpit, that the consciousness of sin renders him doubly guilty in the sight of heaven if he fly not at once to the Cross. If this were more generally done, instead of an occasional revival—a few added to the Church, the rest left over to another time—we should, doubtless, behold a revival of the primitive efficiency of the Gospel, and daily see " added to the Church such as should be saved."

If the sinner bend the power of his mind to contemplate himself as a sinner; if he act upon the mere fact in consciousness, soon will his boasted serenity of mind be gone, and every chamber of his soul be haunted by phantoms from the troubled past and grim spectres that point him with bony fingers to a direful future. Remorse will sit upon the soul, until, banished by the sunlight of the gospel, it gives place to a solemn regret—a "godly sorrow" that "worketh repentance to salvation not to be repented of."

Now the man is face to face with his duty. His conscience is quickened, his mind is enlarged, his sensibilities are in action. If he now keep his eye steadily fixed upon these "sayings" of Christ, and all his powers in frame to do them, the time will be brief until he, his repentance accomplished, shall sweetly rest in God.

Repentance is action, and action of the highest order —action levying tribute upon all the powers of humanity. For if the sensibilities are called upon they must respond; if there is work for the hands it must be done; and it is a somewhat peculiar fact, that at this crisis there is "no help in man," and the soul experiences no consolation from the presence of God. Though friends may be near, yet their sympathies avail not. Though the war-cry of the Church ring in his ear, it awakens no enthusiasm. Though angels may pityingly look upon the struggle from afar, yet they do not "minister" unto him. He is, so to speak, "in the wilderness," and "tempted of the devil." Oh, how fearful the hour! Who that has experienced it can ever forget? It is a conflict in which no bugle note nor scream of fife ever comes to stir the flagging energies of the soul and help it on to victory. All the powers of earth, of hell, and of a carnal nature, in that hour array themselves against these "sayings" of Christ writ on the soul by the Holy Ghost. The pass of Thermopylæ tried men's souls, but not like this. The charge of the Old Guard was fearful, but not so fearful as this. The destiny of a nation often turns upon the issue of carnal strife, but the destiny of the soul always turns upon this. There are none to be found who are unwilling to be saved; few who are unwilling to be Christians. If God would only do away with the necessity for action in the soul—if he would only change the nature of man from sin to holiness without an effort on his part, all would be well (as he thinks), and he would " run up with joy the shining way." But two things are absolutely necessary on the part of man. The first, a complete surrender of self—a voluntary renunciation of his own will, and a controlling desire to devote the whole life to the service of God, together with an humble reliance upon God through the merits of Jesus Christ. The man who does this is saved at this point, if ever saved.

But there may be a sort of mental incapacity for the exercise of this higher faith. The soul, conscious of a full surrender and an earnest desire to be saved from sin, may seem, in some natures, utterly without strength, and it is doubtless true that an abnormal manifestation of God may lift the soul from its despair and give it peace. And yet we cannot but think that if the Savior should speak audibly to such a soul he would use the same tender, yet reproachful, words he addressed to Thomas, "Because thou hast seen me thou hast believed; blessed are they that have not seen and yet have believed." The point is this: While of course the *ability* is from God, yet faith in its exercise is essentially an *action* of the soul, and there seems no reason why he who has faith to begin and carry forward a genuine repentance should not complete the work; that he who believes a *part* of the word should fail to receive it all, and *know* that when man conforms to the conditions God imposes he is always accepted, and accepted at once. Hear Isaiah: "Let the wicked forsake his way and the unrighteous man his thoughts, and let him return unto the Lord who *will* have mercy, and to our God who will abundantly pardon." Here the question arises: What is the test by which the sinner may know that he has reached the point where he may trust in God? Suppose he is tired of sin and heartily renounces it, and in the midst of a "godly sorrow for sin" gives himself with all his powers to God, in a renewed purpose of life, faith at the same time asserting the truth and the power of God. Yet he finds no joy in his trust; no star arises upon the sombre night of the soul. Is he converted? No, we are probably told, for conversion is a change of heart, not merely of purpose. If he die in this condition will he be lost? No; the thought is revolting! But God cannot save in heaven a soul unpardoned; and the conclusion is obvious, that the man *was* converted, or physical death accomplishes that which the grace of God could not do. And with regard to the assertion that conversion is a change of *heart*, and not merely of purpose, we ask, Can there be an entire change of purpose unless the heart is likewise changed? Does not the one spring from and indicate itself in the other?

We think so. And, furthermore, it is true that, while the penitent may not have been able to detect the processes of the Holy Spirit, yet this result—an entire change of heart and purpose—is and can only be a direct result of his gracious influence. For, saith the Savior, "No man cometh unto me except the Father draw him." The spirit of the world draws no one to Christ.

The degree of joy felt in conversion is contingent, not only on the temperament, but likewise upon the heartiness with which man conforms to the conditions—upon the character of his faith. And whatever the attendant emotion, it is generally true that when the excitement of the hour has passed by, a rigid inspection of the consciousness will reveal little more than a changed purpose of life. And this is natural, for he is only a babe in Christ. As the new-born babe is conscious only of *life* and of *desire*, so the spiritual babe is conscious only of a principle of life unknown before and of a desire to possess and feel more than he now does. Here we may be asked, Is the man safe now? We answer, no; nor at any point in the Christian life if he ceases to *do* the "sayings" of Christ. When faith in the soul crystallizes into mere dogma mentally retained, and activity gives place to stagnation, the result is always spiritual death. And if in any given case we are uncertain as to whether the man was converted, or being converted has backslidden, the question is of no consequence, for damnation is no more certain in the one case than in the other. We think it true, in almost every case, that he who intelligently and in all honesty takes upon himself the solemn vows of our holy Christianity *is a con-*

verted man, and if he continue in the path of duty revealed in the word of God the issue is not doubtful. He will "grow in grace," and " go from strength to strength," until the twilight of his spiritual morning gives place to the brightness of perfect day, and the full-orbed glories of the Sun of Righteousness shines away all his fears. He will then be able " to stand and (also) rejoice in hope of the glory of God."

But, under any circumstances, man is to " work out his salvation." He must *do* as well as *enjoy*, keeping always in view the fact that we are saved by "*faith* and not by works." And even admitting that we *do* the *sayings* of Christ, not because we *would* be his, but because we are his, yet, at the same time, we have no sort of confidence in the efficiency of that faith which literally " worketh not at all." Man is not saved by works; and yet it is unquestionably true that our Savior makes these the only tests of faith, and in his delineation of the judgment he approves the righteous because they had *done* certain things, and condemns the wicked because they had failed to *do* these same things, and says nothing whatever of the principle lying behind the action in the one case, or the inaction in the other.

The " doing these sayings" of Christ constitutes the highest test of faith; and more yet, for God will assuredly see the faith if it exist in the soul, and if we only labor to *demonstrate* our faith, the exercise would be useless. But the law of spiritual growth positively forbids inanition, and added to our own spiritual interest is the fact, that the *actions* of others may be largely contingent upon our own. Christ bids us: "Let your light so shine before men that they may see your *good works* and glorify the Father in heaven." Furthermore, this *doing* what Christ enjoins is not to depend upon our *moods*. Our light is not simply to shine during a transient enthusiasm; we are to work and endure as if we *saw* him who is actually "invisible." We are to *work*, no matter how we feel, or, as we have it in the "General Rules," "trampling under foot that enthusiastic doctrine, that we are not to do good unless our own hearts be free to do it."

The young Christian does not always feel inclined to do the will of God. Often he is strongly tempted to do that expressly forbidden. Of course he is not now *joyful* in God; yet the spiritual deprivation of this hour is no proof of a nature yet in the "gall of bitterness."

Now, if one such period is not inconsistent with the Christian life there may be many, and if *many* the whole life may be overcast, and the poor man forever struggling with his fears, and yet be a child of God. If his faith only suffices to keep him at *work* all will be well, and the only loss he sustains is a temporary one—the loss of that perfect repose which inures to the soul dismissing all fear and casting itself upon the mercies of God through Jesus Christ. But it is a reasonable supposition, that if there exist any difference in the feeling of God as he looks upon a rejoicing Christian and a soul struggling in gloom, it must be in favor of the latter; he must look with more interest upon the soul that, beset by all the hosts of hell, and in darkness almost palpable, yet struggles even in agony to do what the Master *says*, than upon the rejoicing obedience of the perfect man in whom this soul-gravitation, "shifting, has turned the other way." The great Shepherd has a tender regard for the weakly ones of his flock; "he will not break the bruised reed nor quench the smoking flax." And if it be true that we are to recognize a Christian as such by'the fruit he bears (Matt. vii. 16; Luke vi. 44), much more may he recognize himself in the same way in the absence of a direct witness of the Spirit. For *he* knows the principle by which he is actuated, and is inwardly conscious of an honest purpose to glorify God, and satisfied that his work will bear the inspection of the Master, his condition is infinitely preferable to that of the man who depends upon an occasional paroxysm rather than a life of steady devotion to the cause of God. Further, for the encouragement of "him that is weak in the faith," we may refer to Mr. Wesley, who says that he does not consider a "knowledge of acceptance essential to justifying faith;" by which he doubtless means that in his opinion one may be a Christian without possessing the "witness of the Spirit." But it would be an anomaly if one should continue long in so low a state, and yet faithfully observe and *do* the "*sayings*" of Christ. The rule is, that he who is faithful over a few things will soon enjoy much of God.

To sum up this part of the subject, we say that salvation is contingent upon a proper exercise of those faculties of our nature we can control, and not upon any paroxysm affecting us involuntarily; upon what is *done* and not upon what is *felt*. Man can *think*, and *will*, and

DOING THE SAYINGS OF CHRIST. 177

act, but he cannot melt to tears, nor lift himself to the hilltops of joy by any effort of the soul. And God requires only that which man can do. Happiness is generally found in connection with personal Christianity, but it is no part of Christianity. Rather it is a *result*, an *accident*. Rarely, if ever, can it be a test of the soundness of our faith.

Through this process of development, so far as we have traced it, but little has been said as to the part performed by God himself. Nor will we dwell upon this point now. Suffice it to say that God either has done already, or will do at the proper time, whatever is necessary in any given case. The soul that earnestly seeks to *find* and *do* the right, if light or faith or strength are failing, will, if persisting in its high purpose, find all the conditions supplied, and that so naturally that only faith can detect it as the work of God. He will abundantly perform his part of the work, and " no good thing will he withhold from them that walk uprightly."

From this position it is clearly seen that the sinner is left without excuse. The man who says, " I would like to be a Christian," but is not, is either dishonest or exceedingly ignorant; for he has the power to conform to the conditions imposed by the Son of God. Let him arouse from the deadly stupor which so long has fettered his faculties, and begin at once to " work out his salvation," looking unto CHRIST for pardon and help.

And if there be a Christian whose religion is but fanaticism, whose faith is an occasional convulsion, and to whom "getting happy" is the surest proof as well as the highest phase of the Christian life, let him remember that saying of Christ: "Not every one that *sayeth* unto me, Lord! Lord! shall enter into the kingdom of heaven, but he that *doeth* the will of my Father which is in heaven."

XI.

THE FOLLY OF SKEPTICISM.

BY REV. J. E. GODBEY,

Of the St. Louis Conference.

"The fool hath said in his heart, there is no God."—PSALM liii. 1.

There are few who are infidels in belief, but many who are so in practice. There are many who would gladly disbelieve the testimony of nature, and shut their eyes to all the evidences she presents of an intelligent Creator. Having a knowledge of God—which, indeed, they cannot shun—they do not like to retain him in their thoughts, and even wish that there were no God.

He who in his heart seeks to crush out his convictions of the existence and authority of his Maker is declared in the text to be a fool. Let us consider the evidences by which this sentence is sustained. That he who denies that there is a God, or, believing in his existence, despises his law, is a fool, we attempt to prove from these premises: He rejects the most obvious conclusions of reason; he delights in low and degrading conceptions of mankind; he glories in his own shame and misery. And, first:

He who denies the existence of God is contradicted by the strongest possible evidence. In the world of matter and of mind we are afforded the most conclusive proofs that there exists from eternity a great First Cause. Such is our conviction of the necessary relation and sequence of cause and effect, that whenever our eyes rest upon any object we cannot but refer its origin to some power or agency; and if we behold in that object design, adaptation to an end, we cannot believe its origin casual or accidental, but are forced to connect with the idea of a cause the farther idea of intelligence or design. From the order and adaptation manifested in all the works of nature, the belief in a Supreme Being is forced upon us. If this conclusion be denied, if it be said that it is as reasonable to suppose all things to have existed as they are, uncreated, as to suppose that there is an intelligent Being who is himself uncreated and eternal, we would meet the denial with such arguments as these:

Allowing, indeed, that matter be eternal, we find phenomena connected with matter which cannot be explained by reference to any power or principle inherent in matter itself. Philosophy will demonstrate that matter is in itself wholly passive and inert. Placed in any given state it has no power in itself to change its state. When I see matter at rest I am assured that it will remain at rest forever, unless some external force shall set it in motion. Set in motion, only external forces can bring it to rest. Such is matter in itself considered. Philosophy declares *inertia* to be one of its natural properties. But in nature I behold these wonderful phenomena: that which is proven to be, in itself, dead and powerless, is constantly changing its state and assuming motion and life. The grass of the field, the forest tree, and all the forms of vegetable life, from the moss of the rocks to the stately fir, but present to my eye the various forms which matter is constantly assuming. Suppose the earth upon which we live was in the beginning a mass of liquid fire, as geologists suppose, or, as others have fancied, a globe of ice, or a chaos of hard clay; adopt any theory which gives us matter alone, without animal or vegetable life, and no principle inherent in matter itself will explain their origin. Admitting that, as they now exist, we see in nature the means by which they are perpetuated, their origin must be still referred to a power which is not found in mere matter. And in all those theories of gradual development which have been in our times suggested, there has been found no theorist who dares ignore that fact. But in this argument we have appeared to admit, what no philosopher dares to claim, that there are discoverable in nature principles which explain the perpetuation of animal and vegetable life, if they do not solve the problem of their origin. But even this, we say, none has as yet dared to claim. The growth of the plant, the blooming of the flower, the perpetual decay and reproduction of animated things, is a mystery too deep for human science, and can only be explained by belief in a God.

The botanist can analyze the plant, describe its structure, tell its species, explain to us the functions of its leaves and roots. Chemical analysis may make us acquainted with its constituent elements, and we may determine what are the conditions of heat and moisture, and what are the properties of the soil essential to its growth, and yet in all these things we do not lay our hands upon the mystery of life. The mode of life we see, but the principle we do not comprehend. The power that resides in the plant puts into action every fibre and vessel to cause roots and leaves to perform their functions, and thus to live and grow is beyond detection. All philosophy teaches that matter alone is powerless, leaving us to the conclusion that all force is spiritual, and that the only answer that can be found for him who asks the cause of such things is, "It is the will of God."

As respects animal life, were even the theory of development by natural selection true, it would in no way solve the mystery of life—life in its primordial, for we must still refer to a Creator, and the law by which it is developed to the ceaseless exertion of his power, and each species thus developed must be viewed as a new creation.

But if neither animal nor vegetable life can spring spontaneously from matter, how shall we account for intelligence, how explain the world of mind? So far from showing intelligence to be the result of any combination of matter, it cannot even be shown to be necessarily associated with physical organism, or at least upon any stated condition of the physical system. Intelligence is not the result of any combination of mere matter, and can only be regarded as produced by an intelligent agent; and, because of the marks of design which appear upon all things, it is evident that in the order of existence mind was before matter, and that intelligence has directed all the work of the natural world. In this supreme intelligence, which is before all things, and by which all things are directed, we have the idea of God.

We talk of the laws of nature, for by this title we are accustomed to designate all the powers by which nature is governed. The effect of these powers is to preserve harmony among all the parts of the universe. Here, then, we behold law and manifest design. But there can be no law or harmonious plan without will. But there is no will in matter, and it can have no design; so we are led to acknowledge a will by which all the conditions and principles of matter have been determined, and so we arrive again at the idea of an infinite, eternal intelligence. Again, in the very relation which we recognize as subsisting between cause and effect, we are forced, in the order of sequence, to place cause first. We also perceive that the chain cannot be endless, and however far we may propose to trace it backward, we must end at last in the belief in a great First Cause, the fountain of all being. Start from whatever point we choose, pursue whatever line or legitimate method of reasoning we may, we arrive always at the idea of the Infinite. Here is the end of all inquiries, the solution of all mysteries. Everything in nature proclaims there is a God. To God every path of inquiry leads, as the rivers run into the sea. The mind cannot advance in any direction of thought and escape this conclusion.

If it could be shown that there are no marks of design upon anything, no evidences of a controlling will, then only would the existence of such a being become a problem, then only would men have an equal ground to affirm as to deny his existence. But who ever surveys through all the objects around him harmony and adaptation, unity of plan in an infinite variety of parts, infinite existence, universal and unchangeable laws, all things controlled by powers certain, fixed, and uniform—who ever beholds all this and yet denies that there is a God, is a fool, and hath not the perception and understanding of an intelligent being. To such an one nature hath denied the gift of reason, or passion and depravity have dethroned it.

The folly of the infidel is exhibited further in the fact that he delights in low and degrading conceptions of mankind. He contemplates himself as the offspring of chance, being without purpose, and left to such destiny as chance may determine. In this view he is no longer superior to the beast. His intelligence ceases to elevate him; yea, rather is he degraded by it. If all things are the sport of chance, what can man presume to know? All our convictions of truth are based upon the recognition of fixed, eternal principles; but with chance nothing is fixed, nothing sure; the mind dares not accept any conclusion, reason dares not advance a single step, for she finds no firm footing anywhere. Unless he recognize the fact that his powers and faculties are bestowed on him by One whose will is sovereign and unchangeable, and who delights in truth, man dares not trust his own senses to give him a proper conception of anything; in short, truth and reason are but fictions, and man is not elevated by his powers of thought, but only made the more subject to delusion, believing in fictions, pursuing shadows, his own existence being but a fitful dream. Viewed as the child of chance, man is but a piece of animated clay, subject to no certain law; having no mission to fulfill, his cares, his hopes, his fears, his toil, are for naught. Even intelligence, which is his glory and boast, does not elevate him above inanimate matter, but sinks him below it; for if there be a higher intelligence by which he is governed, then the existence of a God is acknowledged. But if there be no such superior intelligence, then human intelligence is but the result of a certain combination of matter, and subject to those blind, mechanical laws, which are, under such a supposition, recognized as inherent in matter itself. Intelligence being thus the offspring of mere matter, and controlled by it, becomes clearly inferior, and matter is superior to mind, and man by his intelligence is only degraded below inanimate things.

The belief in a God gives to man a nobility above all the creatures and objects around him, for he perceives that he is endowed with faculties which place him in intimate relation to his Créator. He recognizes in himself will and intelligence as attributes of divinity which he possesses only in an inferior degree. While he feels these powers he cannot but claim kindred with the Deity, and know that there is imparted to him some part of that nature which constitutes the glory and perfection of the Eternal, and which is itself, therefore, imperishable. With what exalted hopes, what glorious aspirations, do these convictions fill the human bosom! Mind is no longer inferior to matter, man rises above the visible and material—the great globe, the vast universe, is nothing to him; and, secure in his own existence, he smiles at the thought that all these may perish and be dissolved.

Upon these convictions is founded all that is great in human character, all that is sublime in human achievements; for there is no longer anything to call forth our admiration if the highest motives which it is possible for man to feel have their origin in his own passions or desires, or result from the fear and authority of a being like himself.

Who is he, then, who would tear from man the crown of divinity, forbid these desires, and destroy that faith which is the source of his happiness, and degrade him lower than the very dust upon which he treads? From the inspired king of Israel an answer comes down to us through living ages, confirmed by every testimony of nature and of reason, declaring that "he is a *fool.*"

Nor is it possible upon any ground for the skeptic to escape the conviction of his folly. For even if it be granted that man's belief in God is but a delusion, his hope of immortality a vain dream—that man, with all his varied powers, is but a chance creation, brought into being and destroyed by some blind, relentless power, still would it be the highest folly to seek to destroy those beliefs, which in every age he hath cherished, and without which he is made an orphan and exile. No Father in heaven to watch over him, no light, no counsel to guide him, no purpose or motive to direct his life, finding no object worthy of his love, and himself unworthy the love or sympathy of his kind! Let it not be answered, that it is nevertheless best that man should give up delusions, however dear, in order to know the truth. For if there be no hereafter, then what is truth?—what will the love or knowledge of truth avail? If the present is the whole of life, then it is man's wisdom to make it as happy as he may, no matter if it be by a delusion. Even errors believed are present realities to our own minds, and if it be true that there is no future state, man shall never wake to his errors, or suffer disappointment for having believed falsehoods. Even then, if this hope be a delusion, nothing can be so much to my interest, nothing can so promote my happiness, as that this dream of eternal felicity should still maintain its power over me, soothe the afflictions of life, and charm away my pains and fears when I sink into the eternal slumber.

But it is not for the skeptic even to talk of truth, or pretend to despise error. That view which regards all things as the sport of chance makes the knowledge of truth impossible, as we have already shown; it offers no foundation on which any firm belief can be rested. It gives the same character of uncertainty to every conclusion. It declares that man's inevitable fate is to believe in unsubstantial theories—to pursue phantoms and shadows until he returns to dust. Surely there can be no greater exhibition of folly than that one should profess to despise me for my errors, and yet claim that to err, and err only continually, is the destiny of man.

Last of all, the folly of the skeptic is seen in this, that he glories in his own misery, and seeks, moreover, for knowledge in attempting to prove that nothing can be known. He seeks, we say, to expose his own shame and to increase his misery. He desires to be recognized as possessing no spiritual nature, no moral character, to be governed by no obligation. He claims that virtue and vice are imaginary distinctions. He declares reason to be a liar, and conscience but a bugbear. He laughs at the sacredness of principle, and acknowledges no obligation but the present necessity. The most illustrious virtues and the most shocking crimes are in his sight only distinguished by the conventionalities of society or the caprice of human legislators, and the philanthropist and the highwayman are regarded as worthy of the same destiny. For these sentiments and views the infidel desires to be honored; for, after all, it is manifest that a conceited pride, and a vain desire to appear wise, are the motives which lead men to such a course—they would attract attention by the singularity of their conduct. They openly contradict the common sense of mankind, and for this desire to be called philosophers. They oppose themselves to everything that is sacred and dear to humanity, and for this they would be called benefactors of the human race. They assert that nothing can be known, and spread over man's prospects the shadows of uncertainty, or the gloom of palpable despair; and for this they call themselves the lights of the world. Thus in their shame do they glory, and by their folly do they seek reputation for wisdom. And while they make such effort to win applause or to be esteemed wise by a creature so wretched and miserable as they represent man to be, they prove themselves to be the slaves of creatures like themselves, and thus degraded even below their species.

The skeptic is an open foe to the happiness of man. Even those who scoff at religion, and deny moral obligation to a higher power, have recognized the utility of those laws and restraints adopted among men for the regulation of human conduct. But nothing is more absurd than to acknowledge the importance and necessity of human law, and yet oppose those principles and convictions upon which alone the authority of the law depends. It is only in these convictions of moral obligation that human laws find their sanction and strength. Show that justice is not a fixed, eternal principle, and that there is no being greater than man to whom we shall answer for our conduct, and every power competent to restrain human actions is removed, and no man cares longer either to obey or enforce the law. Remove from man the fear of God, and even the name of justice would be heard no more; confusion, anarchy, treachery, would reign everywhere; the proudest empires would fall into ruin at once; the instinct of self-preservation, triumphing over every feeling beside, would make men fierce and tameless as the tiger.

Such would be the state of man if what the infidel teaches were believed.

When we consider the folly, the absurdity of his doctrine, and the terrible consequences which its belief would bring upon man, he who denies the existence of God appears no longer simply a fool. Nothing but the most fearful depravity could lead to such a course. It is not the weakness of his intellect so much as the wickedness of his heart which impels man to such a course. Greek and Roman fables tell of the Titans who attempted to ascend into heaven and dethrone the Omnipotent, but theirs is a folly more insane and desperate. God hath written his law upon all his works, yea, even upon the human heart. Here is his eternal record, and while suns shine or planets roll, while intelligent beings exist to behold the wonders of this vast creation, there will not be wanting either proof of God's existence or the conviction of his authority.

"Why do the heathen rage and the people imagine a vain thing; the kings of the earth set themselves and the rulers take counsel together, saying, 'Let us break their bands asunder and cast away their cords from us?' He that sitteth in the heavens shall laugh, and the Lord shall have them in derision."

XII.

HEAVEN: ITS INHABITANTS, THEIR CHARACTER AND EMPLOYMENT.

BY REV. S. W. COPE,

Of the Missouri Conference.

"After this I beheld, and lo a great multitude, which no man could number, of all nations, and kindreds, and people, and tongues, stood before the throne, and before the Lamb, clothed with white robes, and palms in their hands: And cried with a loud voice, saying, Salvation to our God which sitteth upon the throne, and unto the Lamb. And all the angels stood round about the throne, and about the elders and the four beasts, and fell before the throne on their faces, and worshiped God, saying, Amen: blessing, and glory, and wisdom, and thanksgiving, and honor, and power, and might, be unto our God forever and ever. Amen."—REV. vii. 9–12.

This revelation from God is a grand disclosure to us of *heaven*. In a preceding vision which St. John had, he saw five angels, four of whom stood over the four corners of the earth (Judea), "holding the four winds of the earth, that the wind should not blow on the earth, nor on the sea, nor on any tree." These angels were the divinely appointed agents to stay the gathering storms of persecution, afflictions, and wild and widespread commotions, which were soon to sweep over the whole land of Judea, like impetuous torrents, or as a fiery deluge, laying waste the country, and totally destroying the memorable, and once holy city of Jerusalem. The fifth angel makes his appearance in the East. He comes in great haste, indicating the importance of his mission. He comes, the white-winged messenger of love, and, as the royal chancellor of heaven, to authenticate the children of God, and to place upon them a mark of distinction as such. With an authoritative and loud voice, he calls to the four angels standing on the four corners of the earth, saying, "Hurt not the earth, neither the sea, nor the trees, till we have sealed the servants of our God in their foreheads." In obedience to the command of the fifth angel, the four angels stay the winds in their howlings, in their commotions, and in their work of desolation and death, until the servants of God are sealed in their foreheads. And the number of them that were sealed were an hundred and forty and four thousand—twelve thousand of each of the twelve tribes of the children of Israel—a great multitude, a definite number, being put for an indefinite. After this sealing comes the vision of the text, the scene of which is laid in *heaven.* It is most sublime and wonderful, as it is a pleasing revelation of God, and of the throne of God, and of the Lamb of God, and of the angels of God, and of the Church of God, redeemed "out of every kindred, and tongue, and people, and nation." Such knowledge of the future is derived only from Revelation. Blot the Bible out of existence, and there hangs a veil between earth and heaven, impenetrable alike to the mind's eye and to the natural vision—impenetrable both to reason and philosophy. Human reason, with all her boasted and acknowledged powers, never discovered nor revealed a single fact in relation to or in disclosure of the future world. Reason is great, and as important as great, distinguishing truth from falsehood, vice from virtue, and yet, having no power, unaided by Revelation, to tell us anything of a hereafter.

Philosophy may explain the phenomena of matter, alike of heavenly bodies and terrestrial substances; may show the reason and fitness of things, visible and tangible; may "teach men their duty, and the reason for it;" and may be a ready assistant in regulating the actions and manners of men in society. She may sink herself, by means of shafts, deep into the mines of theology, physics, history, ethics, and poetry, and bring up thence a hidden treasure of greater price than pearls, or diamonds, or gems of gold. Gathered here and there, from these and other sources, she may sow broadcast literary, scientific, and holy truths and facts, for the instruction, entertainment, and elevation of mankind. But philosophy knows nothing of a hereafter, but by means of a revelation from God. All that we know of heaven as a place, a state, its inheritance, inhabitants, associations, employments, honors, pleasures, joys, triumphs, felicity, glory, grandeur, and immortality, we learn from the Bible. But in the more particular contemplation of this apocalyptic vision I invite your attention.

I. To the Inhabitants of Heaven.

1. *The angels* are native, and the oldest inhabitants of

heaven. "I beheld, and all the angels stood round about the throne." Angels are a superior order of beings to man—superior in dignity and honor, in sublimity of character, and majesty of person—in their intellectual and moral powers and attainments, and in the perfection of their nature, and in their native happiness. They excel man in strength, in grandeur, and in glory. In this contrast I take man as I find him in his sinful and fallen condition, and the angels as seen by St. John in his apocalyptic vision. If we were to contemplate man in his saved state as a child of God—in his redeemed, sanctified, and glorified character in heaven, the contrast between him and the angels would not be so great; but even in this event man would rank a little lower than the angels. But if we concede the fact of endless progression in heaven, in knowledge and happiness, in glory and honor, then the time may come in the annals of eternity, and doubtless will, when the most obscure saint in light shall have risen to the sublimity of character and majesty of person of the tallest angel which now floats in the atmosphere of heaven or basks in its uncreated light and glory, or the brightest seraph "that adores and burns" in the presence of God.

Another fact worthy of notice is, the vastness of their numbers. Daniel says of the Ancient of Days, "thousand thousands ministered unto him, and ten thousand stood before him." St. John heard the voice of many angels, including four living creatures, and the four and twenty elders, and "the number of them was ten thousand times ten thousand, and thousands of thousands." The Psalmist says: "The chariots of God are twenty thousand, even thousands of angels." These angels, so vast in numbers, are divided into various ranks and orders—seraphim, cherubim, thrones, dominions, principalities, and powers. But, for anything we know, there may be thousand thousands of ranks and orders, and ten thousand times ten thousand, and thousands of thousands in each order.

II. Elders and Beasts.

"All the angels stood round about the throne, and *about* the elders and the four beasts." A definite for an indefinite number. By the term beasts in the text we are to understand a high order of intelligent and redeemed creatures. These elders and beasts represent, as some think, the Jewish and Christian Churches. Others are of opinion that the elders are the representatives of the whole Church—Jewish and Christian—and the four beasts the representatives of the ministry, or, perhaps, the ministry itself. My opinion, and so far as I know, as yet unpublished, is this: The elders are the ministry of the Church, including all the different orders of priests, prophets, apostles, and clergy, of every dispensation, and of all time; and the beasts, or, as some render the term, "living creatures," are the martyrs of all ages and countries. Three facts, at least, are clear to my mind: First, the elders and beasts are, in common with others, before the throne, redeemed to God by the blood of Christ. Second, by title, their relation to God, and nearness to the throne, and for the reasons given, and, perhaps, reasons yet unknown, they are distinguished from the multitude who have palms in their hands, and who are "clothed in white robes." Third, in this distinction they represent not only the Church and ministry of the different ages and dispensations of the world, and of all countries and times, but "every kindred, and tongue, and people, and nation."

3. *A great multitude which no man can number.* "*Of all nations,*" Christian and heathen, civilized and barbarous, ancient and modern — the many and great nations of the Roman, Prussian, Russian, and Austrian empires, with the English and French, the American and European nations, not to mention others who have, or may yet exist. "*And kindreds.*" Abel, Enoch, Elijah, Abraham, Isaac, and Jacob are there. Job and David are there. The prophets and apostles, as well as the patriarchs, are there. The martyrs and early Christians are there. Many of our fathers and mothers, and some of our little children, and other loved ones, have passed over the Jordan of death, and are now on "the other bright shore." These all have kindred there who assist to swell the happy throng of the redeemed, even beyond all arithmetical or other powers of computation.

"*And people.*" Noah was righteous in his generation and in his family, though the people of that age, and amongst whom he lived, were corrupt, and the earth itself was filled with violence. Lot lived and preached twenty-three years among the degenerate people of the Cities of the Plain, which were afterward destroyed by "brimstone and fire from the Lord out of heaven." Job was "perfect and upright" in his day, "one that feared God and eschewed evil." When Elijah had come and said to God, "The children of Israel have forsaken thy covenant, thrown down thy altars, and slain thy prophet with the edge of the sword; and I, even I only, am left, and they seek my life to take it away," the answer of God saith unto him, "I have reserved unto myself seven thousand men who have not bowed the knee to the image of Baal." A people cannot be found where God has no witnesses. These that we have mentioned, and thousands like them, from the midst of the greatest wickedness and the most corrupt and degenerate people of all ages and countries, have gone up on high, and are before the throne and in the presence of the Lamb, as seen by St. John. "*And tongues.*" Parthians, Medes, Elemites, Celts, Teutons, Cretes, Arabians, Greeks, and Romans, including all the tongues of Europe, Asia, Africa, and America. Not only these, and all other parent tongues, but the different dialects of each, have their representatives in the company of the redeemed in heaven.

II. THEIR CHARACTER.

The elders are "clothed in white raiment," as St. John elsewhere testifies; and the four beasts, or "living creatures," are redeemed to God by the blood of Jesus. In his blood they have washed their robes and made them white. The great multitude, which no man can number, stand before the throne, and before the Lamb, "clothed with white robes, and palms in their hands." White is an emblem of innocence and purity. These are all partakers of the divine nature, and are filled with the fullness of God. They are "holy, unblamable, and unreprovable in his sight." As to moral character, they are as spotless as the angels themselves. These are they which came out of great tribulation, and have "washed their robes and made them white in the blood of the Lamb." Therefore are they before the throne. Otherwise they could not be there. "There shall in nowise enter into it anything that defileth, neither whatsoever worketh abomination, or maketh a lie, but they which are written in the Lamb's book of life." "The fearful, and unbelieving, and the abominable, and murderers, and whoremongers, and sorcerers, and idolaters, and all liars shall have their part in the lake that burneth with fire and brimstone, which is the second death." These, with every other class and grade of sinners, "shall go into everlasting punishment," the righteous entering into "life eternal." Those only who are cleansed from all sin can find admission into heaven. They must be first clothed with white robes. Then may they enter into the joy of their Lord. To all such the King shall say : "Come, ye blessed of my Father, inherit the kingdom prepared for you from the foundation of the world." They *now* "have right to the tree of life, and enter in through the gates into the city." All the different orders of beings in heaven are holy. Heaven itself is a holy place, and we must be holy if we ever get there. "Blessed are the pure in heart, for they shall see God." "Follow peace with all men, and holiness, without which no man shall see the

Lord." The ungodly and the sinner cannot enter heaven. It is a mercy in God to shut them out—to close the gates against them. If God were to admit them into the kingdom of ultimate glory, of all places in the universe it would be to them the most miserable. There must be a meetness for, in order to, the enjoyment of heaven. That meetness is found only in moral purity.

III. THEIR EMPLOYMENT.

This consists in praising God. Not only extolling God in songs, but in words and deeds as well. Praising God consists in doing his will rather than in the mere utterances of the lips, or in the sound of golden harps attuned to celestial melody. God says to an archangel, go, and he goeth; to a seraphim, come, and he cometh; and to a redeemed spirit from earth, do this, and he doeth it. All ranks and orders of intelligences in heaven do the will of God perfectly, uninterruptedly, joyously, triumphantly, and without pain, weariness, labor, or fatigue. And as they thus go, and come, and do the bidding of God, individually, and in ranks, and in orders, and in great multitudes, which no man can number, they fill all heaven with their shouts and songs of praise. These acts of obedience involve the principles and exercise of faith and love. The achievements of these will be grand and glorious beyond conception. Of their methods we know nothing. Here, our faith in God removes mountains, our love to him is supreme, and our obedience to the divine will ready, active, cheerful, and even unto death; but there, the same in kind, these will be so exalted in degree as to be marvellous beyond the highest conceptions of the human mind, and astonishing, no doubt, to the angels and all the celestial hierarchy. In ten thousand ways the inhabitants of heaven show their faith in, with their love and obedience to, God. There, as here, the mind and heart alike are ever active and ever employed. In heaven subjects of thought, meditation, and research abound in infinite variety. Among these I may mention creation, providence, and redemption. The study of God in the works of creation is a delightful employment of this life. The mind, in its God-like powers, supported by, and all aglow with the fires of immortality, rises in thought and towers in imagination as it grasps the countless mysteries of creation. In its search for hidden treasure it passes from world to world, from one system to another, stepping from planet to planet, from sun to sun, from one blazing comet to another, on and on, through known into unknown regions, traversing the infinitude of space; knowing more and more of God as it receives and comprehends the nature, extent, principles, and properties of the works of his hand. And in this labor, when the mind has reached the utmost limits of the telescopic view of the astronomer, it stands just where these works and worlds, in number and magnitude, begin to open to its astonished vision. Beyond these limits, throughout infinite space, God is; and where God is are the works of his hand, exhibiting his skill, goodness, wisdom, and almighty power. And shall I know nothing more of the creative energy of God, which has called the universe into existence, than may be known in this life? Is this all the knowledge that I shall ever have of the products and glory, the sublimity and grandeur of that almighty power? Shall not the treasures of knowledge arising from this source rather increase with the rolling ages of an eternal future? So I think. Much more will the mind delight itself in God, and in the study of his works, when mortality is swallowed up of life. This work will afford the most delightful employment to glorified spirits in heaven. Each avenue of knowledge will constitute a ready medium of access to God.

But from the works of creation let us turn and contemplate the providences of God. These are mysterious as his works are vast and incomprehensible. Of God's providences we know but little in this life. We shall know more hereafter. Each successive age and development of eternity will bring opportunities and means of increased knowledge. Connected with our history in the past are providences to us now dark and mysterious. On the other side of the river of death, and, it may be, after ages of study and research on our part, these will become intelligible, both to our understanding and our hearts. The divine counsels and government will no longer be hid from our comprehension, but clearly and perfectly understood. Through a duration admitting no limit we shall trace with infinite delight and satisfaction the providences of God in their infinitude of numbers and mysteries. And from this source will arise a knowledge of God, endlessly cumulative, showing the justice and equity of his superintending care over his works, and especially the sentient beings of his creation. Indeed, all the perfections of God, as I conceive, enter into and are stamped upon his providences. To know one is to know the other. To study and understand the providences of God is to know God. And this is the pleasing employment of the inhabitants of heaven. Through this medium they trace in lines of living light the unity, spirituality, eternity, omniscience, omnipotence, omnipresence, immutability, holiness, truth, justice, and goodness of the Divine Being, as these are connected with his works and ways in all the ages past, and in the eternity yet to come. There we shall see the dealings of God with us in a clearer, if not in a new light. All his providences will be shown to be both wise and good, alike just and merciful. And to search out the knowledge of God in these will be an employment at once entertaining as it will be useful and blessed in its results. And with the increase of knowledge the praise of God will wax louder and louder. All knowledge of God, from whatever source derived, must culminate in songs of praise, or in shouts of victory and of triumph, to Him who sitteth upon the throne, and unto the Lamb for ever and ever.

The pealing anthems of loudest note and most harmonious and sweetest melody, however, originate in the study and understanding of the plan of human redemption, as it shall open to the comprehension of those who have right to the tree of life, and who have entered in through the gates into the city. Study to these will be no weariness, but a source of ravishing and endless pleasure. The great remedial scene of redemption, in its fundamental principles, doctrines, promises, exhortations, and threatenings, will constitute so many mines of inexhaustible wealth. To develop and enjoy this treasure is the work of immortal and glorified spirits. To all such the Bible, in its history, poetry, biographies, prophecies, and their fulfillment, will be a theme of immortal thought and investigation, and a source of ineffable delight.

In the process of a study and research such as this will be embraced the *subjects* of redemption, as well as its principles and its Author. These include patriarchs, prophets, apostles, and martyrs, with the great multitude seen by St. John in the vision of the text. Allowing that the character and lives, the experience and history of these may be studied separately, in their relation to God, and as subjects of his saving and redeeming grace, a treasure of infinite knowledge, and of infinitude of variety, is in store for those who shall join the blood-washed throng in heaven. Here again we find God revealed in all the perfections of his nature, in a manner inconceivably beyond human and angelic grasp. And from this standpoint the new song is sung in louder, sweeter strains: "Unto Him that loved us, and washed us from our sins in his own blood, and hath made us kings and priests unto God and his Father; to him be glory and dominion for ever and ever. Amen." Here culminates the love of God in its designs, its workings, and its results.

Reader,
> "There is a world above
> Formed for the good alone."

Let us aspire to be
> "Translated to that glorious sphere."

Many of our fathers and mothers have already crossed "the flood." Some of our dear children, too, are there on the other bright shore. They swell the number and song of the millions of infant souls who compose the family above. Millions more are now on the way. These all expect to die in the faith, and to go up with a shout to heaven. A conquest of greater magnitude *this*, and amidst shoutings of sweeter notes and louder strains than was ever heard on the battle-field in the overthrow of nations, or in the falling of empires before the tread of conquering kings. Amidst the breaking throes and mournful scenes of death, by saints of all ages, the victor's song has been sung: " O death, where is thy sting? O grave, where is thy victory?" And this song will continue to be sung by Christian pilgrims, as one by one they pass over the river of death, to the end of time. Flushed with victory, and all radiant with heavenly glory, the divine plaudit will be received, and the approved soul will enter into the joy of its Lord—a joy which no tongue can tell, no mind conceive, no pen describe—wondrous, ineffable, eternal! One by one we have seen them bid the world adieu, saying, "All is well with me forever." Their testimony was in this, and language like it: "These are the happiest moments of my life." (Leeper.) " I will soon be on the other shore. I will soon be at rest." (Caples.) "O! I am so happy to die. I shall soon be in heaven. They are waiting for me—they are calling me. Don't you see that bright company? They are here, all around me. What a large, beautiful house! What a large gate! What a beautiful place! O what a lovely home! and I shall be there soon. I never was so happy in my life. O mother, it is sweet to die—so sweet to die." (Dozier.) Reader, when our heart-strings are breaking, may we thus die.

> I'm dying, dying!
> Hark! methinks I hear the sound
> Of lyric voice and golden harps,
> Sweet, united strains of praise—
> Rapturous, transporting songs,
> Of angelic melody.
>
> I'm happy, happy!
> Raise me up. I see bright forms,
> All blood-washed and robed in white;
> See their glittering crowns of gold,
> And their palms of victory.
> O glory! glory! glory!
>
> Jesus quickly comes—
> Comes to take his servant home,
> Comes to free from pain and death,
> Comes a glorious conqueror!
> Hail! thou blessed Jesus, hail!
> O glory, halleluiah!
>
> I fear not to die:
> Bear me to yon courts above,
> Ye angelic, waiting bands;
> Let me go. Adieu. I rise
> To eternal happiness—
> To God and to his people's rest.

XIII.
BAPTISM OF JESUS CHRIST.

BY REV. J. A. MURPHY,
Of West St. Louis Conference.

"Then cometh Jesus from Galilee to Jordan unto John, to be baptized of him."—MATT. iii. 13.

There are no obsolete paragraphs in the life of Jesus Christ. In all and every part there are lessons fraught with doctrinal and practical instruction. Some phases of his wondrous life are imitable, others inimitable. When acting in the character and sphere of a man, his life becomes the model of human excellence, the beau-ideal of attainable and imitable perfection, himself the lone exemplar of a numberless race. Any activities which attach to his mediatorial campaign are anomalous—"of the people there was none with him." In this he is alone; no one having preceded him, none to follow after him. Beings create, nor men, nor angels, are like unto him. Assuming a nature a little lower than the angels, yet their highest honor is to do him homage. Though infinitely above us, he bears our image and is one with us. His mission as the God-man in the kingdom of redeeming grace is, in whole and every part, anomalous, and all his actions relating thereto are inimitable, because they are official.

It concerns us to know whether our Lord's conduct at the Jordan was done in his character as a man or relative to his anomalous character as mediator between God and man. In order to reach a conclusion in truth let us inquire:

I. What was the design of the baptism of Jesus Christ at the hands of John?

1. By this solemn and impressive performance it was *not* intended to place upon him the token of the covenant of grace. The general government of God is a sublime, a pure theocracy, whose law is one — supreme love to God and love to one another. This obtains in sinless realms, as subordinate law is germain to regions where the supreme law is violated, and sin thus existent. This sublime government *per se* makes no provision for transgressors. But the kingdom of God is adjunct to it, and in eternal constitution with it. This kingdom is the universal indemnity to the general government, of which it is an original part. It vindicates the Divine goodness in the creation of beings possible to sin, and contemplates the possible extension of mercy to offenders. Over this kingdom the Eternal Son of God presides. In making his kingdom available in the earth, where sin had invaded the divine realm, and cursed by a single stroke the mighty race of human beings, it behooved him to become a man, " that through death he might destroy him that had the power of death—that is, the devil. And for this purpose the Son of God was manifested, that he might destroy the works of the devil," and thus become Jesus Christ the Savior of men. In providing for his incarnation, a cove-

nant was made with Abraham, a distinctive feature of which was that Christ should be born in the line of his numerous descendants. "He saith not, and to seeds as of many, but as of one; and to thy seed which is Christ." Circumcision was the "token of this covenant," and distinctively of this prime feature. When, therefore, God "had performed his promise to the fathers, and remembered his holy covenant," circumcision ceased as a *token*, and baptism substituted it as a *seal* of the righteousness of faith. Observant of their high obligations, Joseph and Mary placed upon Him the covenant taken " when eight days were accomplished for the circumcision of the child." Therefore his baptism could have no relation whatever to his compliance with covenant stipulations, as these had been attended to thirty years before. We must, then, look elsewhere for an explanation of this singular transaction at the Jordan.

2. It was *not* designed to stamp with divine authority either the mission of John or that of himself. At this period of his life he was without the prestige of popular confidence himself. No demonstrative visitation from heaven had distinguished his career since, from the plains of Judea, the angels had taken their upward flight, shouting, "Glory to God in the highest!" The privacy of thirty years was not interpolated by supernatural and extraordinary events, so that by coming to John's baptism his recognition and patronage would give it a divine sanction.

Besides, to have given John the advantage of his example, he should have been among the first to be baptized; but "when all the people were baptized it came to pass that Jesus, also being baptized and praying, the heaven was opened." The last grand and crowning act of John was "to manifest him to Israel, before he was victimized by the revengeful spirit of Herodias, as the last distinctive act of his life. He could have pleaded no divine authority from this to profit withal, as it came too late.

Neither is the divine authority with which Jesus acted relegated to his baptism. Ecclesiastical authority is another thing, and must not be confounded with divine authority. He refers with distinctness to his miraculous works as his credentials under which he acted as the sent from God, saying, "Else believe me for the very works' sake. But I have greater witness than that of John; for the works which the Father hath given me to finish—the same works that I do—bear witness of me that the Father hath sent me." His wondrous works proceed naturally from his wondrous person, which is the one sublime and unaccountable exception to the universal experience of mankind. In divine calmness, and without effort in the realms of the supernatural and miraculous, he moved like the sun above the clouds of human passion and turmoil that sailed in commotion beneath him. It was an inward virtue, and not a borrowed gift, that dwelt richly within him, so that the fringe of his garment was healing to the touch. The unprecedented and matchless order of his life is inexplicable alone from the divinity that dwelt within him. This shone upon his works in dazzling splendor, like the true Shekinah, and satisfactorily accounts for the wonderful phenomena of his history, whether he moved in the din and bustle of the day, the object of Pharisaical criticism, or at nightfall withdrew for communion with the Father in the solitude of the mountain, or where the utterances of tired nature were lost in the murmurs of the sweet-gliding Kedron. Himself being *wonderful*— the greatest miracle in universal history—the miraculous he accomplished as naturally as we perform our ordinary work. These mighty works, then, which did show forth themselves in him, and not his baptismal manifestation by John, are the accredited witness of divine authority, by which his life was rendered a singular and mysterious fact.

3. The sinless character of Jesus Christ precludes the possibility of placing his baptism in common with the multitudes that came to the regions of the Jordan. From the untarnished purity of childhood, through a notable life, which was the glory of friends and the confusion of enemies, we look in vain for a single fact against which an allegation of wrong-doing may be sustained. His worshipers have been untiring in their laudations of his spotless purity, while foes, conscience-smitten, have been forced to say, "I find no fault in this man." His challenge, "Which of you convinceth me of sin?" remains to this day unaccepted. And through all the wonderful transactions attending his passion, unspeaking nature, by symbols that betokened mysterious sympathy, paid an unconscious tribute to the innocence of the condemned and dying Christ. Fearless John, whose denunciations of sin were uttered in unmeasured terms before the con-

course that thronged his ministry, modestly recoiled in the presence of the sinless Savior, saying, "I have need to be baptized of thee, and comest thou to me?" It is a singular fact that can be affirmed of no other being, "in fashion as a man," that he tested all the realities of a true human life where sin abounded, giving forth a transcendent expression of essential virtue in the walks of men, and in the very moment of expiring agony extorted from unwilling lips the just confession, "Truly this man was the Son of God." The heavens do not rise in starry grandeur above the earth as the beauty of holiness in the life of Christ mounts up in infinite splendor above the corruption of a fallen race. How extreme from this high character of pure virtue were the unselected crowds who came in curious anxiety to the preacher in the wilderness. Every hue of moral turpitude tinging the actions of men commingled in that dark stream which suggested the poison of a "generation of vipers." They came "confessing their sins," for they were sinners. He, the Lamb, of God, "knew no sin." To them the mission of the Baptist was, practically, repentance of sin, to which baptism with water was a public pledge; to him this could not apply, for he was "separate from sinners." The mission of John was clearly of dual design. It had to do with the people as toward Christ. It had to do with Christ as toward the people. It is simply impossible that the design of his baptism should fall to the level of theirs, for which reason "John forbade him," not comprehending the limits of his own mission. It could not be that the sinless Christ should come to a baptism of repentance. The action would have been insincere, and of this he was incapable.

4. It is a groundless assumption to say that He was baptized for an example to believers. When one holds a proposition which is utterly devoid of evidence, it is not faith, but *opinion* by which he clings. True faith rests upon evidence; mere opinion exists without it. That there is an opinion, to some extent, made popular by baseless assertion, that the Lord was baptized for our example, none will deny. But that this should be dignified as an article of faith, and held to be an unanswerable argument, that in some way bars the free and universal communion of the saints, is an out-cropping of unsufferable arrogance. As it is not claimed that a negative is susceptible of direct testimony, the *onus probandi* is not with us; but in vain have we sought for proof on the other side. If this transaction has all the exemplary importance its adherents attach to it, the utter silence of the Scriptures is surprisingly significant. Neither the Savior nor his apostles interpreted this action thus. Not a single text, even by doubtful interpretation, sustains it. As a necessary inference from the harmony of Bible truths, it utterly fails the most sagacious of its advocates. It was born in dogmatic assertion, and lives only by constant repetition. Beginning on the outer line of investigation, where alone the evidence could be found, let us approach the centre by steady steps of inquiry. The senior apostle of our Lord declares how Christ suffered for us, "leaving us an example." But it will be clearly seen that the example was in *suffering*, not baptism, in

heroic endurance, not in an outward ceremony. He must ignore the plainest canons of exegesis who can see the waters of Jordan in this. It was just before the Feast of the Passover, at which our Lord was crucified, that he inculcated practically a lesson of Christian love, which he closed by saying, "I have given you an example." But this has no more reference to his baptism than his crucifixion. Indeed, it must be a mental *mirage* that could lift this circumstance within the purview of imagination, so that John and the Jordan could be seen. "Follow me," and we have traveled from circumference to centre of the domain of possible proof, but the evidence of an exemplary baptism in the person of Christ passes like a phantom away. A few points will aid us in the true application of this language: 1. It originated with Christ soon after his baptism. 2. Its first application was to the college of apostles. 3. It could apply to them in a sense in which it could not apply to us, but in every particular its bearing upon us was common to them. Now, if it can be shown that they did not follow him in the *fact* of his baptism, to say nothing of its design, how can it be made an example for us? We are baffled with uncertainty as to the baptism of the original apostles of our Lord. But this lack of knowledge does not frustrate the argument. They were baptized, or they were not. If they were, it must have been in common, when "Jerusalem and all Judea and all the regions round about Jordan" sought the baptism of repentance. Then it follows that they led the way in this particular duty, and He followed them, for he came to John "when *all* the people were baptized." If they were not baptized at all, they were either disobedient to their Lord's command, or baptism was not included in it. In either case, then, they did not follow Christ in the fact of his baptism. Therefore, the call of Jesus, " follow me," did not include his baptism, as shown in the conduct of the apostles; neither can it be rightly claimed as an example for us.

Literally, they followed him in the course of his public life. No theological school can afford such training. Never were men so thoroughly taught in the truths of sound morals and pure religion as these. Three years under the instruction and personal tutelage of the Great Teacher, as a privilege, surpasses the combined learning of all the universities of modern Christendom. Not until they had completed their course, and had been graduated with the endowment of the Holy Ghost, were they sent forth as "fishers of men." For this purpose they were called to "follow him." What a noble example in the careful preparation for the ministry!

5. It *was* a ceremonial washing that inducted him into his office, as High Priest of our profession, according to law. This was official, and, therefore, inimitable. As his death was accomplished by his priesthood, so was his baptism in order to it. They who are zealous to imitate him at the Jordan say but little about following him in the fact of his crucifixion, yet both are on the same line of his marvellous life. Where they *could*, they refuse to imitate his example in infant consecration to God and recognition as a member of the Church, according to the ordinance that then existed; and where

they *cannot*, they are anxious above measure. Truly the divine order is inverted.

His incarnation was for the accomplishment of his priesthood. So grand a stoop to the level of men, "a little lower than the angels," was not needed to execute his office as the Prophet of God; nor yet was it requisite to the reign of the King Immortal. These could have been fulfilled, and the manger have known no child and the cross no victim. But for the purposes of his priesthood a body was prepared him. And in "the offering of the body of Jesus Christ," as he officiated alone at the altar of a ruined world, the dreaded thunders of eternal justice were silenced, and the music of myriad voices sang sweetly, " Worthy is the Lamb that was slain."

Some facts which amount to circumstantial evidence in support of the position taken may be adduced. At two periods of his life the age of Jesus is definitely pointed out. When the superior wisdom of his boyhood astonished the doctors in the temple he was about twelve. At the time of his baptism " he began to be about thirty years of age." It will be remembered that the ceremonial code fixed the age of the consecration of a priest "from thirty years old and upward . . . . of every one that came to do the service of the ministry, and the service of the burden in the tabernacle of the congregation." It is a coincidence of legal significance that Christ, as well as his forerunner, began his public career at the age fixed by the authority of the Jewish ritual. In this view of the subject he gives us a noble example of ecclesiastical loyalty. But if this action be construed as a religious example in joining the Church, his age would encourage the procrastination rather than youthful consecration to God, and his example thus come in conflict with his teaching. Besides, we learn from the case of the twelve Ephesians, that the baptism of John and that by the command of Christ are not one and the same; that the former was a pledge of repentance, the latter the effusion of the Holy Ghost. These men having received the one under the authority and instruction of Paul, submitted to the other. Therefore, in any statement of the case, a baptism by John would fail to be an example for us, as his mission has long since ceased. In fact, this idea is but the chimera of a tottering system, the flimsy figment of struggling error.

The administrator is brought to our view in this line of thought. John was the son of Zacharias and Elizabeth, of the tribe of Levi. Born of the tribe consecrated to the priesthood, his father a priest officiating in the temple when his illustrious career was announced, he was himself a priest. His authority, as vested in the ritual of the Church, was never questioned. He had, therefore, an undisputed right to consecrate our Lord to the priesthood of the Church according to law. The twofold mission of the Baptist was logically convertible. He came to prepare the people for the coming of Christ. This he did by the baptism of repentance. The *converse* is also true. He came to prepare Christ for the coming of the people. This he did by publicly manifesting the Savior in the ceremonial washing of his consecration to the priesthood. To this agrees the testimony of John, "that

He should be made manifest to Israel; therefore am I come baptizing with water."

There is also direct testimony which sustains this proposition. Jesus Christ fully comprehended the whole subject, and his testimony is that he came to John to fulfill the righteousness of law. "Thus it becometh us to fulfill all righteousness." Righteousness relates to law, and there are but two codes of law delivered to men by divine authority—the moral and the ceremonial. There can be no reference in this transaction to the moral law, as it neither declares nor implies any such thing. The absurdity of such a view is too patent to require refutation. It must and does, therefore, have to do with the ceremonial law. Now, as Aaron was the first to be consecrated, and for this reason the head of the line under this law, we will state the law in question, and also its fulfillment. "And Aaron and his sons thou shalt bring unto the door of the tabernacle of the congregation, and shalt wash them with water." This is the law. And here is its fulfillment: "And Moses brought Aaron and his sons, and washed them with water." At first John hesitated from a sense of his personal unworthiness, not seeing the fitness of the sinless Savior coming to a baptism of repentance, nor yet comprehending that branch of his mission which manifested Christ by formal consecration to the priesthood; but when the Savior pointed out the righteousness needful to be fulfilled, the explanation was satisfactory. He comprehended that branch of his mission he had not understood before. Modesty bows before the majesty of law. "Then he suffered him."

It has long been conceded that fidelity to the established order of the Church is in harmony with the principles that govern Christian conduct. Divine authority for any course of life does not contravene the authority vested in the Church. Rightfully exercised, these are in eternal harmony. The High Priest of our profession, acting under authority from God, acted also under authority from the Church. But if this latter authority was not derived formally through the transaction at the Jordan, then when, where, and how did he obtain it? In a single interview with "the chief priests and the elders of the people" he so strongly intimates the source of this branch of his authority as to remove all doubt. He was teaching in the temple when they came to him inquiring, "By what authority doest thou these things? and who gave thee this authority?" His only reply was, "The baptism of John, whence was it?—from heaven or of men?" This is almost equivalent to a declaration. They understood it so, and withdrew in confusion. Thus destroying no law, he fulfilled it all; and possessing all authority, he silenced the cavil of his foes, and came to the sacrifice of himself more like a God than a man. The priest was the sacrifice, and the sacrifice the priest. It was a sublime and blessed mystery. The instrument of his death is the exponent of his work, and the shame of his cross rises to the majestic support of a falling universe. The mourning veil which concealed the face of weeping nature when the Sacrifice was slain was mysteriously rent to exhibit the smile of a ransomed world.

II. What is the import of the certificate of the Father's approval at the ceremonial washing?

1. Involved in this is the anointing of the Holy Spirit, which was given to him not by measure, and symbolized in the descent of the heavenly dove. Another significant part in the ceremonial consecration of the Aaronic priesthood was, to "take the anointing oil and pour it upon his head and anoint him." In the ceremony at Jordan this was omitted. No precious oil poured forth upon the head of Christ, "ran down to the skirts of his garments, as the dew of Hermon, and as the dew that descended upon the mountains of Zion;" but the Holy Spirit, in measureless effusion, proceeding from the Father "and lighting upon him," was the real anointing to which the symbol pointed since the days of Aaron. Of the anointed of God the Scripture saith, "God, even thy God, hath anointed thee with the oil of gladness above thy fellows." But who were the fellows of Christ, our atoning High Priest? Certainly not the mass of mankind, for the relation was official, but the numerous successors to Aaron in the altar-service. These were his fellows. They received the oil, the symbol; he the Holy Spirit, the gift symbolized. They received the oil by meaure, but "God giveth not the Spirit by measure unto him." He stood, not as the representative of a nationality, at the door of a partial tabernacle, to strengthen "the middle wall of partition" between the Jewish and Gentile world, but under the

universal heavens, that he might abolish "the commandments contained in ordinances," gather Gentiles with Jews unto one Church, by the pacification of himself and maintain through perpetual duration the priesthood of a revolted world.

2. The supernatural voice accompanying the descending dove and certifying the Father's approbation closed the wonderful scene. The "oil of gladness" at the Jordan was quickly succeeded by the fearful trial in the wilderness. Crowds of astonished spectators stood within the radius of the mysterious phenomenon. In dignified silence dumb nature gave audience to the signal rustle of the wings of the heavenly dove. "Lo! the heavens were opened unto him." An aureola of solemn splendor encircled his radiant brow, and a voice from heaven proclaiming, "This is my beloved Son in whom I am well pleased."

Finally, we may notice an irregularity in the priesthood of Christ that detracts nothing from the view maintained, but associates him with Melchisedech "after the power of an endless life." The priests of the Jews were taken from the tribe of Levi, their kings from Judah. Our Lord was of this latter tribe, the son of David. He was a king by generation, a priest by consecration. After the similitude of the illustrious Melchisedech, who was both king and priest, Jesus Christ inherits the throne of David, and serves at the altar of Aaron. Blending in himself royalty and priesthood, changeless and to abide forever, "he is set on the right hand of the throne of the Majesty in the heavens." Designated in prophetic vision "a priest upon his throne," he has by the achievements of his cross obtained all authority over the house of God, consecrating through the veil a new and living way into the holiest by his own precious blood; and dividing his honors with his people, he has made them, in "full assurance of faith, a royal priesthood." He the *Royal High Priest*—they the royal priests. And forasmuch as Aaron was consecrated with the *sprinkling of blood*, the symbol of atonement, and the *washing of water*, the symbol of purification, they are advanced to this exalted privilege by " having their hearts sprinkled from an evil conscience, and their bodies washed with pure water."

Now, as the baptism of Christ was his ceremonial induction into his priestly office according to law, and as said law distinctly prescribes the washing of the body with water, it follows that Christ was not immersed. And further, as the great Royal High Priest was not consecrated by immersion, contrary to law, he has ordained that the royal priesthood should enter into the *holiest*, "having their bodies washed with pure water." As partakers of such honor in the presence of wondering angels, let us hold fast our profession of faith in God,

> " Who hears our Advocate, and through his wounds
> Beholding us, allows that royal name."

XIV.
TO THE YOUNG.

BY REV. C. I. VANDEVENTER,

Of the Missouri Conference.

"Seek ye first the kingdom of God and his righteousness, and all these things shall be added unto you.—MATTHEW vi. 33.

The divine Redeemer knew what was in man. He needed not to be told that the thoughts and anxieties which occupy and agitate the minds of the masses everywhere and in every age, find an utterance in the inquiries, "What shall we eat? and what shall we drink? and wherewithal shall we be clothed?" And while he does not, in this place or in any other connection, condemn or discourage suitable attention to the duties of the present life, yet, by so much as things spiritual and eternal are of more value than those which perish with their using, would our Lord have us to put that first which is of the first importance.

We inquire *what* the Savior in the text commands us to seek? Distinct perceptions of the *objects* of religious pursuit, as well as to the *manner* of their *attainment*, are essential to the proper and successful discharge of duty. We understand the Savior to refer to that kingdom which the prophet Daniel declared the God of heaven should set up, which Jesus says, in another place, is at hand, and which imports the reign of truth and grace under the Christian dispensation. This kingdom not only embodies and represents the visible Church of God, but also the spiritual kingdom, which is righteousness and peace and joy in the Holy Ghost, and which cometh not with observation, but is within us. Of this kingdom Jesus Christ is the Supreme Ruler, and all true Christians are the willing subjects, while the statutes and ordinances of inspired truth, as contained in the Old and New Testament Scriptures, furnish its infallible laws. And all who are the faithful subjects of this kingdom will have, in the sequel of their career on earth, an abundant entrance ministered to them into the everlasting kingdom of our Lord Jesus Christ.

By the term or phrase *righteousness*, or *his righteousness*, we may understand, not that which is the essential perfection of the divine nature, but that righteousness of which God is the author and man the recipient, and which includes a right relation to God's moral government, secured and evidenced in the forgiveness of sins; a right state of heart, both in relation to God and to our fellow-beings, effected by the Holy Spirit in our regeneration, in which the answer to the prayer of the Psalmist is realized, "Create in me a clean heart, and renew within me a right spirit." And thus being made partakers of the divine nature, because we are sons, God sends forth the Spirit of his Son into our hearts, crying, Abba, Father. Yea, the Spirit itself beareth witness with our spirits that we are born of God.

This is the righteousness of which many of the Jews were ignorant, especially of the way of its attainment, supposing it to be by the *deeds of the law*, whereas it is *by faith*, for Christ is the end of the law for righteousness to every one *that believeth*. And being *justified by faith*, we have peace with God through our Lord Jesus Christ. But this righteousness implies, as time and opportunity are given, *a holy life*, for *faith* without works is dead. Make the tree good and the fruit will be good also. If we *know* these things, happy are we if we *do* them. Then that which the Savior directs us in this language to do, is to seek to be Christians, in heart and in life, in fact and in profession—to be true and exemplary subjects of his kingdom *on earth*, that we may reign with him in heaven.

This "kingdom of God and his righteousness" we are commanded to *seek*. In our *natural, unsaved* condition, we are the subjects and servants of the prince of darkness—"without God and without hope in the world." And we will never inherit the " pearl of great price" unless we *seek* it; it will not come into our possession by virtue of any unconditional purpose or irresistible influence of the Almighty. It will not drift into our embrace by chance, or by the mere influence of circumstances. The divine direction is that we *seek*, and in the day that we seek the Lord with all the heart he will be found of us.

But *how* may we successfully discharge this very important duty?

1. We answer, in the language of Jesus, "Search the

Scriptures." These point out the way that leads to Christ, that conducts from sin to holiness, and from earth to heaven. Read and meditate upon the Word of God. Study it as God's message to you; apply its truths, its duties, its promises and warnings, to your own case. Read with an intention to follow its light, and without conferring with flesh and blood to obey the heavenly vision.

2. Seek the Lord by prayer. Unconverted though you may be, yet, as a sincere inquirer after truth and the way of salvation, it is your duty as well as privilege to pray; for " whosoever shall call on the name of the Lord shall be saved." The publican prayed, and he went down to his house justified, rather than the hypocritical pharisee who merely said his prayers. Cornelius the centurion prayed, and his prayers " went up as a memorial before God." And Saul of Tarsus, when an awakened and distressed sinner, prayed. And the psalmist prayed, and the Lord inclined unto him and heard his cry. Pray, then, for the wisdom that is from above. Pray that the good Spirit may help your infirmities. Ask and you shall receive that grace you so much need—the pardon, peace, and salvation which only God can give.

3. Seek the Lord with an *humble, penitent* spirit. God resisteth the proud, but giveth grace to the humble. Through the gift of our Lord Jesus Christ the *grace of repentance* has been bestowed upon all—the ability to repent.

There is no pardon, no salvation, without repentance. " Except ye repent," said the Master, " ye shall all likewise perish." And " God now commands all men, everywhere, to repent." Being convinced of your sinful nature, and of your own sins, both of omission and commission, your many sins of heart and of life, open and secret sins, committed knowingly and wilfully against an infinitely good Being. Repentance implies sorrow for our sins, because they are sins, violations of God's holy law, as well as on account of the fearful consequences to which they lead, for the " wages of sin is death." True repentance will lead you to confess and bewail your sins in the sight of God, and, as far as possible, to confess and undo the wrongs you may have practiced toward your fellow-men, as well as subsequently to avoid indulging in either outward or inward sin.

4. In addition to the duties above-mentioned, as important in the work of seeking God, it is further indispensable to our success that we seek him by *faith*. He that cometh to God must *believe* that he is, and that he is a rewarder of all who diligently seek him. Anything, everything, fails in the absence of faith. We still remain out of Christ and in our sins. But when we believe, not only with the head, or give an intelligent assent to the truth of the gospel, not only, also, with the consent of the will to the plan of salvation and to its personal demands, but in addition thereto *with the heart*, with personal and full trust and confidence in Jesus as our Savior, it is in this moment that we are constituted and accounted righteous on account of his merit by faith, and thus prepared with the mouth to make confession unto salvation; by word and deed to acknowledge the Savior before men, to fol-

low him into his Church, his visible kingdom; to take his easy yoke upon us, and seek within the Church, and by the aid of its means of grace, to make our way to heaven.

But the Savior directs us to seek *first* the kingdom of God and his righteousness. The *time* when this important duty should be performed is thus impressively indicated:

1. As religion is intrinsically of the *first* importance, and as man's first and highest relations and obligations are to his Maker and Redeemer, so our first and most earnest efforts should be employed in the work of seeking to know, and love, and serve our God.

2. We ought not to put off attending to this great interest till the days of affliction or the hour of death shall overtake us. It is a good thing to have the consolations of religion in a time of sickness and when called to die, but these are unfavorable circumstances under which to seek the Lord. If rational at such times, yet how difficult and how uncertain the effort to become religious.

3. We should give attention to this important work in the days of youth—in the morning of life.

1. Because it is *right* and proper in view of our relations to God as our maker and preserver, who is the giver of all our mercies, both temporal and spiritual.

2. Because God *commands* us to remember him in the days of our youth, when the evil days come not, and the years draw nigh when thou shalt say, "I have no pleasure in them." This command is as plain and as binding as any of the Divine requirements, and it cannot be innocently neglected.

3. We should seek the Lord first in the morning of our days, because of the *uncertainty* of life. While the old *must* die, the young *may* die. You may not attain to the usual meridian of human existence, much less live to be old. How many of the companions of your early life are now sleeping in the tomb, and how soon, whether prepared or unprepared, you may be numbered with them!

4. You ought to seek the Lord while you are young, because your habits of sin are strengthened every day. Your moral powers, in their neglect or abuse, are constantly weakening, and the reign of sin over your soul and over your destiny is becoming more and more dominant. The surface of the stream upon which you are gliding may be smooth, but a terrible current is underneath, and the maddening cataract is nearing every day.

5. The longer you defer serious attention to this great life-work the more you will have to do, and the shorter will be the time in which you may labor. Think, dear young friend, how the number of your sins is being multiplied!—how the breach between you and your God is widening, while you still neglect the one thing, of all others, the most important.

6. We urge you to obey the Savior's command in the text, because it opens to you the only way of being and doing all that God requires of his creatures, while it suggests an object of life worthy of him who endowed you with intelligent and responsible existence. In this way God may be glorified, your own best interests be promoted, and you may live to bless, by your example and precept, many of your fellow-beings. Oh! how much

good you may secure for yourself and for others, by seeking first the kingdom of God and his righteousness.

We shall speak very briefly in regard to the promise—" all these things shall be added unto you." The divine requirements are generally " commandments with promise." In securing the *higher good* much of that which is less important is *thrown in*.

The nature and effect of true religion, in its practical adaptations, is to reduce the ills and increase the comforts of the true Christian, even in this world; and the divine blessing, by covenant promise, is given to his people, not only in spiritual, but also in temporal things. Godliness is profitable to all things, having promise of the life that now is, and of that which is to come. As a father pitieth his children, so the Lord pitieth them that fear him. Then cast all your care upon him, for he *careth* for you. Your bread and your water shall be sure. And as thy day so shall thy strength be. If God so clothe the grass of the field, which to-day is, and to-morrow is cast into the oven, how much more will he clothe you, oh ye of little faith! In the proper use of proper means, you have the promise of food and raiment —the things that are needful here—with the blessing of God, which is more to be desired than life; and, at last, of an inheritance, incorruptible, undefiled, and that shall never fade away.

Yes, dear friends—you who are just entering upon the rough and dangerous sea of life, especially—seek first the kingdom of God and his righteousness, and all things shall be added unto you. My heart's desire and prayer to

God is, that you *may be saved.* Listen to the words of one who has passed the auspicious period of youth—of one who sought, in the spring-time of life, to heed the Savior's call, and rejoices to-day that he did. Listen to one who speaks to you through these pages, from the fullness of a father's heart, but listen especially to the loving words of Him who tasted death for you. Dear Savior, draw the heart of each one whose eyes may fall upon these lines to thee, and bless thy own word in the salvation of souls for whom thou hast died.

> " Then seek the Lord betimes, and choose
> The path of heavenly truth;
> This earth affords no lovelier sight
> Than a religious youth."

XV.

THE HIDDEN LIFE.

BY REV. B. H. SPENCER,

Of the Missouri Conference.

"Know ye not, that so many of us as were baptized into Jesus Christ were baptized into his death? Therefore we are buried with him by baptism into death; that like as Christ was raised up from the dead by the glory of the Father, even so we also should walk in newness of life."—ROM. vi. 3, 4.

There are few passages in the Bible which have received so many widely different interpretations as have been given to this. Great and good men of all denominations, and even of the same denomination, have differed widely in their views of its meaning. And they have differed honestly. They cannot all be correct. Somebody is mistaken. Even great and good men have sometimes fallen into error. And even a small man on the shoulders of a giant may extend the point of his observation beyond the vision of the man who carries him. We are compelled to dissent from nearly all the interpretations we have seen of this passage. When intelligent and candid persons differ in their understanding of what some other intelligent man has said, who is so proper a person to give the needed explanation as the author of the language in dispute? So here let us appeal the case to Paul. Who so capable to explain? Will he do it? Rather, has he not done it? Most unquestionably he has, fully and satisfactorily! And we now invite attention to the explanation he gives. Let me ask a few questions, and then attend to his answers.

I. What, then, is meant by the phrase, "*Baptized into Jesus Christ*"?

One thing must be evident. If baptized *into* Christ we must be *in* Christ. Now what does he mean by that? Turn to 2 Cor. v. 17, and we get his answer—"If any man be in Christ he is a new creature; old things are passed away, behold all things are become new." To be in Christ, then, is to be a new creature—is to have old things pass away—and to have all things become new. Do we inquire in what sense all things become new? Hear him: "For we are his workmanship, created in Christ Jesus unto good works, which God hath before ordained that we should walk in them." (Eph. ii. 10.) Again, he says: "That ye put off concerning the former conversation the old man, which is corrupt according to the deceitful lusts, and be renewed in the spirit of your mind; and that ye put on the new man, which after God is created in righteousness and true holiness." (Eph. iv. 22.) The substance of the apostle's answer is this: To be "baptized into Jesus Christ" is to be brought into Christ, to be made new creatures in Christ, to have old things pass away, and to be created in righteousness and true holiness. It involves a change in our spiritual nature, and implies the sanctification of the soul by the

Spirit of God. If there be any doubt of this, it may be dispelled by the following statement of the apostle: "For ye are all the children of God by faith in Christ Jesus. For as many of you as have been baptized into Christ have *put on Christ*. There is neither Jew nor Greek, there is neither bond nor free, there is neither male nor female; for ye are all one in Christ Jesus." (Gal. iii. 27, 28.) To be baptized into Christ is to put on Christ; and to put on Christ is to be *invested with his character*, "Who of God is made unto us wisdom, and righteousness, and sanctification and redemption." (1 Cor. i. 30.) To put on Christ is to *imbibe his spirit*, "For if any man have not the spirit of Christ he is none of his." (Rom. viii. 9.) To put on Christ is to *imitate his manner of life*, "For he suffered for us, leaving us an example that we should follow his steps. (1 Pet. ii. 21.) The sum of it is this: we repent *toward* God (Acts xx. 21), believe *on* the Lord Jesus Christ (Acts xvi. 31), are baptized *into Christ* (Gal. iii. 27), and thus become new creatures in Christ (2 Cor. v. 17), by being baptized by one spirit into one body (1 Cor. xii. 13). From a careful and candid consideration of these passages, how can there be any doubt as to the apostle's meaning when he spoke of the baptism of a believer into Christ? How could he more directly and satisfactorily have explained himself? And now the question is, Will we receive the explanation he gives? We come now to inquire, in the next place,

II. What does he mean by the phrase, "*Baptized into his death*"?

And here, let it be carefully observed, the apostle does

not say that we were baptized *into water*, but into *his death!* And the apostle never said *death* when he meant *water*, nor water when he meant death. And, furthermore, let it be observed that there is a sense, here spoken of by the apostle, in which every real Christian in the world has been baptized into the death of Christ. It is impossible to become a Christian, or to be saved in any other way. We must be baptized into the death of Christ, or perish! Nor is this baptism a mere figure of speech. *It is a glorious reality!* To be baptized into the death of Christ is to be made *a partaker of its benefits*, for in this way only can a poor sinner come into Christ, become a new creature in Christ, and be created in righteousness and true holiness. But upon this point let us now hear the apostle. Turn to Col. i. 21, " You that were sometime alienated and enemies in your mind by wicked works, yet now hath he reconciled in the body of his flesh through death, to present you holy and unblamable and unreprovable in his sight." Now turn to Titus ii. 14, " Who gave himself for us, that he might redeem us from all iniquity, and purify unto himself a peculiar people, zealous of good works." Compare Heb. ix. 14, " How much more shall the blood of Christ, who through the eternal Spirit offered himself without spot to God, purge your conscience from dead works, to serve the living God." Come with us to Heb. ii. 9, " We see Jesus, who was made a little lower than the angels for the suffering of death, crowned with glory and honor; that he, by the grace of God, should taste death for every man." Once more, compare Rom. x. 4, " Christ is the end of the law for righteousness to every one that believeth." But why multiply quotations? The Bible is full of such. And since the world began no man was ever brought into Christ, or was ever made a new creature in Christ, or was ever baptized into Christ, except by being baptized into his death by being made a partaker of its benefits. If we turn our eyes to the city of God and survey the shining multitude before the throne, we are told that they " washed their robes and made them white in the blood of the Lamb." And if we listen to their hallowed song of joy, we shall hear them sing, " Unto him that loved us, and washed us from our sins in his own blood," unto him be glory forever! As money builds railroads, by securing the necessary amount of material, intelligence and labor, so the death, the blood of Christ, washes, sanctifies, cleanses us trom all unrighteousness, by securing the agency of the Holy Spirit, by whom we are created in righteousness and true holiness. And thus we are baptized into his death!

But this brings us to the inquiry which, of all others, is regarded the most important to a right understanding of the text:

III. What does the Apostle mean by the phrase " *We are buried with him by baptism into death ?* " And here it is worthy of special notice, that the brethren to whom this epistle was sent were *then in* the buried state here described. Whatever the word to bury may signify, in that sense they were *then buried!* Paul says, we " *were* baptized into his death; therefore, we *are buried*," etc. What then does the words to bury signify? If we turn to Walker, Webster, Worcester, and to all the other lexicons of the language, we shall find that the words *to bury* signifies *to hide*, or to *conceal*. And this is precisely the sense in which the apostle has used it in the text. This will be seen most clearly by a comparison of Rom. vi. 3, 4; Col. ii. 11, 12; and Col. iii. 1–4. Let us compare these passages for a moment. "Therefore we are buried with him by baptism into death; that like as Christ was raised up from the dead by the glory of the Father, even so we also should walk in newness of life." (Rom. vi. 3, 4.) "Buried with him in baptism, wherein also ye are risen with him through the faith of the operation of God, who hath raised him from the dead." (Col. ii. 12.) "If ye then be risen with Christ, seek those things which are above, where Christ sitteth on the right hand of God. Set your affection on things above, not on things on the earth. For ye are dead, and your *life is hid* with Christ in God. When Christ who is our life shall appear, then shall ye also appear with him in glory." (Col. iii. 1–4.) Here we have an explanation of the whole case. To bury is to *hide*, or *conceal*. The thing buried is the *life*. And the place of its concealment is *with Christ in God!* Christians have a buried, or a *hidden life*. In their piety, their purity, their benevolence, and their good works, Christians "shine as lights in the world." In this respect they are as visible as the light of day. Like the candle on the stick, and the city on the hill, they cannot be hid. They so let their light shine, that others seeing their good works, glorify their "Father which is in heaven." But, like the living branch in a living vine, the living members in a living body, and the living body connected with its living head, so Christians have a buried or hidden life. And in this respect "the world knoweth us not, because it knew him not." (1 John iii. 1.) And this also is the reason why " The natural man receiveth not the things of the Spirit of God, for they are foolishness unto him; neither can he know them, because they are spiritually discerned." (1 Cor. ii. 14.) They have not this spiritual discernment, because they have no Christian experience— have not been "baptized by one Spirit into one body;" have not had "the life hid with Christ in God." To the men of the world, in these respects, the Christian is a hidden man. The Christian's love and joy and peace and steadfast hope of heaven are things unknown to the carnal mind. What does such a mind know of the "Love of God shed abroad in our hearts by the Holy Ghost which is given unto us?" Or of "the peace of God which passeth all understanding, keeping the heart and mind through Jesus Christ?" What does such a mind know of the "joy unspeakable and full of glory" which pervades the consciousness of a believing soul? Or what idea does such a man have of the apostle's meaning, when he speaks of "Christ in you the hope of glory?" In these elements of Christian character and life, and which are the very embodiment of Christian manhood, "The world knoweth us not, because it knew him not." The Savior said to his disciples, "I am the vine, and ye are the branches." (John xv. 5.) Now, as the branch derives its existence, life, and fruitfulness from the vine, so it is with Christians in their relation to Christ. And as the very life of the vine pervades the living branch, so the life of Christ pervades the believing soul. Hence it is that Paul says: " I am crucified with Christ; nevertheless I live, yet not I, but *Christ liveth in me;* and the life which I now live in the flesh, I live by the faith of the Son of God, who loved me, and gave himself for me." (Gal. ii. 20.) And as the life of the branch is hid or buried in the vine, so says Paul, " Ye are dead (to sin), and your *life is hid with Christ in God.* And when Christ who is *our life* shall appear, we also shall appear with him in glory." (Col. iii. 3, 4.) The burial spoken of in the text, then, is not *into water*, but *into Christ.* It is not the immersion of the body in the "liquid grave," of which we hear so much, but the consciousness of a life *" Hid with Christ in God!"* There is no water within a thousand miles of this passage. And no allusion to water baptism in any mode. Tell me not of the great names who have understood the passage to refer to immersion! We have appealed the case to Paul. We respect their opinion, but we prefer Paul's *decision.* He knew best what he meant, and has told us his meaning, and that is sufficient.

IV. We come finally to inquire, *By what agency this baptism and burial are performed?*

And here let it be specially noticed, that it is not performed by the hands of a man, or by a minister of the Gospel, or by an administrator of the ordinance called baptism, but "*by baptism.*"

"Buried with him *by baptism* into death; that like as Christ was raised up from the dead by the glory of the Father, even so we also should walk in newness of life." (Rom. vi. 4.) Here we see that it is done by an agency called "*baptism.*" And this agency, or influence, here called baptism, is the same powerful influence by which Christ *was raised from the dead,* here called, "*the glory of the Father.*" (Rom. vi. 4.) Now, the glory of the Father, by which Christ was raised from the dead, in Rom. i. 4, is called, "*the spirit of holiness.*" And how exactly his name corresponds with the result of his influence, as he enables us to "walk in newness of life." But we are not left to logical inference. The apostle has settled the matter by a direct statement. Turn, then, to 1 Cor. xii. 13, and read, "For *by one spirit* are we all *baptized into one body,* whether we be Jews or Gentiles, whether we be bond or free, and have been all made to drink into one spirit. But in Col. ii. 11 the apostle says it was done by "the circumcision made without hands, in putting off the body of the sins of the flesh *by the circumcision of Christ.*" Now, in these two verses the apostle uses the phrases, "Buried with him in baptism," and "the circumcision of Christ," in precisely the same sense. What, then, is this "circumcision of Christ, made without hands, in putting off the body of the sins of the flesh?" Compare Deut. xxx. 6; Rom. ii. 28; and 2 Cor. v. 1, and you have the answer complete. "The Lord thy God will circumcise *thy heart,* and the heart of thy seed, to love the Lord thy God with all thine heart, and with all thy soul, that thou mayest live." (Deut. xxx. 6.) "For he is not a Jew, which is one outwardly, neither is that circumcision which is outward in the flesh; but he is a Jew which is one inwardly; and circumcision is that of the heart, in the spirit, and not in the letter; whose praise is not of men, but of God." (Rom. ii. 28.) These passages speak for themselves; comment is needless. But as he was about to use the word *baptism*, as if to guard people against the error into which so many have fallen, he says that this circumcision, and baptism, were done "*without hands*, in putting off the sins of the flesh." By "a house not made with hands," the apostle means a house built by God himself (2 Cor. v. 1), so by circumcision, or baptism, *without hands*, he means a circumcision, or baptism, performed by God himself. So that the case is now made out. This baptism makes us partakers of the benefits of Christ's death, brings us into fellowship with Christ, makes us new creatures, crucifies the old man with the affections and lusts, creates us in righteousness and true holiness, hides the life with Christ in God, and invests us with the hope, that when he shall appear we also shall appear with him in glory; and in 1 Cor. xii. 13, he has told us what baptism that is which does all these things for us.

But if you take away every other argument on which an exclusive immersionist relies for support, he will flee to Rom. vi. 4, and cry, "*Buried, buried!* And can you bury a man by *throwing a little water in his face?*" And this cant expression does more for immersion than all the arguments in the world! Now, for the benefit of those with whom cant is more potent than argument, it would be easy to exclaim, " Buried, buried! And can you bury a man by *plunging him into the earth !* " Or rather, is it not by digging a grave in the earth, and then by pouring the earth on him? To ask is to answer the question. Even Mr. A. Campbell has said, "Among all the arguments in the world in favor of immersion, this apostolic allusion to a burial is the strongest." Well, he ought to know. And if this be the strongest, then the cause which it is called to support is a failure. For there is not water enough in this whole burial argument *to sprinkle an infant!*

In conclusion, we would not inquire of what Christian denomination you are members, or how you have been baptized?—whether *in* water, or *with* it?—whether *in much*, or with *little?* But, what is of infinitely greater importance, I would ask, Have you been baptized into the *death of Christ?*—are you now *buried with him?*—and are, you *walking in newness of life?*—and are you now rejoicing in the hope, that when "Christ who is our life shall appear," that "we also shall appear with him in glory?"

How radical and divine is the change of moral character indicated in this text! How imperative the obligation to a holy life which it implies! How intimate and sacred the relation between Christ and his people! How unspeakable the consolation which this relation secures! How secure are his people while their lives are hid with Christ in God! And how bright the hope inspired by the promise, that " when he shall appear, we also shall appear with him in glory!"

"Now the God of peace, that brought again from the dead our Lord Jesus, that great Shepherd of the sheep, through the blood of the everlasting covenant, make you perfect in every good work to do his will, working in you that which is well pleasing in his sight, through Jesus Christ; to whom be glory forever and ever. Amen."

XVI.

SERMON.

(Preached before the St. Louis Annual Conference, assembled at Lexington, Mo., Sept. 19, 1866.)

My brethren: If we would right ourselves at the present and guard the future, it is necessary that we have some respect to the past. There is much in the present that can be best understood when read by the light that is reflected from other days. It is thus that wise men read themselves. They keep in mind what they were, how they thought, how they felt, and how they did, under these or those particular circumstances. How they were influenced by the one, and how by the other; and by comparing themselves at one time, under one set of circumstances, with what they were at another time, under another set of circumstances, they arrive at a more perfect knowledge of themselves, and become better prepared to plan and operate for the future. It is thus, also, that men learn each other. They reflect upon what they *were;* they consider well what they *are*, and hence infer what they are likely to be. The same principle enters largely into the operations of all professional men, and of all men of business. In all the departments of life, among all classes of men, we find them attempting to control the present and prepare for the future by the aids of their past experience and observation. And why may we not apply the same principle to ourselves, as denominationalists? May we not form some opinion as to our probable future by a survey of the past, connected with an examination of the present? I think so. What *were we* as a people, and what have we done?—what *are* we, and what are we likely to do? are very interesting and very grave questions. Suppose we consider them calmly and carefully?

It was just sixty years ago this month—this week, and most likely this day—sixty years ago, that a Methodist preacher was first appointed to Missouri. When I reflect upon Methodism as it then was, and then look around me and see what it now is, changes of the most astounding character present themselves—changes in numbers, changes in position, changes in surroundings, changes in manner, and changes in character—changes in almost every respect, and in almost everything.

But if I go back some forty years farther in the history of the denomination, I note yet other changes. Among all the class-leaders of the land I find no Carvosso.

Among all the pious ladies a Ann Hester Rogers, a Mrs. Fletcher, a Lady Huntingdon, a Madame Guyon, are not found. Among all the local preachers few or none such as were the representative men of that class in other days are now to be found. There are also great differences in the traveling preachers of then and now. There are differences in the men, and differences in their modes of procedure. What these differences were, and what the results of their respective operations, may be considered hereafter. At the present we may, perhaps, profitably employ ourselves in a hasty survey of the introduction of Methodism into what is now the State of Missouri, and in noting some particulars connected with its history from that to the present time.

Before the territory now embraced in the State of Missouri came formally into possession of the United States Government, the only preaching by Protestants the people were permitted to hear was done by one Clark—Rev. John Clark—a Southern man, I think a Georgian by birth. He lived in Illinois, on the American Bottom, below where the city of Alton now stands. As the then existing government was intensely and exclusively Catholic, and no one was allowed to preach or teach or hold religious services unless he first took the oath of loyalty both to the State and to the Church, Mr. Clark had rather a hard time of it. His place of preaching was in a neighborhood in St. Louis County then and now called Cold Water; and his plan of procedure was to cross the Mississippi river in a skiff after dark, hold his meetings at night, and re-cross to his own side before daylight next morning. This he did to avoid the vigilance of the officers of the Spanish government. But notwithstanding the difficulties and dangers that attended him, he persisted, and laid the foundations of the Protestant and Methodistic faith so deep that the changes of seventy years have not been sufficient to remove them, and the results of his labors are there to this good day.

The treaty by which Missouri was ceded to the United States was signed the 20th of December, 1803, and formal possession taken by the representatives of the United States Government in March following, 1804. If previous to that period there were any preaching here by Methodists, or by any other Protestants, besides that of Mr. Clark, already referred to, I have not been able to find any record of it. There were a few Protestant people in the Territory, and, possibly, there may have been some preaching; but if so, when, where, or by whom, is now unknown.

On the 15th day of September, 1806, a Methodist Conference, or a Conference of Methodist preachers, was commenced at Ebenezer Meeting House, Greene county, Tennessee, near to which Meeting House I had the honor of being brought up, and at which, in 1830, twenty-four years later than the period named, I looked on the first Conference mine eyes ever beheld; and as I looked on McKendree and Soule and other great and good men, I experienced a feeling in regard to Bishops and great men that a better acquaintance and a closer friction rubbed out long since. But let that pass. At the Conference of 1806 Bishop Asbury was present, and so of the members of the then Western Conference, except those laboring in Mississippi and Louisiana, and such was the condition of the work there it was thought best they should not leave it. At that time the Western Conference embraced all the country from the Alleghany mountains to the remotest settlements of the Southwest— all the great Valley of the Mississippi. At the Conference under notice the minutes say eleven preachers were received on trial—Bishop Asbury, in his journal, says fourteen—among whom was a young man named Travis—John Travis—and on reading out the appointments at the close of the Conference he found himself appointed to *Missouri Circuit*—not Missouri Conference, nor Missouri District, but to Missouri *Circuit*, Cumberland District, Western Conference; and if you take the trouble to examine, you will find that the Cumberland District, as then bounded, included all of Middle and Western Tennessee, all of Southern Kentucky, a large portion of Indiana, all of Illinois, and all the settled portions of Missouri and Arkansas. The cities of Nashville and St. Louis were in the same Presiding Elder's district, without either railroad or steamboat communication between them. Rev. William, afterward Bishop, McKendree was appointed to travel this district, and I recollect to have heard the venerable Thomas Wilkerson, who was then a Presiding Elder in another district in the same Conference, say that, upon receiving the appointment, Mr. McKendree dryly remarked, he would *try* to travel it, and if Mr. Asbury would furnish him with an *immortal* horse, he thought he could succeed. However, he did travel it, and the presumption is he traveled it on a horse of flesh and blood like other horses. It was necessary that the horses used by those men should be good swimmers as well as good travelers, as most of the water-courses must needs be either forded or swam.

Mr. Asbury says of this Conference of 1806, the preachers were in great want, and to help, so far as I could, "I parted with my watch, my coat, and my shirt;" that is, he partially stripped himself, that he might help to clothe his more ragged brethren. The watch was probably sold, and the coat and shirt given to some needy ones, who, doubtless, felt somewhat consequential as they set off for their new circuits, one wearing the Bishop's coat and another his shirt! Such a procedure might be regarded as very unepiscopal in these days; and if any now present should regard those as times of ignorance, I beg you will wink at them, and pass on. The men who went out from that Conference were not clothed in purple and fine linen, nor did they fare sumptuously *any* day. There were no scented oils upon their heads, and as for well-trimmed, cultivated beards, they wore none. Their feet were not covered with lasting, or Congress gaiters, nor French kid boots; but they were shod with the preparation of the gospel. No pearl or golden studs glittered on their bosoms, but they had the breastplate of righteousness. No costly chains or guards dangled from their fobs, but they wore the girdle of truth. And it must be confessed, that with all their poverty and mean appearance, with all their privations and sufferings, the weapons of their warfare were mighty through God to the pulling down of the strongholds of wickedness.

Between the place where young Travis received his appointment and the work to which he was assigned there was a distance of from five to seven hundred miles, according to the route by which he may have traveled, and a large part of that distance was almost entirely without settlement. If he crossed the Ohio river, he most likely did so either at Louisville, at Shawneetown, or at Old Fort Massac, as these were then the principal, if not the only regular crossing-places on the lower river. Then, after leaving the Ohio, there were no settlements on his route until he reached those of the American Bottom on the Mississippi river. So that along the whole of that part of his route his companion was his horse. His quartermaster's and his commissary departments were both in his saddlebags, his bed was mother earth, his covering the starry heavens, and his protector was his God; and how precious to him must have been the promise, "Lo! I am with you always, even to the end of the world."

If he took a more Southern route, and passed through Middle Tennessee and Southern Kentucky, and crossed the Mississippi river at or near New Madrid, the case was no better—worse, indeed, as at that time a large portion of that country was thickly infested by hostile Indians.

But he reached the field of his labors, and, so far as I can learn, reached it in good time, and addressed himself to his work.

The settlements in Missouri then extended from what is now Pike county on the north, to New Madrid on the south, and to a distance of from twenty to thirty miles west from the river. These settlements young Travis was to visit, and among the people do what he could for the spread and upbuilding of the Redeemer's kingdom. It would be exceedingly interesting to us now if we could know where Travis formed his classes, and of whom they were composed; to know where William McKendree held his quarterly meetings on Missouri Circuit during the Conference year of 1806-7, and of whom the Quarterly Conference was composed. And this we ought to have been able to know. Had the preachers and people done their duty, we would to-day, uncontrollable accidents excepted, have a fair and full record of every Quarterly Conference ever held in Missouri; a fair and full record of the names of every man and every woman ever connected with the Methodist Church in Missouri, with the date of their admission and of their withdrawal, removal, expulsion or death, as the case may have been. We also would have a fair and full record of the name of every person ever baptized in the State by Methodist preachers, with their age and date of baptism. But we have little, almost nothing, of the kind. The loss has been great, and now it is remediless. I am grieved and mortified when I think of the past and of the present carelessness and indifference of our preachers and people in matters of this kind. Would that even now an efficient remedy were applied. Would that all which remains would now be gathered up, carefully preserved, and the future marked by a better state of things.

At the end of the year young Travis reported one hundred white and *six* colored members; and instead of one only, he formed two regular circuits, one of which was called Missouri, the other Merrimac. As I stated awhile ago, this appointment was made just sixty years ago this month, and this week, since when appointments have been made annually; and now it devolves on the Bishop presiding to make the sixty-first annual appointment of Methodist traveling preachers in Missouri. May all the appointees be as self-sacrificing, as zealous, as faithful, and as successful as was young Travis.

And, before I pass entirely away from this point, let me ask you if in your soberest judgment you do not think that such men as Travis deserve to be remembered —deserve a monument—more than do earth's conquerors, whose laurels are

"Blood-nursed, and watered by the widow's tears!"

If so, then I propose that, as soon as practicable, we erect somewhere in the State a substantial and commodious house of worship, and call it by his name. And further, that on the occasion of the dedication of that house as many of us as practicable assemble together, each bringing with him whatever he may be able to gather up in the way of official record, scraps of history, either written or oral, and let us see if we may not collect and preserve something of value in regard to the early history of our denomination in this State.

It may now be proper, and somewhat interesting withal, for us to allude, and merely allude, to some of the more prominent and leading points in our denominational history from the days of Travis to those in which we ourselves are the chief actors. And we take for the first period that from 1806 to 1816. This forms the first decade in our history, and its termination was marked by an important change in our ecclesiastical status.

It has already been mentioned that in 1806 Missouri was included in the Western Conference, and its boundaries have been designated. But at the General Conference held in May, 1812, this mammoth-like Western Conference was divided, and one part called the Ohio, and the other the Tennessee Conference. The territory of Missouri fell into the Tennessee Conference, and so remained during the four years next succeeding. Meanwhile the sessions of the Western Conference from 1806 to 1812, were held as follows: 1807, at Chillicothe, Ohio; 1808, at Liberty Hill, in Tennessee; 1809, at Cincinnati, Ohio; 1810, at New Chapel, Shelby county, Kentucky; 1811, at Cincinnati; and in 1812 the Tennessee Conference held its first session at Fountain Head, Tennessee.

The boundaries of this, the Tennessee Conference, as set forth in the Discipline of that date, were as follows: "The Tennessee Conference shall include Holston, Nashville, Cumberland, Wabash, Illinois and Mississippi districts." These were the districts that had previously formed the Western Conference. Some of them had been somewhat lessened, and the work had been extended north and northwest to form the Ohio Conference. The total membership at that time in Missouri was eight hundred and ninety-three, of whom eight hundred and twenty were whites, and seventy-three colored. Number of circuits, five, viz.: Missouri, Cold Water, Maramec, Cape Girardeau, and New Madrid. These, together with one circuit in Illinois (that is, the State of Illinois, for the circuit had then no other boundaries), were included in one Presiding Elder's district, called Illinois District; but why called "Illinois District," when five out of the six circuits composing it were in Missouri, I have not been able to ascertain.

From this time until 1816, when another Conference division took place, the increase of membership in Missouri was but slight, the total in 1816 being only nine hundred and fifty-eight, only sixty-five more than were reported in 1812, four years before.

At the General Conference of 1816, the Missouri Annual Conference was formed, with boundaries set forth in the minutes of that date as follows: "The Missouri Conference shall be bounded by the Ohio Conference on the north, by the Ohio and Mississippi rivers on the east, and by the Arkansas river on the south." As the western boundaries were not specified, the supposition is that the Conference in that direction should be bounded by the farthest settlement, wherever that might chance to be. The Ohio Conference embraced only a part of Indiana; and the remainder, together with all the settled portions of Illinois, all of Missouri, and all of Arkansas north of the Arkansas river, were included in the Missouri Conference. When first formed there were two Presiding Elder's districts in the Conference—one in Illinois, the other in Missouri—the first having eight and the second seven circuits. But largely over two-thirds of the membership of the whole Conference were in the Illinois district.

The first session of the Missouri Conference proper was held at Shiloh Meeting House, in the Illinois circuit, commencing on the 23d of September, 1816, Bishop Roberts presiding. The next session was held at Bethel Meeting House, Goshen Settlement, in the same circuit. And the third session was appointed to be held in Murphy Settlement, in Missouri, near where the town of Farmington is now; but for some reason it was changed, and the Conference was held in Illinois, at the place of its former meeting. At this session, September, 1818, a new Presiding Elder's district was organized on the west side of the river; and three or four new circuits also were formed. The Conference had now three districts—one in Illinois, one in Missouri, and one in Arkansas—each embracing all the prominent settlements in each of these territories respectively. The Missouri district supplied the settlements from Howard and Pike counties on down to New Madrid, while the Arkansas or Black River district extended from Spring River on the northeast to Red River on the southwest, where a large settlement at Pecan Point was regularly supplied with circuit preaching.

I leave you to reflect upon the labors, the zeal, the perseverance of the preachers of that day—upon the difficulties they had to encounter, the poverty, the privations, and sufferings they were called to endure, while I proceed to remark that from 1816 to 1824 (that is, from the time of the organization of the Missouri Conference, by its separation from the Tennessee Conference, to the time of the organization of the Illinois Conference, and the confinement of the Missouri Conference to the west side of the river), the increase of the number of districts, circuits, preachers, and church members was gradual and constant. In 1816 there was one district, seven circuits, ten preachers, and nine hundred and forty-one members. In 1824 there were three districts, seventeen circuits, twenty-five preachers, and three thousand three hundred and thirty members.

Between 1816 and 1824 five of the eight annual sessions of the Conference were held in Missouri—one in Murphy Settlement, as noticed; two at McKendree's Chapel, in Cape Girardeau county; and two in the city of St. Louis.

For several years immediately succeeding the separation of the work in Illinois from that in Missouri there was less of prosperity than had been experienced previously. This was owing to a combination of circumstances, two or three of which it may be proper to note. And first, many of the most able and experienced members of the Conference chose their positions in Illinois or Indiana, and left Missouri weakened, not only in numbers, but in regard to talent and experience as well. A large proportion of these men were originally from Virginia, Kentucky, Tennessee, or

States farther south, which they had left, partly on the ground of their personal opposition to the institution of slavery, and partly, perhaps, under some hope that they might be able in these Territories to do better for themselves and families than they could hope for in older States; and the fact that, after a long and bitter struggle, Missouri was made a slave State, decided them in their preference for Illinois or Indiana. Then again, although it was not so very difficult to induce men to be transferred from other Conferences to this, it was exceedingly difficult, in most cases, to induce them to remain here; and perhaps there is no Conference in the entire Connection whose records show such a popping in and popping out as do those of Missouri. It were, perhaps, useless to inquire into the reason of this, but the fact is undeniable.

In the next place, as is well known, but little of the best parts of Missouri—those best suited to agricultural pursuits—were settled at the earlier periods in the history of the Territory, and when it came under the government of the United States, and specially after the organization of the State of Missouri in 1820, there was among the immigrants here a large class of mere adventurers—persons who were neither prepared nor inclined to remain long at any one place, preferring to go from place to place as circumstances or caprice might chance to direct. To these may be added a large class whose principal object was to seek wealth in the mines. And both these classes were migratory in their habits, and rarely remained long enough at any one place to feel thoroughly identified with the people, or to take much interest in the religious or general prosperity of the country. And then, the fact that in Missouri were the great military posts and operations of the West—that here were carried on the government operations with divers tribes and nations of Indians —through here were the great Fur Company and Santa Fe operations, contributed largely to retard the growth of the Church. The people were, perhaps, less settled in their feelings, had more to excite and disturb them, and more to call their attention away from that which was needful than any other State or Territory in all the West. Under these and other impeding influences the Church moved slowly, so that from 1824 to the close of 1835 (eleven years) the increase of members in the entire Conference, embracing, as it did, Missouri, Arkansas, and the Indian country on the west, was less than seven thousand; and this increase, small as it was, was gained principally in the few years immediately preceding the last named date. At the General Conference of 1836 the Missouri Conference was again divided, and the Arkansas Conference formed. The boundaries of the Missouri Conference were then given as follows: "The Missouri Conference shall include the State of Missouri, and that part of Missouri Territory which lies north of the Cherokee line." As in former days, the lines continued to run west for complement. The number of members in the bounds of the Conference, after the setting off of Arkansas, was: whites, six thousand five hundred and thirty-four; colored, eight hundred and sixteen; Indians, four hundred and twenty-eight; total, seven thousand seven hundred and seventy-eight, and fifty-four traveling preachers. This, you will observe, was just thirty years ago. From this on to 1846, when the Missouri Conference was again divided, the prosperity of the Church was steady and uniform, and the increase in the number of circuits, of the number of preachers, and of members, was most gratifying, although it was, perhaps, not all it should have been. The Sabbath School and missionary interests began to receive attention, the erection of houses of worship became more common, and a better class of houses was demanded. This spirit increased, and spread among both preachers and people, so that from 1846 to 1860 more and better houses of worship were erected, more Sabbath Schools formed, more institutions of a literary character established, and more done in every way toward a permanent establishing of the Church, than ever before, while our districts and circuits had been multiplying many times, the number of our preachers increased from fifty-four to more than two hundred, and our membership from less than eight to nearly fifty thousand. In 1860, six short years ago, we had schools in almost every county of the State, church houses or preaching places in almost every neighborhood, our periodicals and permanent literature were widely diffused, we were at peace among ourselves, and prosperity attended us on every side.

But now I come to the darkest, gloomiest, and saddest period in all our history. And what shall I say? What pen can describe, what pencil can paint, or what tongue could tell the scenes through which we have passed since the close of 1860! Our day and Sunday schools were nearly all broken up. Some of our houses of worship were forcibly wrested from us and seized in the name of the Lord. Others were converted into barracks, and oaths and blasphemies were heard around the sacred altars where Almighty God had been worshiped, and where he had written the "new name" on many a believing heart. Others again were used for hospitals, and, worse than all, some were actually used for stables, while many others were wantonly fired and burned to ashes. Our regular services were broken up, our people scattered, and of our preachers some were killed and others compelled to flee and seek safety in other States or Territories, while of those who were allowed to remain very few were able to perform their regular work; so that at the close of the year we were in a condition about as pitiable as it is easy to imagine a Church to be. I do not much wonder that our enemies regarded us as dead and proceeded to administer on our estate. Almost any other people under the sun would have been dead had the same means been used to kill them that were used to kill us. Our escape from ecclesiastical death is truly a wonder. But one of the most painful aspects in the history of the few years last past is the fact that the persecuting of our Church, the trials and sufferings of our preachers and people, were, in the main, instigated and carried on by men professing a superior patriotism and a superior sanctity. The most violent and bitter of our persecutors were men professing to be the followers and the ministers of the meek and lowly Jesus! While every precept and every prompting of the spirit of true religion would have moved its votaries to sympathy, to condolence, and to extend a helping hand, these men, *professing* the religion of Christ, Ahab-like, were moved by the sight of pleasant little vineyards in the shape of fine church houses, comfortable parsonages, and the hope of large congregations able and willing to furnish large salaries; hence the fierce and bitter persecutions they incited and caused to be waged against us, and which, whenever they can, they still keep up. Such things are painful to contemplate, and, in all sober seriousness, and with, I trust, no bad spirit, I feel constrained to say that the record of the Northern Methodist Church in Missouri, during the six years last past, is a record of duplicity, of injustice, and of outrage. But let this all pass, at least for the present, while we keep our attention fixed upon our own condition. Truly we have been troubled on every side. Our members were sometimes put under bonds, or banished, or sent to prison on the most frivolous pretexts, without serious accusation from any responsible source, and in some instances our preachers were told by men clad in a little brief authority that the fact of their being preachers in connection with the Methodist Episcopal Church, South, was itself enough to hang them! And when the great Episcopal raid was begun, under a famous, or infamous, order from headquarters, some of our church-houses were saved from seizure only by the fact that they were hastily and temporarily sold to private individuals. We have been perplexed, but not entirely in despair—almost, but not quite. We have been persecuted, but not forsaken. No! Thanks be to God, *not* forsaken. We have been cast down—ah, *down*, deep down, but not destroyed—not destroyed! But many had so nearly lost all hope that when the preachers were allowed again to go to and fro, and met them, they literally shouted for joy. When the Church paper was again permitted to visit them there were strong men who wept like children at the sight of its familiar face. They wept because of the recollections called up—wept, oh, such grateful tears, because they there and then had evidence that the Church of their choice, and of their heart's deepest love, was *not dead!* And here I must be permitted to enter the record, that, in my soberest judgment, the history of modern times affords no instance of greater fidelity to true principles, or of stronger and more unflinching attachment to the Church of their choice, than has been shown by our membership in Missouri during the six years last past. Away out upon the prairies, or among the hills and hollows, or the swamps of the sparsely settled portions of the State, where for months after months they heard no preaching, saw no preacher, had little or no communion or companionship with their brethren; where evil reports and evil prophecies concerning the Church were continually poured into their ears; where men wearing the livery of heaven and professing to be messengers of truth solemnly declared to them that the Church was disorganized, disbanded and dead, and that the scattered fragments were being gathered into the motherly bosom of their fold; under all these difficulties and discouragements they remained steadfast—firm and steadfast, as though each and every one of them had firmly resolved in his heart of hearts, that if the ship did go down, he would be the last one to leave the wreck. But she *did not* go down! Honor and praise be to Him who in mercy gave to these people the spirit of such firmness, such steadfastness, such patience, such perseverance, such faith and prayer, the vessel was not lost. For a time she appeared as if dismantled, and tossed and driven by fierce winds and frightful waves, but she was not lost. And my opinion is, that there might be gathered up from the last five years' history of our membership instances of as true moral heroism as those which characterized the days of the primitive Christians.

But let us glance at the present situation. Brethren, during the fifteen years last past I have been identified with you and your work. My position has been such during that time that I have been at least as well informed as to the actual condition of the Church in Missouri as any other man, and it is with a heart filled, burdened and overflowing with gratitude to God that I tell you, that never in the history of my past acquaintance with the Church were her spiritual prospects better or brighter than at this good hour. Never before were our true and faithful ministers so near or so dear to the great heart of the people; never before were they so much respected, loved, or sought after; and never before had they the influence they can now exercise; never were they listened to more gladly or appreciated more highly; and never before have I heard of so many, such glorious and fruitful revivals in the same length of time as I have heard of during the two or three months past. So deep, so rich in fruits, so all-pervading, and so all-conquering are these revivals; and from almost every section the good news thereof comes up. May this reviving spirit continue to be given

> "Till o'er our ransomed nature
> The Lamb for sinners slain,
> Redeemer, King, Creator,
> In bliss returns to reign."

Brethren, I have shared in your kind Christian friendship, shared in your sympathies, shared in your prayers, and to some extent have had the honor to share in your sufferings; and I beg you will now grant me the privilege of sharing in your songs of triumph to Him who hath said, "I will never leave nor forsake you." And let me join with you in one earnest, fervent, deep, long, and grateful Alleluia to Him that liveth forever and ever because of the great things He hath done for us.

But I remember that with Him to obey is better than sacrifice, and it becomes us to inquire with the psalmist, "What shall I render to the Lord for all his benefits toward me!" And this leads to a few suggestions in regard to the future, and in reference to the course proper to be pursued by us. And,

1. Whatever others may or may not do, whatever they may or may not have done, let us remember, and always remember, "Vengeance is mine; I will repay, saith the

Lord." And remembering this, we should not seek by deed, by word, or by feeling in any way to avenge ourselves. On the contrary, we are required to bless and curse not. We are most positively commanded to "love our enemies, to do good to them that hate us, to bless them that curse us, to pray for them that despitefully use and persecute us, and to be merciful as our Father also is merciful." We are to forgive, that we may be forgiven. We are to take Him for our exemplar, who when he was reviled reviled not again; when suffered he *threatened* not, but committed himself to Him that judgeth righteously. And this we must do, brethren—we *must do*—else we cause the light of his countenance to turn away from us and we be left in darkness, and become like them by whom we are persecuted and caused to suffer. If any man have not the spirit of Christ he is none of his; and the same mind must be in us that was also in Christ. To preserve this will be our greatest difficulty, and the losing of it our greatest danger. Few people ever had a better opportunity for cultivating and manifesting the excellent graces of the true Christian character. The patience, the forbearance, the fortitude, the longsuffering, the forgiveness, and the perseverance of the true Christian may all shine forth now more conspicuously and more brilliantly than ever before in all our lives. We may now live by faith indeed; labor on, toil on, suffer on, amid all the darkness and discouragement, relying on God, who, as we believe, is working out his sovereign will, perfecting and developing his divine plans; and however bitter to us the bud may be, the flower will be sweet. May all our privileges and opportunities be sanctified to his glory and our good.

2. In the second place, we should now, more than ever before, heed the injunction given to Peter, "Feed my sheep." What a wide meaning there is in this, and how applicable to us at the present! *Feed my sheep.* They are scattered and torn, weak and wandering; the dogs and wolves of hell are in pursuit; their baying is heard on every side. Through long fasting the sheep are faint; feed them quickly lest they die. Hearken to their plaintive cries for help, and for a pastor's care, and as freely ye have received freely give—feed them bountifully.

Brethren, ye who have heard the cry of our scattered flocks, will ye not think of these things! This is no time for us to stop to inquire what we shall eat, or wherewithal we shall be clothed. The king's business requires haste, and with Methodist preachers now the best appointments are those where lie the greatest probability of doing good and saving souls. To do our full work at the present will require greater sacrifices of personal ease and worldly comfort than we have ever yet made. We must also encounter severer trials, greater dangers, and more hardships than ever before, so far at least as we have been personally concerned. But, my dear brethren, here is the command, plain and unequivocal; here are the men to whom the command was given; yonder is the work in a wide field whitening to the harvest; and the consequences of a performance or non-performance of that work have been plainly set before you. What will you do? Will you suffer with your Master, and for your Master's sake, or will you flee as an hireling? Will you stand upon the watch-tower and continue to warn the people, or will you say, my lord delayeth his coming, and begin to eat with the glutton and drink with the drunken? In a word, will you suffer affliction with the people of God, or will you seek to enjoy the ease of the world? Woe to them that are at ease in Zion! Woe to them that are full, for they shall hunger! Woe to them that laugh now, for they shall mourn and weep! Curse ye Meroz, that came not up to the help of the Lord against the mighty! Solemn words are these; may we ponder them well.

Finally, the history of the past, the condition of the present, and the prospects for the future, all conspire to assure us that if faithful to our high and holy calling we will not, we cannot, fail. The fires shall not consume, nor shall the waters overflow us. God is our refuge, a very present help in time of trouble, therefore will we not fear. We may go to prison and to death, but the word of the Lord shall not return unto him void, but shall accomplish that whereunto he hath sent it. All flesh is as grass, the wind passeth over it and it is gone, but the word of the Lord abideth forever; and his mercy is from everlasting to everlasting upon them that fear him.

XVII.
FAITHLESS HUSBANDS AND DISAPPOINTED WIVES.

BY REV. J. W. CUNNINGHAM,
Of the Missouri Conference.

"Husbands, love your wives, and be not bitter against them."— COL. iii. 19.

Marriage is a religious and civil contract by which a man and woman, subsequently known as husband and wife, obligate themselves before God and the civil law to live together in mutual affection and fidelity till separated by death. The first marriage occurred in Eden. Adam and Eve were the plighting parties. God gave the woman "unto the man," and the recipient of the boon said, "This is now bone of my bones, and flesh of my flesh." . . . . "Therefore shall a man leave his father and mother, and shall cleave unto his wife, and they twain shall be one flesh." (Gen. ii. 23, 24.)

The sacredness of the marriage relation, thus instituted by the great Creator in the early morn of the world, was enforced by him in the VII and X Commands, delivered in the wilderness through Moses. There was, however, a privilege allowed to husbands under the law of Moses which is not allowed under the Christian dispensation. A husband might put away by a bill of divorcement a wife who became distasteful to him, though guilty of no crime against the connubial state. (Deut. xxiv. 1–4.) But our Lord Jesus Christ repealed that law, and has made the marriage relation so sacred and binding that it can never be dissolved by divine consent except for a single crime.

Jesus said: "It hath been said, Whosoever shall put away his wife, let him give her a writing of divorcement. But I say unto you, that whosoever shall put away his wife, saving for the cause of fornication, causeth her to commit adultery: and whosoever shall marry her that is divorced, committeth adultery." (Matt. v. 31–32.)

Jesus further said: "A man shall leave his father and mother, and cleave to his wife, and they twain shall be one flesh: so then they are no more twain, but one flesh. What, therefore, God hath joined together, let not man put asunder." (Mark x. 7–9.) Marriage is, therefore, eminently a religious contract. Christian States, to insure such protection as the State may afford to those entering upon the marriage relation, have enacted laws pertaining to it. But it is to be deplored that some of the States of our American Union have, by their laws concerning marriage and divorce, encouraged matrimonial infelicities and applications for bills of divorce, and caused many to enter the married state, not "wisely, discreetly, and in the fear of God," but as a mere experiment, to find its remedy, if not approved, in a divorce court.

Concerning the duties of husbands and wives, the apostles of Christianity have left some wholesome counsel. St. Paul said: "Husbands, love your wives, even as Christ also loved the Church, and gave himself for it. . . . . So ought men to love their wives, as their own bodies. He that loveth his wife loveth himself. For no man ever yet hated his own flesh, but nourisheth it and cherisheth it, even as the Lord the Church. . . . For this cause shall a man leave his father and mother, and shall be joined unto his wife, and they two shall be one flesh." "Husbands, dwell with them (your wives), according to knowledge, giving honor unto the wife, as unto the weaker vessel." "Husbands, love your wives, and be not bitter against them." (Eph. v. 25; 1 Peter iii. 7; Col. iii. 19.)

The counsel to wives, husbands may seek for their own edification and comfort.

Women, as a class, are much better than men, as a class. There are many more good wives than good husbands, and many more bad husbands than bad wives. There are a great many drinking, swearing, gambling, virtueless and cruel husbands, but not many wives of either character. There are a thousand words of rebuke and reproof needed by the former to one by the latter class. Therefore,

The faithless husband and the disappointed wife will be chiefly the theme of discourse in the pages to follow.

With professions of sentiments akin to those announced by the apostles in the quotation made, do men usually woo and win a maiden's young affections, and many, after the marriage rite is solemnized, and till death severs the bond, endeavor to discharge the duties of true and loving husbands, blessing the object of their affections. But all are not true to their vows of love and professions of fidelity and devotion made in the wooing days, nor to the obligations assumed at the marriage altar; and of the latter I will speak.

Behold a maiden young and fair, a joy to her parents, a bright star in her childhood's home, an object around whom the affections of parents and brothers and sisters fondly cling. A young man seeks her hand in marriage. He woos her, not with the words of bitterness with which his unfeeling neighbor daily afflicts his sorrowing wife; not by cold indifference when in her presence, as if he cared not for her; not by furnishing her unmistakable proofs that he prefers other places and companions to her society, but woos her with honeyed words of love and vows of undying devotion, and thus wins her heart's warmest affections.

Yielding to his enticing words of love, she loves him in return, and, full of hope for a life of unclouded happiness, promises to be his. Her love blinds her eyes to defects in his character which others behold, and of which she is warned; or, seeing them, she hopes to correct them when "they twain are one," and, against the remonstrances of her parents she marries him, and, to accomplish her purpose, perhaps flees her childhood's home, forsaking father, mother, and all for him. Or he, deceiving her parents and friends, as well as her, as to his real character; or, having never yet exhibited traits afterward developed, or contracted habits subsequently rendering him odious, parents and friends regard with favor his attentions, and cordially assent to the marriage proposed, and, with the benedictions of all, he leads the trusting and hopeful one to the bridal altar, and promises before God and man a life-long devotion to her. And the nuptials are celebrated with tokens of approval becoming the circumstances of the parties.

That nuptial day she thinks the happiest of all the days of her life, the dawn of a new and happier life to her, the epoch of the brightest and most joyous era of her history in the world. And, aside from religion, such it is to many, but not to all. Many a disappointed woman has realized that on her marriage day she "passed under the rod." Many a wife has, from the first year of her married life, groped her way amid the cheerless gloom of a starless night, so far as connubial happiness is concerned. It is of a disappointed one I speak. Let us contemplate the trusting and hopeful maiden described a few years later, when burdened with the cares of a family, and her eyes are opened to the unhappy realization that she is the disappointed wife of a faithless husband.

On her marriage day she left the home of her youth and all the loving and loved ones there, and put herself under the care of a new *protector*. (?) She dreamed then of happiness she has never known (or knew but for a honeymoon period), and is now painfully awake to the delusiveness of her dreams of the past, and the non-realization of her young heart's hopes of happiness in that life on which she has entered.

Cares have come upon her of which she previously had no thought; duties have now to be performed of which she had only heard before, but never knew; physical sufferings are endured to which she had been a stranger; mental disquietudes and heart sorrows are realized, of which, in all her youthful days, she had never dreamed. Every look of love, every word of tender sympathy, every kiss of affection, every act of caress and kindness that a faithful husband can bestow, are needful to keep up her sinking spirits, to suppress the swelling sigh, drive back the rising tear, soothe the aching heart, chase away the clouds, and keep the sunlight of a cheerful smile upon her once joyous countenance. She finds whims, and fancies and caprices, all unlooked for in the man whom she expected to find almost, if not entirely, perfect as a husband—whims and fancies so eccentric and exacting that it is impossible to humor them. She finds clouds of displeasure on that countenance which, in the wooing days of the past, always beamed upon her with bright and approving smiles. She sees anger flashing from eyes in which she never expected to see aught but beams of love. She beholds carelessness and indifference where she expected warm caresses, hears words of petulance, bitterness, and unkindness from lips that once kissed hers with vows of undying affection, and spoke to her only with burning words and in melting tones of love. She finds that he will forsake her company as she watches wearily beside the wee little one in the cradle, or gives attention to older children as they toss fretfully or in pain upon the bed of sickness, that he may mingle with the votaries of the dance till the small hours of the night, squeezing the hands in the dance and encircling in the waltz the yielding forms of other women, married and single.

In the great city she finds that the club-room, the beer-garden, the bar-room, the billiard saloon, the gambling-house, and, what is to her infinitely worse, the house of infamy, where fallen beauties and painted harlots reign, are preferred to his own home and hers. And the society of drunkards, gamblers, and harlots is preferred to her society, and to that of her children and his.

Or, in her lone country home, on bleak prairie, or in dense forest, with none to protect in case of danger, she and her helpless ones are often left through cheerless hours of gloomy nights, while he, all unmindful of her and them, riots in sin and revels in debauchery in village and country haunts of vice miles away. With tearful memories of father and mother, her early home, and the short-lived pleasures of her early married life, she wearily waits, and watches, and prays for, yet fears, the return of her erring husband, heralding his approach as he comes with oaths and blasphemous utterances that proclaim the presence of the ruling demon within him. The very sight of his home intensifies his drunken frenzy. The mother hurriedly hides away the unoffending children, suddenly aroused from their slumbers, to save them from the worse than brutal violence of their father, while she tremblingly awaits the storm of wrath that is to break upon her. The beast that has borne him to his home is cared for, but the wife who has wearily and anxiously waited his return is requited for her watchfulness and concern with oaths, words of abuse, and acts of violence. The stalwart arm, on which she trustingly leaned as so hopefully she walked with him to the marriage altar, is raised against her in anger and in wrath. The masculine hand that held her trembling hand, so confidingly given to him while he solemnly pledged himself before God and men to be to her a true and faithful husband, now smites her fair cheeks with violence, or with rod or club beats the feeble form that crouches piteously pleading at his feet, and to protect whom he should sacrifice, if need be, his own life.

Does she, when he is less inebriated, venture a remonstrance against his faithlessness and cruelty, he responds according to the mood he is in—sometimes with penitence and sorrow, and with promises of amendment, but at others with words of unkindness and bitterness that pierce her heart more painfully than would the dagger of an assassin. Would she seek consolation in religion for her sorrowing soul, he, it may be, plays the part of a petty tyrant, by denying her a right to a place in the church of God, and refusing her the privileges of the sanctuary of the Most High; or, allowing her such privileges, all unattended by himself, he preferring the synagogues of Satan to the house of God, yet he detracts from her enjoyments by often reviling the Church of her choice, and ridiculing her prayers, her piety, her faith, and her hope.

He is a drunkard, a gambler, a libertine, a tyrant, a monster!—a *faithless husband*, with perfidy to his marriage vows, and a long list of crimes against his wife, blackening his soul and making him a fit companion for demons in perdition; and she, a deceived and disappointed wife, abandons him in despair, or worries through a miserable existence with him, dying at last with blasted hopes and a broken heart—dying, it may be, from neglect and cruel treatment—dying, perhaps suddenly, by violence at the hands of her cruel husband.

This picture is not overdrawn. The records and proceedings of police, criminal, and divorce courts would furnish enormous volumes of proof that it is truthful in all its details, and that many cases immensely transcend it in enormity, while thousands of families whose inner life has never been revealed in the courts, and is unknown to the public, would furnish similar pictures, sad and sorrowful to behold, were they presented with the simple details of fact and the plain coloring of truth.

But there are bad husbands, who are neither drunkards, gamblers, nor libertines.

There are some who are sober and industrious, but they do not properly appreciate a wife's trials and troubles; do not sympathize with her in her numerous vexations and worryings as housekeeper without help, or with help that worries rather than relieves; as the wife of an exacting and fault-finding husband, and the mother of fretful and ill-tempered and unmanageable children, who in their defects resemble their father more than their mother; do not give her the words of cheer she covets when overwhelmed with cares and sorrows and vexations, but are cross-grained, ill-tempered, rude in speech, and disagreeable in many respects, often by word or act wounding her sensitive feelings to the very quick. An absent button, a rent garment, an undarned sock, a slight failure in the culinary department, or anything for which a wife might be remotely held responsible by a querulous husband, is the occasion for rebuke or complaint, while words of praise and cheer for her industry and commendable qualities seldom fall upon her ear.

A son of Ethiopia chastened his wife severely with a rod. His employer remonstrated with him, and told him he "ought to love and *court* her," instead of beating her. With a look of astonishment he replied: "I did my courting before I was married." There are too many white men in all the ranks of society who seem to conclude, with the Ethiop, that the days of courting are ended at the marriage altar, or with the "honeymoon," and thenceforth they play the part of a querulous *master* or exacting *superior* toward their wives.

And many a good wife, painfully conscious of the want of congeniality on the part of her husband, in the desperation of utter hopelessness as to future happiness with him, induced by his unsympathetic and censorious character, abandons him for the sympathy of loving hearts in her parental home, or, with no such home to return to, seeks sympathy with strangers, or lives out a miserable life with the unsympathetic master she calls her husband.

Some husbands treat their wives as if they were idle mendicants, and not their own helpmeets. It is "I," and "me," and "mine," and never "we," and "us," and "ours," when speaking of the family possessions, and the wife is made to feel from youth to old age her utter dependence as an *attache* of his household. She dare not make an expenditure for herself or children, give to her church or a charitable object, without consulting him and obtaining his consent, and she is required to render an account of all the money grudgingly furnished her. Many a husband is too penurious in his dealings with his wife to give her a nickel to cast into the treasury of the church she frequents, while he will spend three times the amount for the cigars he smokes as he loiters about the streets on the Sabbath day, and five or ten times the amount for those he distributes to others who loiter with him, while she goes penniless to the sanctuary of God.

Some husbands indicate by their actions that neither wife nor children have any attractions for them. Absent during the day, except when eating the meals a wife's industry has prepared for them, they forsake their homes as soon as supper is ended. In the country they ride over to a neighbor's house, the cross roads' store, or the neighboring village. In the village, town, or city, they stray away to stores, shops, offices, bar-rooms, or taverns, and spend their time with men of like character, while the lonely wives of the idle, gossiping conclaves are sighing for the society of their respective husbands, who only return to their homes when drowsy powers induce or closed doors compel. Like the swine in the fields or streets, they only go home to eat and sleep.

At the risk of rousing the ire of " Bishops and other clergy," as well as of Christian brethren in the Churches, I will venture to say that *he is not a model husband* who subjects his wife to the nuisance of quids, cigars, and pipes, and smoke, and stained saliva, and an odorous breath which finds its equal in offensiveness only in the whisky-scented breathing of the habitual drunkard. That which is so nauseating and offensive to a multitude of men who, in their daily associations with men, are brought in hourly contact with the offensive smell of pipes and cigars, and the yet more offensive breathings of tobacco-scented lungs and mouths, must be an offense to a wife who is compelled to endure it in her own home and husband. A wife who could endure such an offense on the part of her husband, be he sinner, saint, or clergyman, herself not addicted to the habit, without an open and earnest protest against it, must be a most amiable-spirited woman and a long-suffering wife, whatever may be said of him or his good qualities.

There are various things which conspire to make the *worse* class of *bad* husbands heretofore described, at which I have hinted, but to which I will, by way of emphasis, again refer.

One is the drinking saloon.

Within richly-colored and elaborately-ornamented windows of fashionable drinking-houses in the great cities and larger towns, where wealthy and pretentious men seek to gratify their thirst for strong drink at a high price; within rudely-shaded and less ornate establishments, where poor men seek their gratification at a less cost; in the village dramshop and country " grocery," where villagers and countrymen resort; and in some " drug stores," where more body-killing and soul-destroying liquors than health-restoring and life-preserving medicines are sold and drank, drunkards and bad husbands are being continually made. Former generations of inebriates have passed away, but their places are filled by another generation of like character, and, as one by one they perish, others will take their places. In these drinking-houses once loving and beloved husbands are transformed into unloving and unlovable monsters. No grade of society in city, town or country is exempt from the ruinous process. To homes of wealth, where elegance, fashion and refinement reign, intoxicated husbands are sent from the gilded saloons, where, by frequent visits and the persistent habit of dram-drinking with friends at intervals of leisure during the business hours of the day, they have become drunkards. In their homes of wealth wives are enduring great sorrows, on account of the intemperate habits and the cruelty of their husbands. Drunken husbands, once wealthy but now impoverished by their intemperance, are sent from saloons of lower grade, to which they have descended, to homes of poverty, where refined and accomplished wives sigh and weep and sorrow over lost fortunes, departed pleasures, blasted hopes, and a ruined husband—a curse instead of a blessing to their families.

To humble homes, where wealth never abounded, but where comfort prevailed, and intelligence and sensitiveness reign in the persons of amiable wives, as well as to ruder homes, where uneducated and unrefined, but virtuous and worthy women abide in their scantily-furnished apartments, with little ones whose main dependence is on their mothers for the food they eat and the clothing they wear, many once industrious, temperate and loving husbands are sent from the lower grade of dramshops, where, in exchange for their money and their wits, they have received the spirit of a demon, and under its inspiration abuse and maltreat the wives that should be dearer to them than life. And thus from the most lowly homes to mansions of affluence and elegance, fallen and faithless husbands and disappointed and unhappy wives are found, and chiefly through the agency of our licensed "breathing holes of hell."

The family grocer who sells whisky by the gallon to dram-drinking farmers, and thus enables them to become intoxicated in their homes, and causes them to abuse their wives every day of the week, "adds fuel to the fire" the saloon-keeper has kindled in the men whom he thus supplies; and if the *dram* seller is the occasion of sorrow and tears to the wives of his patrons, the *gallon* seller increases their tears and multiplies their sorrows, as the gallon exceeds the dram in quantity, or as habitual drunkenness, induced by the gallon supply, is worse than an occasional *spree*, occurring only on occasional visits to town or city.

Another cause for bad husbands is found in the billiard-saloons and gambling-houses that are found in all the cities and towns, and which entice into their precincts so many men from rural districts, as well as from the cities and towns. Many men become so infatuated with billiards, and other games more secretly practiced in more private apartments of the same establishments, and with the class of men frequenting such places, that they become more attractive than wife and children and home. If they chance to escape the love of strong drink, which is rare, they become by their habits and associations demoralized in all the loftier and nobler qualities that should adorn the husband of a worthy wife, and she cannot be otherwise than unhappy in the contemplation of the wretched character who has fallen so far below the noble being she fancied him to be when he wooed and won her young affections. Many a wife is dying of neglect whose husband is wedded to "billiard saloons" and "gambling hells;" is sighing, weeping, and grieving her life away, while with despicable characters he is driving the ivory balls in the billiard room, throwing cards on the gambling table, or, in gamblers' phraseology, is "fighting the tiger" behind the curtains—playing at games more exciting, more hazardous, and more demoralizing than those more publicly participated in.

Another abomination conspiring to make men forget their marriage vows, win their affections from their wives, and make them heartless libertines and faithless husbands, is the house of infamy were fallen women reign. These dens of iniquity are found in all the cities and larger towns. The inmates thereof, arrayed like the daughters of kings, glittering with golden ornaments, go forth and tread unblushingly the streets where chaste wives and daughters walk. At times they affect the modesty of true virtue, and again shamelessly reveal their real characters to susceptible men in public places. Through the agency of these fallen ones in city, town, and country, many a man is lost—lost to wife, and lost forever.

Sometimes a wife may trace the faithlessness of her husband and the wreck of her own hopes and happines to her own early or later indiscretions, or to the agency of some indiscreet maiden or matron. The facts may be stated in the following paragraphs :

A young lady invites an abstemiously-inclined young man, at a fashionable party or at a little friendly gathering in her own or a friend's house, to drink with her from the sparkling wine cup. He has been taught by a temperate father and mother to "look not upon the wine when it is red, when it giveth its color in the cup," and he has thus far done honor to his parental teaching, but he yields to the temptation of the captivating maiden; he drinks the proffered draught, and thus *she initiates* him into a pernicious habit, into which a male associate might never have ensnared him—a habit which grows stronger as he grows older, and which ultimately gains the complete mastery over him; makes him the patron of drinking saloons, a drunken and a faithless husband, and a curse to her, or to some other fair woman less culpable but more unfortunate than herself.

A young man learns his first game of cards under the tutorage of a fascinating maiden, and repeats the amusement with her in his frequent visits as her suitor, and thus initiated he is led on in the mysteries of gaming by his fair preceptor. In time he becomes a gambler, and with his gaming associates becomes a drunkard, and curses her as a faithless husband for her agency in instructing him in the diabolic art, which he might never have learned under a masculine preceptor.

A wife, by the frequent display of her home-made wines and cordials, inducts her own husband into the habit of intemperance, and sees him fall from the position he occupied as a sober and useful man and devoted husband, when first she put the temptation before him, to the deep degradation of an abandoned drunkard, and a faithless and cruel husband.

A wife accustomed to "trip the light fantastic toe" in the dance, and enjoy the embrace of masculine arms in the waltz in her maiden days, forgetful of her marriage vow, to forsake all others for her husband, persists in attending dances and balls, and inducing her domestically-inclined companion, against his wishes, to accompany her, till at last he becomes enamored of the amusement, and, what is still worse, enamored of some other maiden or married woman. The electric touch of her hand in the dance, her yielding form in his close embrace in the waltz, the languishing look of unlawful love in her eyes, are too much for him. The wife, too busy in her flirtations with other men, fails to see the inroads that are being made on her husband's susceptible heart, till startled by the announcement of his elopement with another woman, or has her soul kindled into a flame of furious jealousy, while yet he remains at home and is professedly true to his marriage vows. The same results have transpired when the wife, forsaking all others for her husband, eschews the dance and remains in her own home, but whom he forsakes for the sensual attractions of the ball room.

Inebriating draughts are almost universal accompaniments of balls and dancing parties, and in connection with such parties many a husband, escaping the charms of other women, acquires the habit of imbibing intoxicating drinks and becomes a drunkard. Thus the dance is a prolific source of libertinism and of drunkenness, and has wrecked the character of more women and blasted the hopes and destroyed the happiness of more wives than all the sensual pleasures it affords its votaries will ever compensate for. When a man and woman marry they owe it to each other and to themselves to forsake all other men and women for each other. No married woman should surrender herself to the embraces of another man in the dance, and no married man should take the liberties with other women, married or single, which the rules and the morals of the dancing-school and ball-room authorize, and which have ultimated in the ruin of many thousands.

The substance of the foregoing discourse was first prepared for a funeral occasion—the funeral of a wife who had been murdered by her husband. It was a portrayal of his character and her sorrows. It portrays the characters and sorrows of many now living. It is given to the public through this medium, for the benefit of all to whom it may apply.

XVIII.
THE LIMITS OF HUMAN RESPONSI-BILITY.

BY REV. C. D. N. CAMPBELL, D. D.,

Of the St. Louis Conference.

"Am I my brother's keeper?"—GEN. iv. 9.

Two difficulties have long stood in the way of a proper consideration of this question and a satisfactory solution of it. The first is six thousand years old, and is connected with the blood-stained lips which first uttered it. We see the question in the lurid light of that first murder. It shocks and appals us. There is a seeming profanity in making it our own; as if we sympathized with that dark soul who sought to hold it as a blinding lie between his crime and the searching voice of God. It seems, even yet, as if gory with the stains of that original crime, to pollute the hand that lifts it. It is a haunted theme, and a retributive ghost affrights us from its threshold.

But there is another and graver difficulty: the ages have passed upon it; and we have learned to repeat their answer by rote. The venerable authorities of Eld have said one same eternal thing, and we dare not contradict them. "Yes," they have replied, " every man is his brother's keeper—the janitor of his body and his soul. He may save or destroy him, both for this life and that which is to come." And this answer, I repeat, we have learned by heart, and roted to our children, and preached from our pulpits, and proclaimed to all the world as the simple, final truth; and yet this answer is a lie; and, what is more, every truthful instinct of our nature has risen up in revolt against it all our lives long, while yet we have suffered our souls to be crushed and chidden into submission by the iron despotism of its long supremacy in the minds of men.

It may therefore be well, though late, to inquire, for once, in what we are *not* our brother's keeper. And I reply, we are never the keeper of our brother's positive virtue; or, in other words, it never depends on us whether the character of our brother is finally virtuous or vicious. It is never true that, but for us, the character of a man now permanently good would have been as consistently bad; nor that, but for us, the bad man would have been a good one. This depends, in every instance, upon the pure contingency of his individual and original choice. He has, by divine and gracious endowment, a self-moving power which determines always the direction of his soul to virtue or to vice. The functions of this power lie in the very springs of all moral being. In the soundless deeps of his nature, and far below the winds of motive and the waves of circumstance, lies this conscious ocean of hidden and intelligent power. The storms of surrounding and impending life may agitate its surface, but its tremendous tides yield only by their own preference to the attractions of good or evil planets. It is this, and nothing else, which essentially distinguishes man from "the brutes that perish." No extraneous inflence ever *determines* him to good or evil. Of the soundness of this proposition a very little thinking will convince us. If he might be so determined by surrounding influences, then his determination would depend, it is plain, upon those influences and not upon himself. If the influences were favorable to virtue, he would be helplessly inclined in that direction; and all the merit of his seeming choice would be justly attributable not to him but to the influences which moved him. So, if the influences were favorable to vice, he would be as helplessly impelled in that direction; and all the demerit of his seeming preference for evil would be as justly attributable not to him but to the external forces which swayed him. Then he would be as responsible for his seeming choice of good or evil, as a piece of driftwood floating upon the surface of a stream is for its inclination towards either bank, and not one particle more so. Then, also, in effect, he would be neither virtuous nor vicious, but the living lie of Nature and Revelation. Therefore with all confidence we may affirm, that no man is the keeper of his brother's positive virtue: it rests with no man to say that another shall be finally either virtuous or vicious.

And with equal confidence, and upon the same grounds of immutable truth, may we affirm that man is never the keeper of his brother's immortal life. No man can save or damn another's soul. This rests, like his positive virtue, upon man's individual sovereignty. Either he has no soul to be saved, or, after divine provision made for its salvation, he alone must determine its destiny. If he have a soul, it is a limited spiritual independency; a sovereign trinity of intelligence, conscience and will. Within its sphere, it is the very "image and likeness" of the sovereignty of God. Otherwise, it is not a moral soul, but a calculable and almost material thing. For such a thing there can be no right or wrong, no good or evil. If man's personal salvation be not in his own sovereign keeping and control, then the merest and most inconsequent accident may defeat it, without his fault and against his will. It will lie at the mercy of every malignant contingency. Men and devils may sport with it. The breath of a human, infernal or Divine caprice may waft it to heaven or to hell. It may be endlessly rewarded for another's virtue, or punished for another's fault. Can any one contemplate, without horror, the monstrous injustice of making the immortal salvation of one man dependent upon the purely contingent and precarious goodness of another man?

But it will be objected that this teaching narrows too much the scope of human influence; and, in particular, it will be asked, if parents may not reasonably indulge the hope that their faithfulness may be blest of God so as to effect the salvation of children who would otherwise be lost; and if they may not as reasonably entertain the fear that their lack of faithfulness may result in the perdition of children who would otherwise be saved; and if both the hope and the fear are not warranted by those words of Inspiration, "Train up a child in the way he should go, and when he is old he will not depart from it." To this it may be replied, that the authority of Scripture is absolute and final as far as its real meaning goes; but in this case it does not go so far as is supposed. It is beyond question that a child trained up "in the way he should go" "will not depart from it;" for this is made certain by Divine testimony. But is it equally certain that we can always succeed in so training him? God has not said this, and all history and experience are against it. Then there is no warrant in the Scriptures—since this is confessedly their most absolute passage bearing on this point—for the belief that parental conduct may effectuate the salvation of a child who would otherwise be lost, or the perdition of one who would otherwise be saved. And if this opinion has no warrant of Scripture, what ground of reason can be urged in its behalf? In what essential quality does parental influence differ from any other outside force which affects the characters of men? Who endowed it with this incommunicable majesty and potency of Godhead that it should save or damn immortal souls? Is the Almighty incompetent or unfaithful, that He has committed an error so deadly and irreparable? Is He such a bungler that He did not know how to plan more wisely, or so feeble as to be unable to effectuate wiser and safer schemes? There is no such thing rationally supposable. The wisest and best parent never succeeded in saving a child that would otherwise have been lost, nor the worst and most foolish one in losing a child that would otherwise have been saved.

But the objector will inquire, if the same thing is true of pastoral faithfulness; if the purity, sincerity and devotedness of the Christian pastor do not save men who would otherwise be lost, and his lack of these qualities cause the loss of souls who would otherwise be saved; if there will be no soul-stars in the faithful minister's "crown of life," which but for his fidelity would have been wandering meteors in a world of woe; and no blood of murdered souls, who would otherwise have been living in glory, on the hands and garments of the ministerial hypocrite; and especially if the words of Christ and many passages in the Apostolic Letters do not warrant this conclusion. No; I reply, unequivocally and fearlessly, no. I can find no passage in the Word of God whose legitimate interpretation goes so far. It is true that we are therein, by many expressions, encouraged to hope and warranted to believe that our pastoral faithfulness will be rewarded by the salvation, through our instrumentality, of some souls, but not of any soul that would otherwise have been lost; and we are therein as frequently admonished to fear lest our pastoral unfaithfulness should be attended with the perdition of some souls, but not of any soul that would otherwise have been saved. And would it not be strange, and revolting to reason, and an outrage to justice, if it were so? That God should make one man's ultimate salvation dependent upon the uncertain faithfulness of another man is simply inconceivable. He has not done it, and He can not do it, because it would be partial, cruel and unjust. But this lie, which would stain the very purity of God—

we learned it from the lips of bloody Rome, sucked it in with the mother's milk she gave us in the infancy of our Protestant being; and it is time that we discard it with the rest of her "vain traditions," and walk by the Word of God and the rules of common sense and sound reason.

But the objector would urge a final question: Is there, then, no power in the preaching of the Gospel to save men who would otherwise be lost? Are all the visible institutions of Christianity non-essential to salvation? Do all the light and warmth of true religion save no soul from everlasting death? Does not sending the gospel to the heathen prevent the perdition and accomplish the salvation of many souls otherwise dead and doomed to die forever? I reply again, the preaching of the Gospel is blest to the salvation of all who embrace and hold to it; but among these is not one who would have been lost if he had never heard of the Gospel. The visible institutions of Christianity are utterly non-essential to salvation. True religion—the religion of Revelation, as we understand it—saves no soul from everlasting death that would not have escaped that death had he never heard of true religion. And sending the Gospel to the heathen changes immortally the destiny of not one single soul that receives or rejects it. And all this is true from the plainest considerations. The preaching of the Gospel, the visible institutions of Christianity, the religion of Revelation, and missions to the heathen, are all influences extraneous to the soul, and can not be made conditions of its salvation without rendering it liable to perdition by the accident of destitution. To render this still plainer, if we say that the preaching of the Gospel saves any who would have been lost if they had never heard it, then we make the salvation of those persons to depend, not upon their own choice or conduct, but upon the occurrence of an accidental or providential circumstance over which they had no control, and concerning which they could not possibly have entertained a preference, for the simple reason that they had no conception of it even as a possibility. This dogma of the dead creed of the Augustinian Catholics is, I repeat, unworthy of our Protestant manhood. There is good enough in the Gospel, in the religion of the Bible, and in Christian missions, to justify more enthusiasm than they have yet kindled in our souls, without resorting to the exaggerations and fables of a false and effete ecclesiasticism.

There is something in this truth effectively trenchant and powerful. It strikes down with a blow illusions that we have deemed virtuous, and even sacred. The vanity of goodness and the vanity of evil fall dead before it. The extremes of self-righteousness and extravagant remorse meet in a common ruin. We are neither so good, nor so bad, as we had deemed ourselves. We have neither murdered souls, nor redeemed them. Unwise and wicked parents as we are, God will not let us damn our children. Unfaithful and inefficient pastors as we are, God will not suffer us to ruin the souls of our people. Covetous and idolatrous holders of the treasures of Revelation as we are, God will not let the heathen perish by our neglect.

THE LIMITS OF HUMAN RESPONSIBILITY. 291

If we will not work with Him for the salvation of men, He will save, by other men or means, "whosoever will."

We have next to inquire in what we *are* our "brother's keeper." And I reply, we are the keeper, in a clearly limited sense, of the degree of his virtue. While we can neither make him positively virtuous or vicious, nor constrain him to be more or less so, yet we can influence his whole progress in either direction; and our influence affects both the beginning and the continuance of his career. If our own character and conduct be virtuous, and he consent, we can occasion his earlier, more intelligent and decided choice of virtue. So, on the other hand, if we are vicious, and he is disposed to vice, we can occasion his speedier and more complete devotion to evil. Thus parents can win their children, pastors their people, and Christian nations convert heathen nations, if they are willing to be won and converted. And thus parental wickedness, and pastoral unfaithfulness, and ecclesiastical indifference and neglect, can postpone the conversion of children, people, and the heathen world, if they are willing, of their own accord, to postpone their own salvation. More than this it is not given man to do, towards hastening or delaying the work of God in the souls of other men.

In the matter of progress, also, man can exert some influence upon his brother. He can encourage or discourage him, in virtue or in vice; he can help or hinder him, in either. By ministering to his daily needs, physical, mental, or spiritual, he can impart to him, so to speak, along with these gifts, something of the virtuous qualities of his own nature, and thus aggrandize him in purity and power. By the same means, one viciously disposed may win the confidence and affection of another and send, disguised in seeming kindnesses, the fruitful germs of his own vices to the willing soil of his brother's soul. Indeed, the "ways and means" are numerous and endless. Example is powerful; precept is powerful; kindness is powerful;, unkindness is powerful. There are ten thousand modes by which we may help or hinder our brother in the ways of life or death; but start one in either path who would not have trodden it without our impulse—or hold one to either course who would not have been steadfast without our aid—this we cannot do; for this is more than God has left even Himself at liberty to do for the salvation or perdition of a human soul.

As a consequence of what has been already advanced, we shall easily see that we are, to some extent, the keeper of our brother's rank in the immortal state. The state itself we cannot fix. He goes to heaven or hell on his own motion, and without our effectual help or hindrance. But his rank in that state—the height he reaches or the depth he explores—may depend upon our influence, or even upon our force. To instance, we may strangle him in infancy, or murder him at any later stage of life. In either case, having diminished the factors of immortal rank, we have perforce lessened their result. And what may thus be accomplished by the hand of Violence is still more plastic to the touch of Influence. We cannot send our children to heaven or hell; but we

THE LIMITS OF HUMAN RESPONSIBILITY. 293

can exalt or degrade their rank in either place. As pastors, we cannot save or lose our people. They will be saved or lost in spite of us, and independently of our utmost power or weakness; but we can seat them on thrones of intelligence and glory, or exalt them to corresponding eminences of woe; we can sink them to the rabble of heaven, or the *canaille* of hell. As churches, we cannot hold in our niggard hands the " Bread of Life," without which the heathen world must perish by immortal inanition; for God will feed them from the granaries of heaven, if we do not; but we can, by our beneficence given or withheld, make them richer or poorer forever. This is the sphere of human influence. Here lie the eternal boundaries of man's power over his brother. And some have complained of their extent. While we contract them too much for the uses of superstition and imposture, they are naturally too wide for the convenience of skepticism and sin. It has even been objected to the Divine justice, that man's temporal welfare should lie so much at the mercy of his fellow. The inequalities of life, the contagion of example and sympathy, and the sweep and rush of those surrounding influences whose force is measured by universal induction, are but other counts in this profane and blasphemous impeachment. All these, it is true, are overthrown by the concurrent testimony of common sense and sound reason, backed by the Divine Sovereignty. But now that we have gained the cause and vindicated the purity of Divine Justice, by *quashing* the indictment of its prosecutors in their chosen court and on the evidence of its own looseness, wildness and inaccuracy of statement, shall we turn around and become ourselves the effectual accusers of that Justice by teaching that God has committed to frail and fallible hands—our own or others'— the destiny of immortal souls? Can it be a matter of legitimate surprise that thoughtful men are everywhere perplexed or driven into skepticism, while intelligent Protestant pulpits continue to utter the false and blasphemous assumption, that they can save or damn the souls of men? Then the worst of men may dismiss his vain and exaggerated remorse when assured, as he is from the lips of infallible Truth, that all his wickedness never caused the loss of a soul; and the best and most useful of men may dismiss his humble-seeming pride when assured, by the same unerring authority, that all his goodness never caused the salvation of a single soul. The bad man's account with God is dark and bloody enough, without this false and needless aggravation; and the good man's record is full and fair enough, when purged of this glittering fiction.

But again, it will be objected, that this doctrine takes away our thunder; that the ghostly terrors of the pulpit and the platform will vanish before this tremendous exorcism; that we can no longer scare the preachers into a frenzy of earnestness and fidelity, nor convulse the people with an occasional spasm of liberality, by telling them that souls will perish if they fail to rave and give; that it diminishes numerically the motives to a virtuous life, and weakens those that remain; and, finally, that it contravenes the universal belief of the Christian world. If it did all this, that would be nothing to us; because it is the truth, and we must receive all truth as from the lips of God; it is God's universal voice; it is sacred, and we cannot palter with it; we must simply receive it and believe it. But the objections, when carefully examined, may have more apparent than real force. Let us see if this will not be found true in detail.

It is objected, first, that this doctrine steals the thunder from the pulpit and the platform. But will not these engines of the Church have thunder enough left, even after so large a depletion of their sonorous powers? Is it so absolutely certain that the noise and terror of religion effect its highest and best ends? Have not the light of truth and the warmth of love something to do with saving and moving men? Then it is just possible, as it seems to me, that the pulpit and platform of Christianity may get along at least equally well with a little less thunder and terror, and a little more light and heat.

It is objected, secondly, that this doctrine lessens the number and impairs the strength of existing motives to a virtuous life. I freely concede that if this objection were valid, the doctrine would be proven false; since they contradict each other flatly, and therefore cannot both be sound. But to tell me that my brother's absolute salvation is in my keeping—that it depends upon me whether he shall dwell forever in heaven or hell, is to overwhelm me with a responsibility too vast for even the Almighty himself to assume. It is to paralyze, by the force of utter despair, every rational effort of which I should otherwise be capable to save and bless my brother. There is such a thing as putting too much upon a man for his strength to bear, and thus destroying his efficiency by over-tasking his powers. And this is precisely that thing. Many a parent has been discouraged from attempting anything for the spiritual welfare of his children, by being told that their salvation depended upon him. Many a pastor has felt this terrible paralysis shearing through all the strength of his efficiency for good. Many a Christian man has buttoned up his pocket and his purse because he was told, from the missionary platform, that the salvation of the heathen depended on his charity; and he had sense enough to see that, if this were true, he would be as guilty if he failed to give all he had in the world as if he gave them nothing. The fact is, that this thing is so ineffably and outrageously false, that nobody in the world believes it heartily; and try how we will, we cannot make ourselves or others the consistent dupes of such a monstrous imposture. So far, then, is it from being true, as objected, that the doctrine of this discourse weakens and impairs our motives to virtue, it is rather true that, in proportion as we receive and inwardly digest it, will our souls be emancipated from the long-worn fetters of despondency and inefficiency; we shall rise to a higher life; we shall breathe a purer atmosphere; the light of a kindlier truth will shine upon our heads, and the warmth of a better hope gladden our hearts.

But it is objected, finally, that this doctrine is in contravention of the belief of the Christian world. If by the Christian world the objector means all the nominal Christians in the world, except, of course, this preacher, then I answer, simply and bluntly, such is not the fact. If he means a large majority of the nominal Christians of the world, this may be conceded without harm; for that large majority is composed of Catholics; and the error which I am controverting is a favorite and fundamental dogma of their creed. But if he means the Protestant part of the Christian world, then I reply that, in my humble opinion, he is very much mistaken; and if he were not, his objection is quite aside from the merits of the question. The doctrine is either true or false in itself, and its general or partial acceptance in the Christian world touches not at all the question of its truth.

I conclude with an exact and specific statement of what, as it seems to me, is the simple truth in the whole case of the mutual responsibility of men. We are the conduits to others, if we please, of a divine influence sufficient, if they please, to accomplish their salvation; and we are responsible for the whole measure of our capacity thus to do men good. If we fail, either wilfully or by evitable ignorance and carelessness, to acquire and transmit to others this gracious influence, which might, if they chose to have it so, be the means of saving them, we are debited to the death of those souls—that is, we are charged with the crime which we would have committed if we had not been forcibly prevented. So, if we keep on hand and transmit to others, as well as we can, the Divine influence which might save them if they would, we are credited by the salvation of such souls—that is, we are rewarded for the virtuous purpose and effort, as for the accomplished deed. This is the perfect rule of the Divine administration, as taught by the Master of life; and even men, in their fallible systems of justice, try to imitate it as well as they can. And is not this enough, and the best? If any man intend evil, he will be punished for the evil intended, though he could not accomplish it; if any man intend good, he will be rewarded for the good intention, though he failed to compass it. Who would have a heavier responsibility than this? Who could wish for a sweeter and more perfect consolation? Success is nothing, failure is nothing; these have might only in human and fallible standards of merit. God reads the heart; and "as a man thinketh in his heart, so is he;" and so is he written down on those imperishable records which will confront him at the judgment-seat of Christ.

XIX.
SERMON.

DELIVERED ON EASTER SUNDAY, APRIL 5, 1874, IN THE SECOND
METHODIST CHURCH, SOUTH ST. LOUIS.*

BY REV. D. R. M'ANALLY,

Of the St. Louis Conference.

"But now is Christ risen from the dead and become the first fruits of them that slept."—1 COR. xv. 20.

If Christ be not risen from the dead, then, saith the Apostle, our preaching is vain, the Christian's faith is also vain, and ye are yet in your sins. The Old Testament Scriptures taught, Christ himself taught, and his Apostles taught, that the resurrection of the Savior was as necessary a part of the redemptory scheme as was his life or his teaching or his death. "It behooved him to suffer and to rise from the dead, that repentance and remission of sins might be preached in his name." That

*Two or three sermons expected for this volume were not furnished. The book had been promised at an early date, and at the urgent request of the compiler this sermon, hastily prepared and written, without any idea of its publication, was furnished. This much is due to the author.   PUBLISHER.

is—neither repentance nor remission of sins could have been offered to guilty man had he not risen as well as died.

From the general character of this chapter we may reasonably conclude there were some at Corinth who denied the resurrection of Christ, and the Apostle proceeded to discuss these following questions:

1. Whether there be any resurrection of the dead? This is done from the 1st to the 35th verse.

2. What will be the nature of the resurrected bodies? Verses 35 to 51.

3. What will become of those who are found alive at the coming of Christ in judgment? Verses 51 to 57.

At present we are concerned with only the first of these questions—whether there be any resurrection, or whether Christ be raised, for it all depends on this? If Christ be raised, then is there a resurrection of the dead, but not otherwise. This is the hinge on which the whole turns. Settle this, and we settle all.

The Apostle, in the chapter under notice, proves the resurrection of Christ: 1. From the Scriptures, declaring he himself had preached to the Corinthians that which he also received, or which had been revealed to him by the Spirit of inspiration, how that Christ died for our sins — according to the Scriptures — that he was buried, and that he rose again according to the Scriptures, thus indicating that he had the same Scriptural or written authority for Christ's resurrection that he had for his dying for their sins; and from this he could legitimately and justly argue that if Christ had not risen from the dead, then he had not died for their sins; and if he had not died for their sins, they were yet in their sins, and Christ was to them as nothing at all. In reality, he was no Christ—no Savior—no Redeemer.

It is here worthy of note that both Christ and his Apostles frequently referred to the Scriptures, seemingly taking it for granted that the authenticity and credibility of those Scriptures were unquestioned and unquestionable, and that their Divine origin and authority were admitted by all. But to what did they refer by the term Scriptures? None of the New Testament Scriptures were written until after the death of Christ; it is not probable, therefore, that they referred to them; nor is it probable that more than two of the gospels had been written previous to the date of this letter to the Corinthians. It is *possible*, not probable, I think, that the Apostle here refers to the testimony of Matthew and Luke in regard to the resurrection. I say *it is possible* this may be so, but I know of no single instance or proof in the New Testament where *its writings*, or any part of them, are called the Scriptures—nor do I think such proof can be found.

The reference both by Christ and his Apostles was to the Old Testament Scriptures. Of this we may be sure —because these were called, by way of eminence, *the* Scriptures or writings, and the aggregate of them was, also by way of eminence, called *The* Book, and all were regarded and esteemed by the Jews and Jewish teachers as containing God's revelation to man. But Christ and his Apostles referred to the writers of many of these

Scriptures by name, as Moses, David, Isaiah, etc., etc., acknowledging them as holy men, who spake as the Holy Ghost gave them utterance, and from time to time made quotations from nearly or quite all of these canonical books, always referring to them as of Divine authority. This was the way in which the Apostles contended with the Jews in reference to Jesus, "arguing and proving *from the Scriptures* that he was indeed the Christ."

But, it may be said, the Old Testament Scriptures in no place state in express terms that Christ should rise from the dead on the third day. To which I reply: If not stated in so many words, it is clearly taught by the many types which were admitted to refer to Christ. Instance two only: that of Jonah, which the Savior himself recognizes and applies—and that of Isaac, who was a very expressive type of Christ. As his being carried to Mount Moriah, bound, and laid on the altar to be sacrificed was an admitted type of Christ's death, so his being brought *alive* from the Mount on the third day was a type of Christ's resurrection.

It is very clear, at least to my mind, that both Christ and his Apostles, not only recognized the authority of the Old Testament Scriptures, but regarded them as part and parcel of the redemptory scheme and the system of God's revelation to man, which revelation was to culminate with that of the Apocalyptic vision. They acknowledged the importance of these Scriptures, and by their testimony the Apostle here proves the doctrine of Christ's resurrection. These Scriptures taught the necessity of that resurrection, and foretold its occurrence. Then the *fact* that it did occur the Apostle proves by eye-witnesses. " He was seen of Cephas, then of the twelve, then of five hundred brethren at once, of whom the greater part " remained or were *alive* when the Apostle wrote; hence he could easily have been confronted by many had he dared to utter what was not strictly true.

"Then," continues the Apostle, "was seen of James, then of all the Apostles, and, last of all, was seen of me also." That is, "these all saw him *after* his resurrection and I *saw him*. I saw him! I know he is alive; I heard his voice and felt his power; and the fact was so clear, so demonstrable, and so undeniable, that from a hater I became a lover, from a violent persecutor I became a willing and patient sufferer in the cause of Christ. I *know* whereof I affirm; I *know* whom I have believed; I follow no cunningly devised fables—I teach none. It is a Divine reality, an incontrovertible truth, that will endure forever, and on which the hopes and destinies of millions upon millions yet unborn will securely and safely rest."

If, my brethren, Paul were the only witness of the resurrection of Christ, I do not see how the evidence could be overthrown. Consider his talents and learning—his peculiar temperament of mind—his strong will—his earnest zeal—his unconquerable energy—his indomitable perseverance! Then think how earnestly all these were consecrated to the work of opposing Christ and destroying his disciples. With a zeal above his fellows—more than any one else did he persecute the infant Church! And why? Because he thought he ought to do things contrary to the name of Jesus of Nazareth. He looked upon that Jesus as an *impostor*—as a bad man—as disloyal both to the Jewish and Roman governments—as a disturber of the public peace and a disquieter of the Church. He regarded him as having been justly condemned and executed, and that it would be doing service both to God and the country to put an early stop to the delusion he supposed the disciples to be under. He was honest, but was mistaken, as many others have been.

On his way to Damascus, "breathing out threatenings and slaughter against the disciples of the Lord," he suddenly saw a light, which was greater, or above that of the mid-day sun—greater than that of the mid-day sun in the unsurpassed clearness of a Syrian sky. He heard a voice saying, " Saul, Saul, why "—for what reason, for what purpose, or with what intent—"persecutest thou me ?" Using a form of expression then common when superiors or even equals were addressed, he replied, " Who art thou, Lord ?" " *I am Jesus* whom thou persecutest."

I need not proceed with the details. But now consider the subsequent life of the same man. What earnestness, what zeal, what fidelity to the cause he then and there espoused! What patient perseverance, what incessant labors for the good of others! What toils, what sacrifices, what privations, and what sufferings were his! How fully did he prove that in deed and in truth he counted all things but loss for the excellency of the knowledge of Christ! All, too, because he had seen Christ, heard his voice and felt his love.

Whenever called upon to defend himself and his course —before either the ecclesiastical courts of the Jews or the civil or military courts of the Romans—he invariably referred to the scene on the way to Damascus, and gives its facts as the reason for his hope and conduct. Before high priests and before kings he unhesitatingly and unqualifiedly proclaimed, "*Jesus is the Christ.* He *was* crucified, *was* dead, *was* buried, but he *is risen*. I *know* he is! I felt his power! I heard his voice! I *saw* him! He is alive for evermore!"

Brethren, could *that* man, with such a record of preaching and writing, of laboring and suffering, of living and dying, have been deluded! Is such a thing probable. Nay, is it possible.? Could his whole life, subsequent to this event, with all its profound reasonings, all its pure and healthful precepts, all its uprightness and consistency, and such a death as his—have resulted from a mere flash of lightning, followed by a distempered imagination? Do deluded fanatics talk as he talked, write as he wrote, live as he lived, or die as he died? If Christ did not rise from the dead, and if Paul did not really see him *after* the resurrection, then Paul was certainly one of the most mistaken men of whom I have ever read, and was, beyond doubt, the most reasonable, philosophical, profound, upright, consistent and useful under that delusion! But we are not left to rely solely on his testimony as an eye witness of the resurrection of Christ. There are others. Examining the subject carefully we find a record of not less than ten open and unmistakable appearances of Christ after his resurrection. They were as follows:

1st. To Mary Magdalene, as she stood at the sepulchre, weeping over her disappointed, blighted, and, as she supposed, ruined hopes. After talking with the angel she turned herself, and seeing one whom she supposed to be the gardener, said, "Sir, if thou hast borne him hence tell me where thou hast laid him, and I will take him away." As if she had said—He did much, ah! very much for me; did what none others could do—I owe him everything. I know he was an innocent, good —and no common man! Why he suffered himself to be crucified, and his body to be laid here—I do not know—cannot even conjecture. But I can neither forget nor cease to revere and love him, though cold in death he be! Tell me where thou hast laid him, and, weak woman as I am, I will take him away! Jesus said, "*Mary!*" and there was something in the tone, in the manner of utterance, that thrilled every nerve, that went to the inmost depths of the soul! It was *more* than the electricity's shock! As it thrilled, it dispelled darkness—removed all doubts and revealed the most glorious truth the world ever heard: and, in ecstacy, she exclaimed, *Master! It is he! It is he!!* He told her not to touch him, but to go and tell his disciples he had risen. She went and reported accordingly.

2d. Next he appeared to certain women who had gone to the sepulchre, and been told by the angel that Jesus was not there, but had risen. While on their return to

Jerusalem, Jesus met them, saying, "All Hail!" and they held him by the feet, and worshiped him! This was evidently a separate case from that just mentioned.

3d. The next appearing seems to have been to the penitent and sorrow-stricken Peter.

When Cleopas and the disciple that was with him returned from Emmaus to Jerusalem, the others told them, " The Lord hath risen indeed, and hath appeared to Simon." This was the *third* appearing, and it is remarkable and *very suggestive* that his first appearing of all was to that once bad woman out of whom he had cast seven devils; and the first *man* to whom he appeared seems to have been Peter, who had so basely denied him only a few hours before the crucifixion. A manifestation this of most wonderful love and mercy, pity and tenderness.

4th. The fourth appearing was that on the road between Jerusalem and Emmaus, to two disciples, one of whom was Cleopas. The account of this, as given in the 24th chapter of Luke, is very instructive and exceedingly touching. I may not stop now to dwell upon it. They walked along the way, and in their deep sadness talked of what had so recently occurred. A stranger joined himself to the company—it was Jesus, but they knew him not. He asked of the things about which they talked so sadly. They informed him of what had occurred, and also informed him of their once buoyant, but now depressed and ruined hopes. Then Jesus, beginning at Moses, expounded to them all the things, in all the

Prophets, concerning himself. He went further. He opened their understandings that they might understand the Scriptures, and, finally, was made known to them in breaking of bread, and then vanished out of their sight. With unspeakable joy they hastened back to the city to tell of what they had seen and heard, and were at once met with the intelligence that the Lord is risen indeed, and hath appeared unto Simon!

It would be useless to attempt to draw anything like a full picture of the feelings of the sorrow-stricken few, as the deep darkness of their midnight gradually gave place to dawn, and then to a bright and blissful day. The news, first of the empty sepulchre, then the rumor that Jesus had risen, and been seen by Mary; then by another, and another, and yet another! How it must have excited, then astonished, and then overwhelmed them! But soon all doubt was at an end. The disciples had gathered together at the same place; talking, no doubt, of what had been reported, hoping, yet doubting; wondering how such things could be, or what would be the result of the then existing state of affairs; when suddenly

5th. Jesus appeared to all, with the blessed annunciation, "Peace be unto you!"

This was the fifth appearance of the risen Savior—all made during the same day, and that, too, the day of the resurrection!

6th. The next and sixth appearance was, if I read correctly, one week from the day of the resurrection, when the disciples were *all* in one place. Thomas was not present before, and, notwithstanding the testimony of the others, he persisted in his disbelief of the fact of the resurrection, declaring he must see for himself, and even then he would not trust his eyes alone, lest some optical illusion should mislead him. He must feel as well as *see* the prints of the nails and of the spear, and he must put his finger and his hand therein, ere he could believe such an improbable story. Well, at the sixth appearing, and on the eight day after the resurrection, Thomas was present, and invited to judge by his own rule, and test by his own standard. He was satisfied; and thenceforth we hear of no more doubts among the disciples on that subject.

7th. The seventh appearance, counting the whole number, was made to the *eleven* at the Sea of Tiberias.* At the suggestion of Peter, they had gone fishing; toiled all night, but taken nothing, a circumstance very unusual in that water, celebrated for the abundance and excellency of its fish. In the morning Jesus appeared on the shore, and by his direction an extraordinary draught of fish was made. The disciples went on shore, and after they had partaken of food, then occurred that interesting and touching interview between the penitent Peter and his forgiving Master that is recorded by St. John.

8th. The eighth appearance seems to have been that made to the more than five hundred brethren, most of whom were alive when Paul wrote this epistle. And the

*In the record (John, 21st chapter) this is called the third appearing of Christ, by which I think we are to understand the third *general* appearance to the disciples as a body.

9th. Was that made to James, but at what particular times, or places, or under what particular circumstances these were made we have no direct information.

10th. The tenth and last appearing before the ascension was made to the eleven on Mount Olivet, near Bethany, where Jesus gave to them the great commission to go into all the world and preach the gospel to every creature; and whence, as he finished speaking, he was parted from them, and ascended up to heaven. Some time after the ascension he personally appeared to Saul, otherwise Paul, while on his way to Damascus, as already alluded to.

Now, if any event, natural or supernatural, can be established by human testimony, then we must admit we have witnesses enough on this subject; and to my mind there are but three suppositions concerning them. Either,

1st. That they were impostors, and, as such, knowingly and willfully deceived the people; or,

2d. They themselves were deceived, and honestly believed Jesus had risen when he had not; or,

3d. Their testimony is true, and Jesus is indeed risen from the dead. Now, to one or the other of these conclusions we are bound to come. One or the other we must admit, for one or the other—and *only* one, must be true. If the first be true, the others are necessarily false. If the second be true, then the first and third are false; and, if the third be true, the first and second are false. One *only* can be true, and one *must* be true—which is it? To suppose that the first was true, and allow that these witnesses knowingly and wilfully testified to what was alse, in order to deceive the people, is to suppose a miracle at least as great as that of the resurrection itself. What possible motive had these witnesses, or what motive could they have had, to pursue such a course? They knew that, in a worldly sense, their testimony was in every way adverse to their interest; they knew it would be in direct conflict with the opinions and wishes of both the civil and ecclesiastical authorities; they knew it would subject them to the loss of all religious standing among the Jews, on the one hand, and of all civil privileges on the other; knew it would render them liable to trial and punishment for treason, as supporters of another King than Cæsar; they knew if they bore false witness there were hundreds of people at hand to convict them of perjury, and make them suffer according to the Mosaic law—and, if they still contended, though convinced of its truth, that Jesus had risen from the dead, they might be liable any day to be put to death as he had been. Yet they seem to have made no secret of the matter, from the day of the resurrection to the day of the ascension—and soon after the ascension they boldly proclaimed the fact to congregated thousands in the streets of Jerusalem, and, that too, in sight of the places at which the crucifixion and burial had occurred, and while the circumstances were still fresh in the minds of the people! Were they confronted? Were the facts denied? On the contrary, thousands of the hearers were convinced, and received the truth. The disciples had nothing to gain by the propagation of such an error, if this had been an error—but had everything to lose; and it is positively contrary to human nature, contrary to human reason, and contrary to human experience, that men should deliberately and persistently propagate falsehoods, when they know that by doing so they will lose all and gain nothing. Yet these disciples bore this testimony at all times, under all circumstances, and many of them suffered violent deaths, rather than recant it! Such is not the course of men who know they are in the wrong.

But were these witnesses mistaken? Were they a company of honest, but deluded men? Had they been, by some means or other, imposed upon, deceived and misled?

In answer to this, suppose we look calmly and carefully into those masterly discussions of Paul; and those profound discourses of John; or the logical histories of Luke; or the plain and simple, yet sublime and truth-like narratives of Matthew and Mark; and then ask ourselves if this were the kind of men, and this the character of mind likely to be easily imposed upon! The idea is simply preposterous! That these men were the real authors of the works that bear their names, there can be no reasonable doubt. The books are clear indices to the character of the minds—and the character of the minds is a sure guarantee against all such impositions.

Now, finding as we do, that the first and second of the suppositions named are untenable; we are compelled to fall back on the third, and admit that Christ *is* risen from the dead. This is the only supposition in the case that coincides with the universally received laws of evidence. There is no Scripture—there is no process of sound reasoning—there are no rules of logic—no laws of philosphy, by which we can legitimately reach any other conclusion. *It must be so !* Christ is indeed risen, and having risen he is the first fruits of them that slept.

By first fruits, as the phrase is here used, reference is had to the ceremony under the Jewish law of presenting the first ripe fruit of the annual crop, as an offering to the Lord, in acknowledgment of his supervising providence, and as a token of gratitude for the same. At the sheaf offering there was, 1st. A passover. 2d. The day following was a Sabbatic day. 3d. Then the day following that, the first fruits were offered. With these circumstances the resurrection of Christ agrees; there being a passover, following which was the crucifixion, then the next day was a Sabbatic day, then following that was the resurrection, or the first fruits from the dead; and the conclusion of the Apostle is : that as the first fruits were sure proof of the coming harvest, so surely was the resurrection of Christ proof of our resurrection. As the first fruits were followed by a glorious harvest, so the resurrection of Christ was to be followed by the resurrection of myriads from the dead, whose triumphant song should be " O grave, where is thy victory ?"

There had been resurrections from the dead previously to the resurrection of Christ. The daughter of Jarius had died and been raised from the dead; so had the son of the widow of Nain, and so had Lazarus the friend of Jesus; and it is worthy of remark, and withal very suggestive, that of these the first had been raised from the bed whereon she had died; the second from the bier on which he was being carried to the grave, and the third, from the tomb where he had lain four days. These particulars have their significance, but may not be noticed now.

There are also recorded in the Old Testament Scriptures several cases of resurrection from the dead. But in all these cases, whether recorded in the Old or New Testament, there was no material change passed upon the bodies raised. They were simply brought back to life, to dwell a while longer on earth, and then to return to dust. But the resurrection of Christ was different. His body, though preserving its identity, was raised a glorious body. The corruptible had put on incorruption, and the mortal had put on immortality; so that in his case, to the fullest extent of its meaning, death had been swallowed up in victory: in his body was fully verified what the Apostle declares shall be verified in all, "It was sown in corruption and raised in incorruption; sown in dishonor and raised in glory; sown in weakness, raised in power," and the victory he thus gained *is* a victory which, through him, God will give to us all; and for which we may with the Apostle well say: "Thanks be to God." We may also take to ourselves the exhortation with which he followed this inimitable argument, and "be steadfast, immovable, always abounding in the work of the Lord, knowing that our labor is not in vain in the Lord."

The Lord is risen indeed He is the first fruits of them that slept. We also shall rise from the dead — "for the hour is coming in the which all that are in their graves shall hear his voice, and shall come forth; they that have done good unto the resurrection of life, and they that have done evil to the resurrection of damnation." These are his own words; to them let us take heed, for

> "Now, only now, against that hour
> We may a place provide;
> Beyond the grave, beyond the power
> Of hell—our spirits hide."

And now, in view of all, we may safely say, with Dr. Edward Young:

> "In that blest life
> I see the path, in his death the price,
> And in his great ascent the proof supreme
> Of immortality. And did he rise?
> Hear it, O! ye nations! hear it, O! ye dead!
> He rose! He rose! He burst the bars of death;
> Oh, the burst gates! crushed sting! demolished throne!
> Last gasp of vanquished death! Shout, earth and heaven!
> This sum of good to man! whose nature
> Took wing, and mounted with him from the tomb.
> Then! then I rose; then first humanity
> Triumphant passed the crystal ports of light
> (Stupendous guest) and seized eternal youth—
> Seized, in our names; e'er since 'tis blasphemous
> To call man mortal. Man's mortality
> Was then transferred to death, and heaven's duration
> Unalienably sealed to this frail frame,
> This child of dust. Man, all immortal, hail!
> Hail heaven! all lavish of strange gifts to man!
> Thine all the glory, man's the boundless bliss!
> Hallelujah! Amen!"

XX.

PIETY PROGRESSIVE.

"Therefore leaving the principles of the doctrine of Christ, let us go on unto perfection."—HEB. vi. 1.

By the phrase "the principles of the doctrine cf Christ," the Apostle means the rudiments or elements of Christianity. The margin reads, "the word of the beginning of Christ." Verses one and two enumerate these elements: Repentance, faith, baptisms, laying on of hands, resurrection, and eternal judgment. These are learned first, and serve to initiate the man into the kingdom of heaven; but they are only initiatory and rudimental.

Have we well learned even these? Before we contemplate progression it is well to be assured that we are soundly initiated. How much less proficient could one be than ourselves and be any Christian at all? Let the question be meditated. The "repentance" of some has hardly sufficed to turn them from sin overt. The "faith" of some is hardly at all justifying. The "baptism" of some has hardly been appreciated or understood as a formal obligation to a godly life; and possibly they have sought only one, the outward, and know nothing of the "sprinkling of the heart from an evil conscience." And so of the rest.

How reproachful to have it said of us, as our Apostle writes in chapter five: "For when for the time ye ought to be teachers, ye have need that one teach you again which be the first principles of the oracles of God; and are become such as have need of milk, and not of strong meat." Of how many of us is this reproach true? Again ask, have we well learned even these first principles?

But *there is a higher life*—perhaps I should say a deeper life. There is a life for us beyond the initiating principles. We are obligated to look on sin, not only as a thing to be *pardoned*, but as a principle from which we are to be *cleansed*. Our religious life must go through justification, by regeneration, into sanctification. Our Savior pardons his prisoner, then releases.

"He breaks the power of canceled sin,
He sets the prisoner free."

According to the text, this advanced life is a moving on in religious experience—improving, becoming better; acquiring spiritual life, strength, enjoyment, discernment. "The natural man receiveth not the things of the Spirit of God. . . . . But he that is spiritual judgeth all things"—his discernment is so quickened, having grown wiser by growing better; "yet he himself is judged of no man," is not known or understood by any. "The world knoweth us not." This life is such a moving on that the first principles—repentance, justifying faith, baptism, etc.—become rudimental, as the alphabet, tables of weights and measures, and the like, to the scholar. They become so incorporated in his mental constitution that they are, unconsciously, ever with him—a part of his being. The mere letter of the law is well nigh forgotten to the advanced Christian, the spiritual vision being so far extended beyond. The root of the matter is in him, while he plies his soul to higher phases of truth.

The higher life is progressive, like the day, which first dawns, then expands, and shines brighter till the noon. It is like the shooting plant, which first germinates in the seed, then throws up the blade, then the ear, then the full corn. It is like the growing child: first the infant, then the youth, and then the man of full stature and maturity of mind. All these are Scripture figures of illustration. Let us not be content to stay in the twilight of our day, in the germ of our growth, in the infancy of our being in Christ. Our growth must be an escape, like that of Lot, who was commanded to escape for his life—neither stay in all the plain. We should not linger in any condition at all contiguous to our former death, but go to the utmost verge from it, becoming as religious as it is possible to be, both inwardly and outwardly. It is a development of religious principle, evolving the principle of eternal life out of the soul by the grace given unto us. " Therefore leaving the principles of the doctrine of Christ, let us go on unto perfection."

Quitting the rudiments, the novitiate, what blessed

discoveries we make! We come anon upon an abiding confidence, a complete self-mastery, an exhilarating joy, and "full assurance of hope." And the joy is ever new. It does not satiate. Carnal pleasures grow dull, and even nauseous.

> "But thy words, with grace divine
> Imbued, bring to their sweetness no satiety."

In this state of grace unimpaired everything about us touches the springs of joy, and God is seen in everything. The voice of a friend falling on the ear, the beauties of the landscape greeting the eye, the wings of the wind fanning the cheek, the rising or the setting sun, the thunder-cloud or the rainbow, rest or motion, work or waiting—everything has its power to spring the gushing joy within and bring the ineffable One to view. Not in terror, but in joy, the soul reads everywhere: "Thou, God, seest me." There is an abiding conviction, not only of acquittal from guilt, but of acceptability of state. God has cleansed the temple, it yields him ready occupancy, and he approves its furniture. And his assurance is not based on a supposed purpose of God to save him whether or not, but from a faith, a living, appropriating faith, bringing "the witness" of God himself.

Such a believer is not ever reasoning and probing to see if I have repented, if I have true faith, if I have been baptized aright, etc. These first principles were settled long ago, and now his language is: "I know whom I have believed, and am persuaded he is able to keep that which I have committed to him against that day."

> "Not a doubt doth arise
> To darken my skies,
> Or hide for a moment my Lord from my eyes;
> In him I am blest,
> I lean on his breast,
> And, lo! in his wounds I continually rest."

Like Moses on Pisgah, he views the promised land, and becomes familiar with the heavenly world by daily observation from his commanding standpoint.

Living faith and joyous hope make us superior to the petty annoyances of time. This experience arms us against the temptations common to men and defends us against the snares of the enemy. It frees us from the vexatious cares of a carnal life, and from the enslaving "desires" of a worldly heart. It brings content in poverty, and shuts out avarice in wealth. It opens the eyes of the soul to the beauties of God's creation, the wisdom of his providence, and "the riches of his grace." The man is emphatically "a new creature." With what truth he can say: "Old things are passed away; behold, all things have become new!"

> "A bleeding Savior seen by faith,
> A sense of pardoning love,
> A hope that triumphs over death—
> Give joys like those above."

The gospel is still "the power of God unto salvation to every one that believeth." Jesus is still "able to save unto the uttermost all that come unto God by him."

> "No fable old, nor mythic lore,
>   Nor dream of bards and seers;
> No dead fact stranded on the shore
>   Of the oblivious years;
> But warm, sweet, tender, even yet
>   A present help is He;
> And faith has still its Olivet,
>   And love its Gallilee."

On this subject of a higher or deeper religious life many of us err in two particulars. First, in not recognizing the *fact* of a higher life. If it is not denied, it fails often to be admitted and confessed as desirable. It is ignored. This is a sad error. (The Scriptures teach spiritual maturity, Christian perfection, freedom from sin, sanctification of heart and life.) It is highly important to recognize the fact, to make it a point in our theology.

The second error is in failing *to go up to it*, as a necessity, when it is recognized. We content us with meagre attainments, with mere initiation. We need appetite for it; we have moral dyspepsia, and spiritual food is sickening to the carnal taste. Holiness is unrelished, unpleasant. The fault is theirs who have destroyed a better relish by indulgence in the "forbidden fruit." And so there is no advancement beyond first principles. Some never see anything more important than repentance, justifying faith, baptism, and such rudiments, and talk only of these. Baptism, a mere outward rite, is likely to be the most cherished matter, and this, with kindred rudiments, will be vehemently discussed, but no mention of "righteousness, peace and joy in the Holy Ghost."

Yet the Scriptures contemplate *advance* by believers, and enjoin it. "*Add* to your faith" is the constant tenor of Divine instruction. "Desire the sincere milk of the word, that ye may *grow* thereby." "And he gave some apostles, &c., for the perfecting of the saints, for the work of the ministry, for the edifying of the body of Christ, till we all come in the unity of the faith, and of the knowledge of the Son of God unto a perfect man, with the measure of the stature of the fullness of Christ; that we henceforth be no more children, tossed to and fro, and carried about with every wind of doctrine; . . . but, speaking the truth in love, may grow up into him in all things, which is the head, even Christ." Where is our growth? Can we show it? Happy is he who can point to the unmistakable marks, the increased gentleness, kindness, benevolence, work, faith and hope, and thus prove his advancement.

Now, we should not rest in the rudiments, for two reasons: First, because we will decline from that state if we aim to stop there. It is a law of all growth, that when increase is stopped decay sets in. Christian life will stagnate when it ceases to improve. (The perfection we have spoken of is not one where no growth is needed more, but a reaching of that maturity where freedom from sin is vouchsafed.) The virtues and capacities must be ever deepening and augmenting. If not so, there will be retrogression; the salt will lose its seasoning power.

A second reason for not remaining in that novitiate is, that there we have little power for good. It is very rare that one without the happy experience of advanced Christian life is either zealous or efficient. If conscience impel to zeal, there is apt to be wanting the alacrity which gives tact and effectiveness to the work. "The joy of the Lord is your strength." Every Christian should strive for that joy, that he may be useful. This is our duty and life-work—*to do good*. Salvation is equally for ourselves and others—that we should *impart;* "that they which live should not henceforth live unto themselves."

We have little heart to work, because we are weak and sickly; and are weak because we do not seek the milk and meat of the word, and grow. The heart is not enough set upon God. "If any man love God, the same is known of him." Do men "take knowledge of us," that we are taken up with the Divine love? Does your religious life exhibit itself in godly deeds? (Do you say you are *too busy* to do Christian work?) You are not too busy to die! A merchant sat at his desk, immured in his papers and books. A Christian man entered and begged his attention to a matter of interest to the Church of which both were members. "I am too busy," replied the merchant; and with this word the entreaty of his Christian brother was repelled, and he compelled to retire. Another visitor entered that office, laid a cold hand on his shoulder, and demanded that he go with him. He arose with dizzy head and went. The visitor accompanied him to his own chamber, laid him on his bed, and placed a chill hand on his heart. Then the busy man knew his visitor was death! He was too busy to do the work of the Master, but not too busy to die! In the midst of unfinished business, my friend, you shall have to lie down in the grave.

> "Make haste, O man, to do
> Whatever must be done;
> Thou has no time to lose in sloth,
> Thy day will soon be gone.
> Make haste, O man, to live!"

You are not too important to work for your fellows, even the lowliest. If your culture isolates you from your fellows, your culture is unchristian; if your wealth, your wealth is wickedness; if your honor and superior greatness cut off your sympathy and aid from the neglected, you honor is false. JESUS is our exemplar. He "went about doing good;" and of him it was said, in ever-blessed reproach, "This man receiveth sinners, and eateth with them." Go thou and do likewise, and receive the same creditable reproach from those whose censure is commendation.

We must *acquire the life* that will qualify and impel us to such work; it will not flow from dead hearts and palsied hands. The highest style of life—outer life, will flow only from the deepest life within. The deeper the purity of heart, the more active the hands will be in all good works. "Pure religion and undefiled before God and the Father is this: To visit the fatherless and widows in their affliction, and to keep himself unspotted from the world." Is *this* pure religion? Then how few have it! Who of us *inquire* and *seek* after "the fatherless and widows," that we may visit them in affliction, and thus show our pure religion? Had we *the life* acquired by leaving the rudiments and going on to perfection, would we not exhibit it more?

With this life enjoyed, *worship* will also then be a delight; we shall then love the place where God's honor dwelleth." We shall also more truthfully sing:

> " Beyond my highest joy
> I prize her heavenly ways,
> Her sweet communion, solemn vows,
> Her hymns of love and praise."

The Church must "come up out of the wilderness, leaning upon the arm of her beloved, fair as the moon, clear as the sun, and terrible as an army with banners." And to this end individuals must inquire, *am I alive to God?* Am I " going on unto perfection?" The nearer one approximates "perfection" the more abundant he will be in all "good works." Purity of heart does not stand alone; the perfect man is no recluse; he neither refrains his lips nor his hands; he works. If his life is barren of good deeds, it contradicts his claim to purity; if filled with love, he is ready for every word and work; he is generous and benevolent, gracious and good, one whom the poor will bless and the Church will honor. So allied are grace within and deeds without: they attest each other.

www.ingramcontent.com/pod-product-compliance
Lightning Source LLC
Chambersburg PA
CBHW030737230426
43667CB00007B/747